MO...
UNHOLY COMMUNION

Think Agatha Christie meets Stephen King, and you'll have the formula for Thomas Rumreich's Unholy Communion. *A spine-tingling tale of one man's revenge delivered as long-delayed justice.*

—Craig MacIntosh, publisher of Pugio Books and author of *Wolf's Inferno, Wolf's Vendetta, McFadden's War, The Last Lightning*, and *The Fortunate Orphans*

Unholy Communion *is a chilling vigilante tale that takes you on a ride through authentic Minnesota, both rural and urban. The people and the places are vivid and real, and the core of the story is both shocking and heartbreaking. If you appreciate a narrative that dwells in the gray area between right and wrong, this is a book for you.*

—PJ Tracy, *New York Times* and *London Times* bestselling author of the Monkeewrench series

UNHOLY
COMMUNION

THOMAS
RUMREICH

BEAVER'S POND
PRESS

ISBN 13: 978-1-64343-926-6
Library of Congress Catalog Number: 2019905816
Printed in the United States of America
First Printing: 2020
28 27 26 25 24   6 5 4 3 2

Cover art by Margarita Sikorskaia
Edited by Angela Wiechmann
Project Manager: Laurie Buss Herrmann
Designed by Mayfly Design

BEAVER'S POND
PRESS

Beaver's Pond Press, Inc.
939 Seventh Street West
St. Paul, MN 55102
(952) 829-8818
www.BeaversPondPress.com

Additional copies of this book may be ordered on Amazon.com.

To the survivors of child abuse

PART I

MEA CULPA

With shame and repentance, we acknowledge as an ecclesial community that we were not where we should have been, that we did not act in a timely manner, realizing the magnitude and the gravity of the damage done to so many lives. We showed no care for the little ones; we abandoned them.

—POPE FRANCIS, AUGUST 20, 2018

CHAPTER 1

*L*ow November clouds obscure the waning moon. The wind howls through mostly bare branches. The road to the old cabin is a tortuous half mile. It's difficult to navigate with my headlights off and little ambient light, but I will get there. I have to. I have planned this for a long time. Years, in fact.

The man has a dog. A golden retriever. I know that because I have seen them in town together at the vet's office next to the little market, where he buys his groceries.

When I was ten years old, my old man shot my dog. It still breaks my heart. But I will kill this one if it's necessary. I won't hesitate. My hope, though, is that the juicy treat in my pocket will buy the dog's silence.

I have a different treat for his master.

Before the last turn to the cabin, I stop the car, step out into the starless night, and put on my booties. I pull back the slide on my Beretta, ensuring a bullet is chambered, and let it close quietly. With fingers covering the lens of my flashlight, allowing just enough light to see, I walk the rest of the way.

I arrive at the cabin and quietly move through the thick brush to the back. The rear window is nearly covered by thorny branches. I stand there watching him.

What I see confirms what I read in the letter. It described what went on in that basement office. The priest's office. Below *the auditorium, where he taught speech to vulnerable and trusting young men.*

I am sickened. Bile bubbles up in my throat. I want so much to believe in God, the tenets of the church, the eternal happiness promised if I just obey. (And, of course, pay.) Yet how can I, when the church protects those who defile the virginal children of God? The masters of spiritual incest. After all, they are called Father.

I'm conflicted. These men of the cloth are supposed to be good people. Most of them are. Even the vile ones have done some good things. But the evil they do lasts far longer—and perpetuates itself.

I know that all too well.

Enough reflection. It's time to complete my task.

The front porch is old. I'm careful not to make a sound as I creep up the rotting steps. My vinyl-gloved hands noiselessly open the screen door and the heavy door behind it. Sounds from the speakers in the den drown out my entry as well as my soft steps down the dimly lit hallway.

The dog comes around the corner and pads toward me. He is uncertain at first, but then he happily accepts his bribe.

The priest is still sitting, eyes riveted to his computer screen. He is naked except for silver-rimmed bifocals, a clerical collar, and black leather slippers. And an erection.

His bald pate, surrounded by an annulus of white hair, reflects light from the disgusting images displayed on the screen. Haze from a recently smoked cigar hangs near the ceiling of the small room.

Sensing my presence, he looks up, surprised. Instantly, he is embarrassed by his erect penis and by the horrible images I see on his computer. He is too stunned to speak.

"Looks as though you've forgotten some of your religious regalia," I say, referring to his near nakedness.

He tries to cover himself with his hands.

I brandish my Beretta. "Do I look familiar?"

He nods. He thinks he recognizes me, but I can tell he's not quite certain. For good reason—we've never met before.

But I know about him. I know too much.

"Your clerical collar, Father. Does that make you feel holier when you masturbate? More powerful? Sinless?"

His trembling fingers reach up and touch his collar. He looks away.

"Do you remember, Father? Do you remember the private speech lessons you used to give in your small office in the basement of the college?"

His eyes feign confusion. His body tenses.

"Do you remember, Father, masturbating while you looked at young boys' bodies? And touching them?"

His face becomes ashen. Once again, he looks away.

"How many did you abuse, Father? Do you even remember?"

His computer has timed out and gone into sleep mode. He stares at the blank screen, unable to look at me.

"Would you like absolution, Father? Would you like God to forgive you?"

He nods.

"God has forgiven you many times, but after absolution by your priestly friends, you continue to offend him."

He lowers his head in shame.

"The Act of Contrition would cleanse your soul, wouldn't it, Father?"

"Yes. Please, may I—"

"There's no time, Father."

He begins to cry.

"Now it's time for Communion. Do you see the irony? You must take Communion, even though your soul is heavy with mortal sin. Your church forbids that, Father. It dooms you to hell."

I point at the floor and make him kneel. Under the threat of my gun, he receives Communion—a special Communion I have carefully prepared for him. It's difficult for him to swallow this sacramental offering, but what option does he have? Water from my bottle helps him wash it down.

Not only a priest, it seems, can give Communion.

I feel omnipotent, powerful, controlling. How different from years ago, when he was in control. His victims dared not tell anyone how he abused his power.

The time has come. I command him to stand and face me.

He frowns, his eyes wrinkling at the corners while his brain sorts through his memories from years ago. He's trying to re-member me, but so many had succumbed on the cot in that small basement room.

Finally fear gets the best of him. His bladder lets go, and he pisses on his slippers.

"Please, mercy. I'll do anything," he pleads in a high-pitched voice.

"Mercy, Father? Not today."

I grip the Beretta tightly. It tends to jam if held too loose, although I doubt a second shot will be necessary. His hands reach up to cover his face, as if they will stop the projectile that's about to rip through his skull.

I nearly have an orgasm when the muzzle kicks upward and the bullet plunges through his forehead. For several seconds, I watch the contents of his head slide down the wall and over the items on his desk. Then I dip my gloved finger in his blood and scribe my message on the blank computer screen.

Priestly Father James Doyle is now burning in hell with his other boy-fucking friends.

For a moment, I tremble as a painful memory that has existed for a very long time washes over me.

The dog lies in the corner, shaking. He looks up at me, his head between his forepaws, ears lowered. His brown eyes blink.

I tell him I'm sorry.

I leave another memento before vanishing into the dark.

CHAPTER 2

Eighty-two-year-old Delbert Peltier was looking forward to being done for the day and going home for his midafternoon nap. His last Meals on Wheels delivery was to Father James Doyle.

It required navigating his white Cadillac Seville down a sinuous gravel road that wound its way through a copse of mature oak and leafless birch. Weeds had grown between the tracks on the narrow lane. It was only noon, but his failing eyesight made the road seem dark.

Arriving at his destination, he parked next to Father Doyle's minivan, on the uncut grass near the wooden steps. Always wanting to look his best, Del pulled down the visor and looked in the mirror, inspecting the deep crevices on his cheeks that disappeared into the white beard framing his thin lips. He noticed the sadness in his eyes.

His wife of sixty-one years had died a year ago. They had married shortly after high school. Since her passing, the lines on his face had intensified, and his hazel eyes had grown dim. His irises were clouded by cataracts and ringed by milky gray halos. The thick black plastic frames of his tinted glasses called attention to his sad eyes, making him appear even older and frailer than his years.

Like his aging body, the Seville had nearly given up the fight as well. The rocker panels were rusted, and the exterior paint was peeling, leaving dysmorphic black splotches. The left headlight was broken, but that was only a cosmetic issue. His vision was so poor he only drove in the daytime anyway.

The red leather seat on the driver's side was shiny and cracked. The gray backing was visible where the leather had stripped away. On the passenger side, where his wife used to sit, was a soft red corduroy cushion, a reminder of their annual trip to Florida. Del wasn't about to part with that particular artifact. Nor with the simple gold wedding band he still wore on the third finger of his left hand.

He missed her terribly.

Resting on the back seat was a beat-up, duct-taped Styrofoam cooler where he kept the meals for his deliveries. He reached over the seat, flipped open the cooler, and removed the last bag.

It took considerable effort to push the heavy Caddy door open. The hinges squealed their resistance; his arthritic elbow ached in unison. As he unfolded his lanky body from the four-door sedan, he was overtaken by a fit of coughing, thanks to pulmonary disease from years of smoking—a habit long abandoned but continually regretted. Pulmonary disease had left his voice a loud whisper, requiring sharp, difficult inhalations when he spoke and pursed lips when he exhaled.

After the coughing abated, Del raised the collar of his flannel jacket and headed for the cabin. He struggled up the old steps, his thin legs barely sufficient to support him. With one arthritic hand, he grasped the loose railing as tightly as he could. With the other, he held the brown paper bag of food.

Most days, the elderly recipient would be at the screen door anxiously awaiting his meal. The rescue dog, Brodie, would be right alongside, expecting a biscuit.

This day was different. The heavy inner door was open, but no one was standing behind the screen. The morning's *Pioneer Press* was still lying on the porch in its orange plastic wrapper. Peering through the screen, Del could see rusty-black paw prints mottling the old birch floor.

Del knocked.

The golden retriever barked loudly from a room in the back of the cabin.

Del knocked more forcefully. Then, in a loud, wheezy whisper, he called through the screen, "Father? Father Doyle! It's me, Del, with your dinner."

The effort to speak loudly provoked another fit of raspy coughing, which further roused the dog. Brodie howled and came running from the rear of the cabin to the front, then back to the rear again, as though beckoning Del to follow.

Del opened the door and followed the dog through a small living room and down a hallway. He cautiously stepped around the trail of rusty-black stains. A grimy ceiling lamp lit the hallway, casting a dim splash of yellow light.

"Father Doyle," he called out again. "It's Del. You here?"

The door to the small carpeted den was open.

Del's sense of smell was the first to respond. Instantly,

he was sickened by a fetid, coppery odor mixed with cigar smoke. Other smells assaulted his nose too, but he couldn't identify them.

Then he felt a sticky, spongy softness under his right foot.

And then he saw it—a few feet away, Father James Doyle lay faceup on the carpet, naked except for slippers and a clerical collar. His glasses lay on the floor alongside the remainder of his head.

Del dropped the bag and stumbled out of the den, groping the hallway walls for support. He lurched outside just in time to vomit over the porch railing. He looked down to see his bloodstained foot.

Once the retching had subsided, he wiped his mouth and beard on his handkerchief, then tottered as fast as he was able to the Caddy. He found his cell phone.

"Nine-one-one State Patrol—what is your emergency?" a brusque, clipped female voice asked.

"I'm at Father Doyle's, and . . . it's . . . it's terrible." Del swallowed convulsively, gasping and wheezing. "My God, there's blood everywhere." He doubled over, leaning against the door of his car.

"Sir, I can barely hear you. Take a deep breath, calm down, and speak up, please."

More loudly and slowly: "I said, I am at Father Doyle's, and something terrible has happened here. He's lying on the floor. Blood. Lots of blood."

"Is the person breathing?"

"I . . . I don't know."

"Can you check, sir?"

"No!" he said as loudly as he was able. "I can't go back in there."

"Is anyone with you?"

Del paused to take a breath. "No. I'm alone."

"OK, I see this is cellular call. Sir, I need your location." After waiting a moment with no answer, the dispatcher asked again, "Sir, where are you? And *please* speak louder! I can barely hear you."

Through another fit of coughing, Del retrieved the delivery list from the back seat. "It's Two-Three-Two-Two, Melanie Trail North, Scandia." He could hear computer keys clicking. "It's hard to find. Off County Road Three. Back in the woods. On Goose Lake. I was just delivering his dinner, like I always do, and—"

"Sir," she interrupted, "I've dispatched a deputy and the EMTs. Stay on the phone with me until they arrive, OK? It's busy here, so I'm going to put you on hold, but I'll check back with you every minute or so. *Do not hang up!*"

"Yes, ma'am."

Del shook his head, took another deep breath, sighed, and kept the phone to his ear. The urge to vomit was rising again.

Minutes later the dispatcher had come back on the line to check with Del when he heard a siren and saw emergency lights flashing through the trees. He disconnected, set his cell phone on the hood, and doubled over.

CHAPTER 3

At the same time that Del was arriving at Father Doyle's, Deputy Ron Grafton was northbound on Highway 95, on routine patrol in his new black Ford Police Interceptor SUV.

Ron, a fifteen-year veteran of the Washington County Sheriff's Office, was one of the few lucky patrol deputies to score an SUV. At six feet five and many pounds too heavy for his frame, Ron suspected his size had landed him the vehicle. But he was happily willing to accept that consequence.

Ron loved duty in northern Washington County. There was less crime and fewer calls. Because of his weight, he did not have a penchant for hard work—or perhaps it was the other way around.

Most of his work that day was follow-up on juvenile crime and completing paperwork. Some of the report writing could be done in his vehicle.

It was time for lunch, the best part of his shift. Or any shift, for that matter. He was headed to Meyer's Bar and Grill in the northern Washington County town of Scandia, a small community with just under four thousand people within its borders.

After lunch, he planned to park behind the Scandia fire station or in the shadows of the maintenance shed next to the community center to write reports and complete some paperwork. More importantly, a brief snooze would be in order—his first chin resting comfortably on the bulbous second chin beneath. As always, though, he would keep his clipboard on his lap, just in case a supervisor happened to show up.

Arriving at the restaurant, Ron backed the Interceptor up to the building, parking beneath the large kitchen exhaust fan. Next to his SUV was a beat-up Chevrolet sporting so-called whiskey plates. These special license plates all began with the letter *W* and were assigned to certain DUI offenders—hence the "whiskey" reference. Sure enough, Ron recognized the Chevy as one he had stopped several months earlier on Highway 95, when the driver had earned himself a DUI and a trip to jail.

With a tug on the duty belt that encircled him and cut a trough around his obese belly, Ron stepped out of the SUV and onto the concrete veranda that bordered the street. Wrought-iron tables and chairs once sat on the patio. Now they had been removed for the coming winter and replaced by a blizzard of leaves.

As he opened the front door, the hinges creaked, cuing a trio of men to swivel on their ratty barstools. They nodded at the officer, then sheepishly turned back to their too-early-in-the-day beers. One drinker seemed more sheepish than the others.

Ron chuckled to himself. He knew his uniformed presence would curtail another round for Mr. Whiskey Plates.

The bartender, white shirtsleeves rolled to his elbows, was washing glasses behind the old lacquered bar. He smiled and nodded at Ron.

A bar and grill since the early 1950s, and a meat market before that, Meyer's was a longtime institution, a gathering place for locals where much gossip and little truth were exchanged over popcorn, beer, burgers, and, on Saturday nights, prime rib.

They gave Ron free burgers when he was on duty. He liked that. Almost as much as he liked Brenda, the well-endowed and thin-waisted waitress. She often leaned over when taking his order, allowing him a peek into her blouse and its ample contents.

The bar area had nine stools bolted to the floor. Other than the three early drinkers, the bar was empty. In the dining section, six booths abutted a knotty-pine wall. The button-back booths were upholstered with well-worn and cracked black vinyl. Tables with fake-wood-patterned Formica filled the remaining space.

The redolence from years of deep-frying was embedded in the walls. The wood-lath ceiling housed several mostly working recessed lights, which illuminated the warped oak strip floor. Beer signs, a Minnesota Wild schedule, and historic photographs of the meat-market days hung on the walls. At the far end, a blackboard advertised drink specials and upcoming events that had been handwritten with multicolored chalk.

Brenda emerged from the kitchen and gave Ron a smile. "Ronnie! It's been a while! You must be busy. We don't see you here much anymore."

He nodded and sighed. "Yeah, I've been working in the southern part of the county, near Hastings. It's a lot busier down there. But I caught a lucky break this shift. Slower here, up north."

"Can it ever be *too* slow for you?"

"C'mon. You know patrol work is tough on me. I put in for a desk job in Stillwater. But even if I get it, I'll still come up for lunch, just to see you, Bren." Using the shortened name made him feel emotionally connected to her.

Brenda grinned. "Hope so, Ronnie."

He beamed, hoping she really meant it.

"Pick your own seat," she added.

"Thanks." He made a mock bow. "Think I'll take one with cracked vinyl."

Brenda laughed. "Diet Pepsi and the double cheeseburger again?"

"Yup. Crispy fries and extra pickles too. Kind of hungry today. Guy works up an appetite driving around all morning with no one to talk to other than the dispatcher."

She looked at him for an extra second, shook her head, then left to get him his soda. Returning with the Diet Pepsi, Brenda leaned over longer than necessary while she placed it in front of him. She straightened when she was sure he was sated.

I feel sorry for you, she silently thought to him. *Gained all that weight after your wife died. You used to be so handsome.*

She shook her head again. "I'll put in your order. But the way you eat, one of these days you're going to drop over dead," she opined. "I'd hate to see that happen." She meant that more than she was willing to admit.

"Yeah, I'd hate to see that too, Bren."

"By the way, Ronnie, I meant to ask you—did they figure out who vandalized the new Speedway station? Those kids from Hugo?"

He winked. "Well, I can't be specific, because no one's been charged ... but you're a good amateur detective. You did your homework."

"I should have gone into law enforcement," she said with a smirk.

"You would have been good at it. Very intuitive. We could have been partners." He raised his eyebrows and smiled, indicating *partners with benefits*.

"Ronald Grafton, you're too much!" She tried to look offended, giving him a fake glower.

Despite her playful reply, he immediately regretted the innuendo. He quickly moved on. "Dumb-ass kids these days have too much free time. They ought to raise the price of spray paint. That'd cut down on some of the graffiti. Of course, then they'd just start stealing the paint."

"So true!" With a laugh, she leaned over and kissed his pockmarked cheek—giving him one more peek down her blouse. "I'll be back when your order's done."

His cheeks flushing more than a little pink, Ron removed the radio from his duty belt, adjusted the squelch, and set the unit on the table. He paid only cursory attention to the staccato chatter, whereas he paid a good deal of attention to Brenda as she glided around the booths and tables, her sassy bottle-blond ponytail swaying back and forth. He didn't like it, though, when she leaned over for other male customers, just as she did for him.

He of course understood that her peekaboo routine was good for tips. But still. Seeing her flirt with the other patrons, he couldn't help but wonder if he was reading too much into her flirting with him.

But with further scrutiny and much relief, he noted that while she gave other men glimpses down her low-cut pink blouse, she did *not* give them kisses.

Just then, he recognized 279—his squad number—from the radio chatter. He turned up the volume, leaned toward the radio, listened intently, and nodded at no one. Time to move out. There'd be no double cheeseburger, crispy fries, and extra pickles. He gulped his Diet Pepsi, wiped his lips with a napkin, cleared his throat, and tossed five bucks on the table.

Brenda was waiting on customers in the back of the restaurant. She looked up in surprise as Ron headed for the door.

"Sorry, Bren," he said. "No lunch for me today—emergency. Gotta run."

"Come back soon, all right?" she said with an affectionate grin.

"You bet," he replied, hoping it would be sooner rather than later.

Ron walked quickly to his vehicle, speaking into the microphone on his epaulet as he hurried to his car. "Two seventy-nine," he announced.

"Male, unknown breathing status, Two-Three-Two-Two, Melanie Trail North, Scandia," the dispatcher reported.

"Ten-four, two seventy-nine," he answered, climbing into his SUV.

"Twelve twenty-two," replied the dispatcher, time-stamping and terminating the call.

Ron activated the emergency lights and siren. Within seven minutes, he was coursing up the gravel lane, his red and blue LEDs pulsing.

Arriving at a shabby cabin, he saw an elderly gentleman and two old cars. All three had seen better days. He exited the squad and approached the man bundled up in a red flannel jacket, hugging himself tightly and leaning against the hood of a rusted Seville.

"You the guy who called nine-one-one?"

"Yeah. Name's Del. It's horrible in there." His voice was quaking and wheezy. "I think I stepped in blood. Got some on my shoes." He held out his foot as proof. "Dropped the bag of food in there too. And then I dropped *my* food over there." He nodded to the vomit on the ground near the porch.

"OK. Anyone else in the cabin?"

"Didn't see anybody other than Father Doyle, but I really didn't look." He coughed into his handkerchief, then resumed. "I only went to the den in the back. First time I'd ever been back there. I just wanted to get the heck out. Oh wait, I forgot—there's the dog."

Ron raised an eyebrow. "The dog gonna be a problem?"

"I doubt it. Golden retriever. Brodie's his name. Nice dog. Kinda crazy right now, though."

"I need to know," Ron said, "do you have any weapons on you, sir?"

"No. Nothing."

Ron nodded. He didn't feel it necessary to pat the old man down.

"OK. Let's keep you safe while I check things out. Have a seat in my car." He opened the back door of his SUV and motioned Del inside. "Just sit tight here."

It was difficult for Del to tuck his arthritic body into the back seat. Before Ron could close the door, he put his hand out. "Wait—are you arresting me? I mean, I just got here and found him."

"Nope," Ron replied. "I just want to keep you safe while I check the place."

He pushed the door shut, locking Del in the squad car. He then walked across the grass to the wooden stairs. The steps creaked under his massive weight.

As soon as Ron opened the screen door, Brodie jumped on him, his front paws leaving wet rusty streaks on Ron's khaki shirt. The deputy grabbed the dog by the collar and led him outside. He secured the dog with a leash looped over the porch railing, then he tied the other end to the trunk of a small birch tree.

Heading back inside, Ron hastened down the hallway, taking care where he stepped. He could see the rusty, chaotic trail of paw prints leading to the den as well as Del's single bloody footprint heading away from it. As Ron neared the doorway, he noticed a cigarette butt flattened on the floor.

After one look into the den, he squeezed the button on his microphone and radioed dispatch to send an investigator. The scene demanded expertise beyond his level of training.

Swallowing hard and trying to forget what he had just seen, he turned back down the hall to check on the other rooms. He found no other occupants in the cabin.

There didn't seem to be any signs of robbery. Then again, it was a bit hard to say if the place had been tossed. Father Doyle obviously wasn't a neatnik. With boxes of stuff everywhere, the house sort of looked like a landfill.

In the distance, Ron heard the siren for the Scandia fire department's EMTs. He headed outside as the vehicle pulled into the yard. He raised his hand in a halt position and approached the driver, who put his window down.

"Sorry, fellas," he said. He instantly corrected himself when he saw a woman sitting in the passenger seat. "Oops, pardon me. Didn't see you, ma'am." He nodded to her. "Anyway, this guy's long past any help you can give him."

"You sure?" the driver asked. "We can have a look if you'd like."

Morbid curiosity, Ron thought.

"No, I've got it under control," he said.

As the EMT made notes on a clipboard, the driver began to pull into the parking area to turn around. Ron stopped him again.

"I'd appreciate it if you could just back out of here. The less contamination of the area, the better."

"Got it," the driver said. He backed down the road.

Ron glanced over at his SUV and saw Del staring back at him. Hiking up his duty belt, Ron walked over and opened the door.

"Sir, let's sit at the table over there." He motioned to a rough-hewn picnic table next to a stack of firewood. "I haven't even gotten your full name. Things happened sorta quickly."

"It's Delbert Peltier. I deliver for Meals on Wheels."

"Nice to meet you, Mr. Peltier."

While Del slowly made his way to the table, Ron pulled out the small tablet he kept in his shirt pocket and began taking notes.

"We'll get your other particulars later. I'm Deputy Ron Grafton, Washington County Sheriff's department." He extended his hand across the table.

Del's hand quaked a bit as he accepted it.

Ron gazed around, noticing the moss-covered underpinning of the old log cabin. He wondered how much longer the structure would stand. Torn screens, peeling paint, a crumbling stone chimney, and warped cedar shingles also spoke to that issue.

"Looks like this cabin has been here a long time," he said to Del. "The fieldstone foundation is sinking."

"I've never seen any maintenance. Place is as old and beat up as I am." Del gave a wheezy laugh.

Ron chuckled with him. "An investigator's on his way, Del. He'll want to talk with you. Meanwhile, think about anything in the cabin you might have touched. He'll want to know that."

Del visibly shivered. Ron knew the last thing the old man wanted to think about was what was inside the cabin. For that matter, Ron didn't want to think about it either.

As if in agreement, Brodie whined and pulled on the leash. A flock of chickadees skittered noisily amid the branches of an old oak tree.

CHAPTER 4

Thirty minutes later, Investigator Chris Majek arrived at Doyle's cabin. Chris always looked on top of his game: shirt stiffly starched, pants creased, shoes highly polished, mustache neatly trimmed and sporting a hint of gray, and muscular body stressing the seams of his uniform. He had earned a reputation for doggedness when investigating crimes.

"Hey, Ron," Chris said.

As he slapped the deputy's back, Chris silently took note of odd stains streaked on the front of Ron's shirt. Knowing Ron did not have a reputation for neatness, he decided to forego asking him about it.

"I keep meaning to call you about our hunting trip," Chris said. "Almost time to head to South Dakota and kill us some pheasants." He smiled for a moment, then let it fade. "What do you have for me here?"

Ron grimaced. "You go have a look. It's pretty messy."

"Suicide?"

"Your call. The old man over there, Del Peltier, found him." He nodded at Del, still sitting at the picnic table, staring at the lake. "He's pretty rattled. I feel sorry for him. Says he stepped in some blood and dropped a bag of food in there as he ran out. Made it outside just in time." His eyes darted toward the vomit.

"What was he doing here?"

"He delivers for Meals on Wheels."

"He clean?" Chris asked, though he knew the answer.

"He's fine," Ron confirmed. "Actually, I didn't even feel the need to check him."

"Got it. I'll get to him in a minute."

As Chris took a step toward the cabin, a dog started barking. He looked over to see a golden retriever looking eagerly back at him.

"Oh, yeah," Ron added. "Be careful where you walk. The old man's bloody footprint is in there, and the dog tracked blood all over the place—and me." He pointed to his shirt. "The deceased is in the back of the cabin. Down the hall to the den. Just follow the trail."

Chris glanced over at the retriever. *Nice-looking animal*, he thought as he pulled on a pair of booties.

Inside, Chris followed the rusty prints down the hallway and to the doorway of the den. He, too, noticed the cigarette butt.

Peering into the den, he found Father James Doyle. Already attracted to the nutritious plasma, blowflies were busy creating their next generation.

Skull fragments, high-velocity blood spatter, and brain matter had found purchase on a flat-screen computer monitor, the wall, and the ceiling.

Thick blackening blood had spread amoeba-like some distance from the body, soaking the once-beige carpet nearly to the doorway. Inside the bloodstain was a distinct footprint and a brown paper bag. The footprint turned and tracked back to the front door of the cabin, where it became barely visible. Blood had migrated up the side of the bag and had terminated with a rusty tinge, not unlike the pattern of paper chromatography.

Without going farther into the room, Chris squatted down to look at the body. Doyle's left eye was partially open, as if savoring one last glimpse of life before his soul departed. The right eye was closed. The face was distended.

He had been shot in the forehead, but from Chris's position, he couldn't see a contact wound. For that matter, he couldn't see a gun.

There was a mostly dried puddle soaked into the carpet beneath Doyle's black slippers. The smell of urine was unmistakable.

Chris also noted the cupric odor of blood, the pungent remnants of cigar smoke, and the distinct scent of cordite. Cordite, smokeless gunpowder, always seemed to linger in a small room such as this.

Chris left the den and exited the cabin, taking care not to disturb anything. Ron looked up expectantly.

"I can take it from here," Chris told him. "Why don't you head out to secure the road? Leave your Christmas lights on." Then he added, "And let's talk soon about the trip."

Ron nodded. "Ten-four, buddy."

As Ron slid into his SUV, Chris strolled over to Del, who turned his attention from the lake.

"Hello, sir," Chris said. "I'm Investigator Chris Majek. Thanks for your patience and cooperation. I'll be with you in a moment." He gave the older man a warm but authoritative smile.

Del's face was tight and weary, but Chris's smile did seem to put him at ease. He nodded without a word, then set his eyes back on the lake.

From his spot by the birch tree, the dog lifted his head and ears as Chris looked his way. Chris gave him the same smile too.

Walking over to the front steps, Chris punched the BCA number into his cell phone. The scene required more-sophisticated forensic analysis than his department could provide. As the phone rang, he took a moment to prepare himself. He knew who would be on the other end.

"Bureau of Criminal Apprehension, this is Marty," a woman answered.

"Chris Majek, Washington County," he announced, trying to start things on an appropriately professional note. Of course, he knew it was futile.

"Oh, hey, Adonis!" Marty exclaimed. "Haven't seen your handsome face in a long while!"

Chris let out a silent sigh. Even in the current cultural climate, Marty didn't understand—or perhaps chose to ignore—the nuances between flirting and friendliness in a professional setting. She was married, as was Chris, so it all seemed harmless. Still, each and every interaction with Marty required his careful—and slightly uncomfortable—navigation.

"Say, you still got that mustache?" He could hear her smiling and maybe even winking as she spoke.

"Yep. Gives me authority!" he tried to joke. He cleared his throat. "Anyway, it looks like we need some expertise on a case we have up here in Scandia."

At last, that seemed to send the conversation in the right direction.

"I'll see who's working investigations," Marty said. "They're in and out so much these days—I never know for sure who's available." She paused to check the log. "It looks like Agent Phil Walker is still in. Hang on just a sec. I'll put you through to him." With one last parting shot, she added, "Don't be a stranger, eh?"

He shook his head. She couldn't hide her Canadian heritage. Nor her affection for him.

On the first ring, the raspy voice of a longtime smoker answered. "This is Walker."

"Hey, Phil. Chris Majek."

"Chris!" Phil responded in recognition. "Last time I saw you was on the Lindstrom case."

"Yeah. Couple winters ago."

"If I recall, you also helped search for that girl ..." He tapped the desk with his fingers. "What was her name ... Janicke?"

"Close. It was Jelinek. Danielle Jelinek. Actually, the Chisago officers found her body. We just assisted. Tough one, searching that swamp."

"I remember when the boyfriend was arrested."

"Schnagl was his name," Chris added. "I remember— the girl OD'd on drugs he gave her. He let her wander off on her own half naked. Nice guy."

Chris could hear the distinct sound of paper tearing—most likely packets of sugar for a coffee, judging by the slurp that followed.

"Nice of you to assist the Chisago officers," Phil said. "Your people should be proud."

"Thanks. Did you know they found her body on her parents' wedding anniversary?"

"Ouch. That's a bitch. Great gift."

"Anyway," Chris began, "the reason I'm calling is because we've got ourselves a dead priest in a cabin on Goose Lake. The scene's strange. I'd like you guys to assist with forensics."

"What's strange?"

"A couple of things. Looks like he pissed himself before he died. He was wearing slippers. They're soaked, so it seems he was standing when he pissed. But now he's on his back. And there's a good-sized hole in his forehead too, either a nine millimeter or a forty caliber. Probably forty."

"Suicide maybe?" Phil offered.

"I suppose it's possible, but personally, I'd be surprised. No gun, unless it's under the body. And he was shot in the forehead, but I didn't see a contact wound. I'd expect one if it were suicide."

"What else is odd?"

Chris leaned against the railing, then quickly realized he was asking too much of the rotting wood. Instead, he meandered over and propped himself against his squad car.

"Well, the guy's buck naked except for a clerical collar and the slippers." He paused. "Oh yeah, the dog did a good job of contaminating the scene."

"Please tell me the dog was removed."

"He was—but not until he jumped on Ron Grafton and messed up his uniform."

"Probably took one look at Grafton and assumed he had some leftover food."

Chris laughed. "Never thought of that!"

"What about robbery? Any sign?"

Chris glanced at the cabin and shook his head. "Don't think so. But the place looks like a mess anyway. Boxes all over."

"Okay," Phil stated. "Give me the address, and I'll be up ASAP with Crime Scene. Within an hour if the place is easy to find. If I recall, GPS doesn't work too well in that part of the county."

"It's a couple miles north on County Three, off Highway 97. I've got Grafton at the end of the drive to make it easy for you. Just look for the lucky bastard's new SUV."

"Have him light up his colors."

With a smile, Chris looked down the driveway at the flashing lights breaking through the nearly bare trees. "Already told him."

CHAPTER 5

While he waited for Phil and the BCA Crime Scene unit, Chris turned his attention back to Del. Apparently, the zen of staring at the lake had run its course. The old man was now pacing nervously around the picnic table, tugging at his beard and coughing intermittently.

Chris retrieved a clipboard and an ICR sheet from the car, then headed to the picnic table. "Mr. Peltier, why don't we sit down? I've got to ask you a few questions while we wait for the Crime Scene guys."

Both men took a seat. Chris took his pen in hand.

"OK, now, let me get your full name."

Del coughed again. "Delbert Allen Peltier. That's P-E-L-T-I-E-R."

"Is that A-L-A-N or A-L-L-E-N?" Chris asked, spelling out the two possibilities.

"With an *e*."

"Got it. Thank you, Delbert."

"Please call me Del. Delbert sounds like a name from some goofy soap opera." He took a wheezy breath. "Wife used to watch those dumb shows all the time."

"Del it is." Chris looked at his watch. "Again, your

patience is appreciated. We should be able to get you home while it's still light."

"Thanks!" Del thumbed at the Caddy. "I don't want to get a ticket for a dead headlight."

Chris chuckled. "We'll make sure that doesn't happen." He glanced down at the report, then back up at Del. "So, what time did you get here today?"

"Right about noon. Father Doyle is my last delivery stop."

Chris leaned forward so he could better hear Del. His voice was fading even more. "Did you see or meet any other vehicles on the road to the cabin?"

"Nope. I was the only one. Of course, Father Doyle's minivan was parked in front, where it is now." Del pointed to the battered Town & Country. Dried leaves speckled the faded blue exterior.

"Does he always park in the same spot?"

Del shrugged. "Guess so. The car's there every time I come."

"How about on County Road Three? Did you see any vehicles?"

Del paused, then shrugged again. "Nothing that seemed out of place. Utility trucks, some SUVs—everybody out here seems to drive an SUV now."

"Anything unusual about the cabin when you arrived? Anything out of order?"

Del thought a moment. "Well, yeah." His voice rose, which of course made him cough. "The newspaper. It was still on the porch."

Chris raised his eyebrows. "That's unusual?"

"Yeah. It's never been there any other time I've delivered."

"Do you know who delivers the paper?"

"No idea. Probably someone from Scandia or near the area."

Chris made a note on the ICR. "Did you notice anything else different?"

"He and the dog are usually at the door when I arrive." The coughs were hard to stop now, but Del tried to wheeze through. "Not this time. And I only had to open the screen door. The inside door was wide open. Before I went inside"—more coughs and wheezes—"I called Father's name several times."

Chris nudged forward even more. "I'm sorry—can you speak up just a bit? Actually," he said, leaning back, "how about I get you some water?"

Del could only nod as the coughs consumed him.

Chris quickly retrieved a bottle of water from his squad. He gave it to Del, who took a long drink.

"That's better," Del said. He wiped his lips on his jacket sleeve. "Thank you."

Clearly seeing the exchange, the dog began barking and whining.

With a smirk, Chris stood up, got another bottle of water from his squad, and found a dish sitting beside the porch. He poured water into the dish and brought it over to the dog. The retriever eagerly drank, then sat up so Chris could pat his head and scratch his ears.

Before returning to the picnic table, Chris motioned for the dog to lie down, which he did.

Obedient, Chris thought.

"Now, Del," Chris continued, "once you were in inside, how about smells? Any unusual smells you detected? Perfume, men's cologne, anything like that?"

Del took a deep sniff, as if that would jog his memory. "Cigar smoke, for sure. And some other smell I didn't recognize, but it was strong." He grimaced.

Chris assumed was the combination of urine, cordite, and blood.

"How about cigarette smoke?" Chris asked, remembering the butt by the den doorway.

Del shook his head emphatically "Nope, just cigar. I'd know—damn tobacco is what got me this COPD. I hate those things." Del scowled, coughed as proof, then took another drink of water.

"Did you touch anything inside the house?"

"I think just the wall, when I ran out. I stumbled. Wanted to get the heck out of there. Pronto."

"How about Father Doyle? Did you touch his body?"

Del reeled back. "Are you kidding?"

"The paper bag on the carpet," Chris continued. "That his lunch?"

"Yeah. I dropped it. Wasn't about to go back and pick it up."

"Not a problem." Chris nodded. "How long have you known Father Doyle?"

Del doubled over with another bout of coughing. "Sorry." He cleared his throat and took another drink. "Um, let me think…three years. That's how long I've been delivering his noon meal."

"You didn't know him before delivering his meals?"

"No, sir."

"You deliver every day?"

Del shook his head. "Nope. Just Monday, Wednesday, and Friday."

"Who delivered to Father Doyle before you started?"

"I think it was Spitzmuller. Jim, his name was. He died a couple years ago."

Chris scribbled the man's name as quickly as he could, not bothering to ask about the spelling. "Does another agency deliver on the days you don't?"

"I really don't know," Del admitted. "But rural areas like this often have local organizations that provide meals—Lion's Club or something."

"Where was your last delivery before coming here?"

"Off Highway Ninety-Five. Pilar Avenue. Mrs. Sweeney. Mildred. Used to be a good friend of my wife's."

Chris noted that this was the second time Del had referred to his wife in the past tense.

"What time did you deliver to Mrs. Sweeney?" he continued.

"Must have been around eleven forty. Wait." He stopped. "It was eleven forty-five. I remember now."

"So you came straight here after the Sweeney delivery?"

"Yes, sir. I did. I like to get done and go home for an afternoon nap."

Chris chuckled. "What did you do before volunteering for Meals on Wheels?"

"I've been retired twenty-plus years now. The wife and me traveled a lot, mostly Florida for the winter."

Chris made eye contact with Del and gave a slight nod of understanding. "Before you retired, what was your occupation?"

"I worked for IBM. Electrical engineer. Down in Rochester."

"Back to Father Doyle." Chris paused. "I'm not sure what happened here, but can you think of anyone who might want to hurt him?"

Del slowly shook his head. "He never mentioned anything like that."

"Did he ever give you the feeling that he was worried about something?"

"No." Del looked over at the cabin as if remembering the man who now lay inside with most of his head missing. "He didn't talk to me much. Quiet guy. When I'd deliver his meals, he'd just say thanks. Never invited me in or anything. I'd never been inside the cabin—until today. Brodie—the dog—sort of led me to the back room."

Chris glanced over at Brodie. The dog was asleep.

"Did Doyle always wear his clerical collar, Del?"

Chris met Del's eyes, but then the elder man looked down. He, too, had seen that the priest was wearing nothing but his collar.

"No. He never wore it when he'd meet me at the door."

Chris set his pen down. "When the crime scene techs get here, they'll test your hands for GSR and get your fingerprints."

"GSR?"

"Gunshot residue."

"I'm a suspect?" Del squawked.

Chris shook his head. "Just routine. If this turns out to be a homicide, defense attorneys will ask why things like this weren't checked. Meanwhile, please call me if you think of anything else. Absolutely anything." Chris gave him his card. "I'll need your contact number as well, in case we have more questions." Chris glanced over at the dog and started to say something else, but then he decided to wait. "Anyway, the crime unit should be here any sec. We'll get your hands swabbed right away. You can wait here or sit in your car. Don't leave until I get back to you."

Del headed for his Caddy.

Minutes later, Phil arrived in his squad, followed by the Crime Scene van. The techs swabbed Del's hands and took his fingerprints. The spectrometer would find no trace of nitrites. His fingerprints were not in the criminal database.

Chris walked over to shake Phil's hand and update him on the situation. The BCA agent was nearly bald, an inch over six feet, and slightly built. His nervous eyes were coal black, matching his black BCA jacket.

Surveying the den, he quickly confirmed it was not a suicide.

Under his direction, the team went to work scouring the cabin for evidence. Technicians shuffling around in booties and white-hooded suits made for a busy scene.

Some of the techs lit the cabin interior with a lightning storm of photographic strobes; others dusted for prints. A blood spatter expert meticulously photographed and measured the angle of blood droplets. Interpretation of the spatter would help determine the position of Doyle's body when the bullet took his life.

Donned with goggles and an alternative light source, another technician looked for fibers and other evidence not readily visible to the naked eye. The cabin was darkened with black drapes, and BLUESTAR was sprayed to detect evidence of blood that may have been cleaned up. The cigarette butt was collected and placed in a paper evidence envelope.

Taking advantage of the activity, Chris went outside and approached Del, who was still sitting in his car. Del lowered the window.

"There's something I need to talk with you about," Chris said in a quiet voice. He looked around and made sure no one could hear them.

Chris's nervousness sparked Del's. After all, he had yet to be released from the crime scene.

"Detective, er, Investigator, I hope you don't think that I—"

"No, no, not at all!" Chris quickly reassured. "Actually, this has to do with the dog."

"Brodie?"

"Yes, Brodie. How long have you known him?" Chris leaned in through the open window.

Del took off his glasses and rubbed his eyes. "Like I said before—three years. He's been here ever since I started delivering."

"And he's not a biter?"

"He's a golden retriever," Del said, as if that were answer enough. "He's always been friendly with me. Only time I ever saw him get crazy was just today."

"Do you think he'd be good around kids?"

"It wouldn't surprise me. Glenda—that's my deceased wife—Glenda and me had a golden retriever before we started to travel. Couldn't have a dog after that. He was real good with the grandkids."

Watching the door to the cabin, Chris spoke with an urgent whisper. "Del, I'm wondering…could you take Brodie home with you?"

Del held up his hands in protest. "I'm too old to take care of a dog. When he has to go outside—"

"No, no—just for a few days," Chris clarified. "Just take him home with you for a few days. When I'm ready to come get him, I'll call you. Then I'll make sure he goes to a good home." Chris paused, choosing not to reveal that the good home would be his own. "There'll be a few bucks in it for you too." He leaned in further and patted Del's back.

"Am I going to get into trouble over this? I mean, won't it look bad if I take his dog home?"

Chris waved his hand. "It's fine. We do this whenever we want to make sure a pet goes to a good home." Chris stroked his mustache. "Otherwise, there's a lot of red tape. Shelters get involved, you know. You don't want to see Brodie go to a shelter, do you?" Chris protruded his lower lip in a pouty face. "What if he were put to sleep?" He stared unblinking at Del.

The thought of Brodie being euthanized was more than Del could handle. He gave a quiet nod.

Chris opened the rear door of the Caddy and moved the Styrofoam cooler to the side. He then went over to Brodie, who quickly scrambled to his feet. Chris checked the dog's feet—the blood was mostly dry now. Not that the Seville was in mint condition, but Chris didn't want bloodstains all over it.

Brodie whined excitedly as Chris took him off the leash and led him to the car. After a gentle nudge to his backside, Brodie climbed into the car and hopped onto the seat next to the cooler.

CHAPTER 6

The first flakes of snow were falling when Chris turned onto the southbound I-35 freeway from Forest Lake. Not yet sanded, the highway was slippery over the bridge decks.

Having just completed a vigorous workout at the Scandia fire station gym, Chris was on his way to Saint Paul to meet with Agent Walker at the BCA headquarters. The radio station was playing "All Night Long," his favorite song by the Mavericks. He was looking forward to their appearance at the State Theatre in the spring. He cranked up the volume, sang along with the music, and settled back for the drive.

After maneuvering around what seemed to be endless and ever-changing road construction, he exited onto Maryland Avenue, crossed over the freeway, and headed east through several blocks of houses and small businesses. Arriving at the modern three-story brick-and-glass building, he parked, pushed through the heavy doors, and stomped the slush off his feet on the entry mat.

At the reception desk, Marty was busy with a phone call. She looked up and broke into a broad, toothy smile when she saw him. She gave him a "be right with you" gesture.

Chris gave her the "take your time" wave in return. He removed his mirrored sunglasses and slipped them into his jacket pocket. This day, he was dressed in Levi's, Converse tennis shoes, and a maroon Forest Lake Rangers T-shirt that stretched across his muscular pecs. When he slid off his brown sheriff's jacket, blue veins could be seen coursing their way up his biceps.

Finished with the phone call, Marty stood to greet him. "Oh my God!" she said loudly enough to attract the attention of others in the lobby. "The Great Investigator is here in the flesh!" She twirled her thick red hair into ringlets. "You look just as good in your civvies as you do in uniform."

Chris involuntarily cringed, though it was easy to mistake as a smile.

"You're too kind, Marty," he replied.

"And I love that mustache! The hint of gray looks good."

Few people knew that as soon as he was old enough, Chris had grown the mustache to hide the scar from a hockey injury.

Marty smiled, sat back down, and swept another wisp of hair from her face. "So, how ya been? You look good." She was outright flirting now.

"You look good too."

A half-truth. Although somewhat attractive, Marty's face showed the fatigue of a party girl. Thick eyeshadow tried to cover up the evidence of late nights and heavy drinking.

"That lucky guy you married must be taking good care

of you," Chris said, more for the sake of the people eaves-dropping in the lobby.

It was Marty's turn to cringe and pass it off as a smile. "Three years now, and we're still married." She held up three fingers. "Second time for us both, you know. Pretty good for a couple of Canadian immigrants. Guess we learned something the first time." The tone of her voice was not convincing.

"I hear the second time around is usually better," Chris replied. Having been happily married for nearly twenty years, he couldn't really relate, but it seemed the appropriate thing to say. "Hey, I'd love to stay and chat, but I need to meet with Walker."

Marty held up a hand. "Quick question before you go. Do you and your friends still go pheasant hunting at that fancy ranch in South Dakota?"

"As a matter of fact, we do. How'd you hear about that?"

"From lots of envious agents around here." She winked, but then she blushed and looked down. "Actually, I was wondering if you'd have a spot for Matt. My husband."

Chris was speechless. He'd never met Matt in his life. He barely knew Marty, for that matter. Chris had been going on this hunting trip for several years with his good friends Paul Thomas and Ron Grafton. The trio had an easy camaraderie. Chris wasn't sure about adding a complete stranger to the mix. But maybe Matt would turn out to be a perfect fit.

Or maybe not.

"Does Matt hunt?" he finally asked.

"He does, yes." She twisted her hair, not flirtatiously but anxiously now. "A weekend away with a bunch of guys might do him some good. He's showing signs of the seven-year itch—about four years early." Realizing this wasn't the most persuasive argument, she shook her head and changed course. "I mean, he's a great guy. You guys will love him."

It didn't take a seasoned investigator to read between the lines. Chris scratched his head. "Gee, I don't know, Marty…"

She reached out and touched his arm. "Please, Chris. You'd be doing me a huge favor." She tried to smile, but her eyes were pleading.

Just then, her intercom buzzed. "That's Phil. He's testy," she added quietly. "Quit smoking a few days ago. On his birthday."

"What brought that on?" Chris asked, relieved to be talking about anything other than Matt. "I recall he was a heavy smoker."

"Doctor told him he damned well better. Something to do with a stress test." She motioned toward the security door. "I'll buzz you in."

The electronic lock clicked open.

"Do give it some thought about Matt joining you guys, will you?" she said. "And come down on a day off. We can have lunch, eh?" Her voice had once again taken on the singsong of a high school girl.

Chris laughed. "You still got that Canadian in you."

As he walked away, the back of his neck bristled with embarrassment at his unintended entendre. He hoped she had missed it. But he knew she hadn't. Not Marty.

Against his better judgment, he turned back to glance at her.

She gave him a coquettish grin.

Phil was sitting quietly at his desk, bending a paper clip, when Chris tapped on his door and entered. He looked up from his desk, an almost childish expression on his face.

"You ever smoke, Chris?"

"Nope. Never took it up. Never appealed to me. Can't stand the smell of 'em."

Chris draped his coat over the back of a chair and sat. He noticed the yellow nicotine stains still evident on Phil's fingers.

"Smart man," Phil replied. "I'm trying to quit. Doc said it's taking a toll. But quitting's a bitch. Three days so far, and it's all I think about. Now I'm trying to satisfy myself with coffee in my sugar." He nodded at a heap of empty sugar packets next to his coffee mug.

Chris smirked, remembering the sound of tearing paper during their earlier phone call.

"I've got the gum too." Phil fumbled in a desk drawer, pulled out a pack of nicotine gum, and tossed it on the table as if presenting key evidence. "But that stuff's expensive. I can drink coffee for free all day long here."

"Hang in there, Phil. I know you can do it."

"Speaking of smoking," Phil said, "one of our guys found a cigarette butt on the victim's floor yesterday. In the hallway by the den."

"Grafton noticed it too."

"Priest smoked cigars, though, so I doubt it's his. Maybe the meal delivery guy. What do you think?"

Chris shook his head. "No way. He's got a classic case of COPD. During the debriefing, he mentioned the cigar smell in the priest's cabin, said it reminded him how much he hated smoking. Have your DNA guys take a run at it. Might get lucky."

"It's already in the lab, but folks there are swamped. All these new DNA techniques mean they're reprocessing old cases. They said they'd get to it soon as they can."

Chris raised an eyebrow. "Can we push them on this?"

"All I can do is ask. We're at their mercy." Phil gave a shrug of surrender, then sighed. "This is an odd case. My gut says there's a lot we don't know about this priest. Being naked and wearing that collar is over the top. Just when you think you've seen it all, something like *this* comes up."

"Kind of weird, if you ask me." Chris shuddered.

"I wonder whether the perp was someone who had a serious motive to kill him or whether it was just a nutcase who did this for fun."

"My guess is, someone had a hard-on for him," Chris ventured.

Phil let out a snort. "So you saw that crap on his computer?"

"No. Screen was blank when I was there. Must have been in sleep mode."

"Well, we activated it. The priest was into teenage boys."

Chris slumped back. "You shitting me?"

"Nope. We confiscated the computer. If there's anything there that'll help us, our guys will find it. Also, something appeared to be written on the computer screen."

Now Chris leaned forward again. "Which was . . . ?"

"Dunno. Nothing that made any sense to me. The lab guys are working on that too."

Chris stood, stretched, and looked absently around the room. His eyes landed on the window overlooking the parking lot. He walked over and looked out. Heavy snow was falling now.

"I envy the guy who runs the plow. Does his job, then goes home to the family." He gazed for a few more moments, then turned back to Phil. "Anyway, what else did you find?"

"A bunch of DVDs stacked on his bookcase—more kiddie shit. The only things on the shelf that weren't dusty. He must've looked at them often."

Chris turned back to the window, shuddering again. "Wonder where he got the stuff."

Phil cleared his throat. "Kiddie porn used to come out of Denmark, Sweden, and the Netherlands. Now, due to statutory changes, most of it originates in Southeast Asia. From there, it's often smuggled into Canada."

"And once it gets to Canada," Chris continued, "there are a million places it can cross our border." He returned to the chair and sat down.

"Right." Phil sighed. "Also, it looks like the priest's read every Sandford novel. He's got at least thirty in his bookcase."

"Interesting irony! Sanford's crime novels were often about 'prey'—just like the kids on those DVDs."

"Sick bastard!" Phil shook his head in disgust. "It takes only a few of these pedophiles to make all priests look bad."

"Yeah. They're the ones who make the news. Unfortunate reality." Chris thought for a moment. "What about the projectile? Any info on that? Was it a forty caliber or nine millimeter?"

"You made a good call. It was a forty, like you thought." He reached for his coffee mug, tipped it toward Chris for emphasis, then took a loud sip. "More specifically, a Federal Cartridge Hydra-Shok, one-hundred-and-eighty-grain jacketed hollow point."

"Pretty good punch."

"Whoever did this wanted maximum damage. Those hollow points expand like crazy when they hit bone. If all our perp wanted was a kill, a twenty-two would have done the job."

"So you found the projectile or just the casing?"

"The projectile. Our crime scene techs dug it out of a wall stud behind the computer. Lucky they found it. If it hadn't hit the stud, it would have gone all the way through the wall, and we may not have found it. Hole in the Sheetrock indicated it was flattened out the size of a nickel before it hit the two-by-four. No wonder his head exploded like that." Phil closed his eyes and gave a faint twitch.

"What about time of death?"

"Yes. Doc McPhearson, our illustrious medical examiner, estimated the time of death to be about ten hours before the old man found him. That puts it around two in the morning. The estimate was based on the temperature in the cabin, the state of rigor mortis, and the livor mortis." Phil stretched his arms out and interlaced his fingers behind his head. "But he emphasized it's just that, an estimate."

"I'm amazed they can get it as close as they do."

"No kidding." Phil cleared his throat again. "Did you see any sign of a struggle?"

Chris shook his head. "Didn't notice that."

"I agree with you, though—it does look like he pissed himself. Also, it was hot in there. Your guys didn't mess with the thermostat, did they?" Phil asked.

"No one touched it. Standard protocol." He paused with thought. "I suppose if you're sitting around naked, you need to keep your house extra warm."

Phil bobbed his head at the theory. "Did your guys come up with anything from the neighborhood?"

"We checked the houses and cabins on either side of the property and across the road. The Meals on Wheels guy said he didn't notice anything unusual—although he is damn near blind. And we talked with the woman who delivers the newspaper."

"Anything?"

"She never got out of her car. Just chucked the paper on the porch, turned around on the grass, and left. Said it was around five a.m. And she was positive she didn't meet another car on the road, coming in or going out."

"What about the rest of the neighborhood?"

Chris gave a dismissive shrug. "Couple of families are gone for the winter. We got in touch, but they were no help. Said they didn't see anyone snooping around before they left."

"So, no one saw anybody checking out the area, no cars going by late at night…?"

"Nothing anyone reported."

Phil picked up another paper clip. "The diocese in Avon said Doyle had been a speech teacher at St. Michael's College, up in Bakerville. They have no record of any family still living. And the diocese owns the property—Doyle was getting a free ride. The diocese just declared bankruptcy, so I bet they sell it quick."

"So does the diocese own the dog too?" Chris appeared to be making a joke, but he was suddenly wondering about a possible complication.

Phil chuckled. "I honestly don't know. By the way, what *is* the deal with the dog?"

"The dog?" Chris stroked his mustache, a nervous habit. "I guess if no one comes forward to claim him, he'll make a great pet. Looks like the Meals guy took him for a while," he added, in case anyone noticed him putting Brodie in Del's car.

Phil worked the paper clip until it broke in two, then he tossed the pieces into the wastebasket. He reached for his coffee, only to find nothing more than a sip left.

His intercom buzzed.

"What, Marty?" he snapped.

"Dr. McPhearson's holding on line three-one. Can you take it?"

Phil sat forward, punched the lighted button, and took the call. "Hi, Doc! You finish the post on the priest?"

As Phil listened intently, Chris watched his face for any clues. Suddenly, Phil's dark eyes widened.

"Well, I do love surprises. We'll be right down." He disconnected and looked at Chris. "You got time to run to the ME's office with me? Doc McPhearson says there's something unusual he wants to show us."

"Sure. Let's go."

Chris grabbed his jacket from the chair.

Phil grabbed the pack of gum from his desk.

CHAPTER 7

Driving westbound on Maryland Avenue for nearly two miles in slow rush-hour traffic was frustrating. However, being in a marked squad car allowed them to move through traffic more easily. They entered the freeway and drove south to University Avenue.

At the stop sign by the University exit, a group of young men sauntered defiantly across the intersection. With attitude, caps askew, and pants barely hanging on, the youths shot hostile looks at the occupants of the squad car.

"Now there's an industrious group," Phil commented. "Success written all over them. They even wear their hats in the 'stupid' position."

Chris gazed at the young men. "I gotta feel sorry for those kids and others like 'em," he said quietly. "I wonder what their lives are like at home. If there is a home."

Phil stretched his fingers, then curled them around the steering wheel again. "You're right. Guess I'm just getting a little jaded after so many years in law enforcement."

They crossed the intersection and parked in one of the few available slots in the well-plowed lot. Because the medical examiner contracted with many jurisdictions, police vehicles from different counties occupied most of the spaces.

"Looks like the ME has a busy day," Chris said.

"From what I hear, they need a larger morgue. A new one's scheduled for construction in the next couple of years."

"Hope they get a bigger parking lot too," Chris added as they climbed out of the squad.

With collars raised and coats held close to their bodies, they leaned into the northwest wind as they made their way to the entrance of the Ramsey County Medical Examiner's Office. Chris was carrying a clipboard, which he instinctively positioned as a makeshift shield against the biting gusts.

The agency was housed in a nondescript one-story brown-brick building dwarfed by the adjacent Regions Hospital. The morgue was windowless except for the conference room and small offices that bordered the parking lot and the back of the building.

Deanna, the devoted protector of the front door, admitted them. Businesslike, adorned with glasses on a gold chain, and not prone to warmth, she slid open the glass window between her and the men. She forced what was meant to be a smile and pointed down the hall to the autopsy suite.

"He's waiting."

She then slid the glass window shut and went back to her computer.

Chris and Phil exchanged smirks as they shook snow from their coats and left them in the reception area.

Neither of the men enjoyed morgue visits. Often a grief-stricken family was present in the small serenity room off the lobby, tearfully learning the disturbing details of a loved one's death. There was also the cascade of vile smells that combined to be something indescribable, often nauseating.

They walked past a small office, where a young technician was eating a sandwich.

"How anyone could eat in a place like this is beyond me," Chris said, swallowing phlegm that suddenly bubbled in the back of his throat.

"We shoulda hit that Culver's before we got here," Phil added. "'Cause I don't think I'll wanna stop on the way back." He reached for a tissue in his pocket, spit out the gum he had been chewing, then wadded the tissue into his pocket.

They approached the double doors to what was generally referred to as the "cutting room." The scream of a Stryker saw could be heard whining, bogging down, and revving up as it separated bone from its deceased owner. The sound escalated when they opened the door. It ceased when Dr. Gregory McPhearson became aware of their presence.

He was a tall, slender, arrogant man with once red but now white-blondish hair and a freckled complexion. Like his guardian of the front door, the doctor was not given to amiability. Any semblance of pleasantry was actually just patronizing pomp.

He removed the acrylic splash guard, pulled the green face mask below his chin, and acknowledged them with a counterfeit smile. It was not a good time to shake hands.

McPhearson pointed to a box of masks and vinyl gloves that sat on a stainless steel sink. Chris and Phil put them on before moving closer to the dissecting table where Father James Doyle's body lay.

"Gentlemen," McPhearson began, "thank you for coming so quickly. I appreciate it. As you can see, I have another client awaiting my skilled hands." He gestured toward the body of a woman on a stainless steel tray, her pubic area covered by a green cloth.

Chris and Phil glanced at each other over their masks, noting McPhearson's arrogance.

Unaware of or perhaps just unbothered by his own tone, McPhearson continued. "As I mentioned on the phone, I found something unusual inside the priest. But before I reveal the surprise, I must go over the basics."

He's gonna milk this "surprise" thing as long as he can, Chris thought. Another glance at Phil revealed that the BCA agent was thinking along the same lines.

"Your victim was shot from just a few inches away." McPhearson lifted the hands of the dead priest. "See the gunpowder tattooing?"

Chris and Phil moved closer to the body, noticing black speckling on Doyle's hands.

"The muzzle was no more than eighteen inches away," McPhearson said. "The firearms experts did the estimate. The residue would indicate he knew he was about to be shot. It would be instinctual to cover one's face in such a situation. The stippling is obvious on his forehead as well." He pointed to the dead priest's left index finger. "And see here? The projectile just nicked it."

"Interesting," Phil said, looking at Chris.

Chris nodded in affirmation.

McPhearson moved on. "Your priest knew death was imminent. His bladder let go. He was standing when he was shot. There's evidence of dried urine on his legs, feet, and slippers."

Chris was jotting on his clipboard. "Fear, right?"

"Very good, Investigator." McPhearson's chest puffed. He enjoyed interacting with his audience.

"I'm surprised that's *all* that let go," Phil added.

Chris stifled a laugh.

McPhearson ignored the comment.

"Sorry, Doc," Phil apologized.

McPhearson also ignored the apology. "Another thing I'd like to point out is the livor mortis." The doctor pointed to the purple skin visible on the underside of the priest's body.

Chris tapped his pen on the clipboard. "Isn't that because the blood—"

"Yes." McPhearson did not let him finish. "It's also called postmortem lividity." He smiled, demonstrating his knowledge. "It is because the blood settles in what we call the dependent position, the position of the body that is closest to gravity at the time of death."

"I also see discoloration on the back of his arms," Chris added.

"Very observant, Investigator." McPhearson smiled broadly. "You've been paying attention. I have taught you well. Now, let's take a look at the little surprise I have for you, shall we?"

Chris heard Phil let out a sigh, tiring of McPhearson's self-importance.

"Before the surprise is removed, I wanted you to see it in situ, meaning right where I found it." He smiled again as he demonstrated his medical expertise.

As McPhearson activated the overhead halogen lamps, Doyle's skin took on a ghastly pallor in contrast to the dark-red cavity that had been stripped of its thoracic organs.

"The surprise, gentlemen, is inside this." He pointed to the stomach, which was neatly incised by the blade of a scalpel. "I first noticed it on the x-rays. Didn't know what it was until I opened his stomach, which was otherwise empty."

With gloved hands, he parted the incision, inviting them to peer inside.

Phil and Chris reluctantly leaned inward, both grimacing at the smell of the internal organs. Inside the stomach was what looked to be a puddle of blood with lumps in it.

"What are we looking at here?" Phil asked. He glanced at Chris, who just shrugged.

McPhearson continued to enjoy every minute of his dramatic production. "Let's take a closer look, shall we?"

Using tissue forceps, he probed into the incision. With a flourish, he pulled out the mystery item and held it aloft. The toothed grips of the forceps held a short chain of small red orbs.

Chris and Phil both took a step forward.

McPhearson held the chain over the dissection table and rinsed it with a spray of distilled water. The water ran toward the drain, carrying clotted blood and particles of tissue. McPhearson then held the object up to the lights.

Hanging on a silver chain were ten small evenly spaced

stones, each with multiple facets. They glowed bloodred under the bright halogens.

A decade of a rosary.

Phil gasped. "What the hell?" He poked Chris with his elbow.

"You've got to be kidding me!" Chris exclaimed. "You mean someone forced that down his throat?"

McPhearson shook his head crisply. "Definitely not forced down. There's no evidence of oral or pharyngeal injuries. I have to assume he swallowed it."

"Why in the world would anyone swallow *that?*" Chris wondered aloud.

With the air of a great observer, McPhearson gazed at the chain. "I know very little about these ... *doodads*"—his word choice reflected his opinion of religion—"but I do believe this one is rather unusual. It's almost a work of art." He paused, then drew a breath. "In any case, I need to photograph it. Then you may take it with you. Just give me a minute."

He rinsed the chain again, shook off the water, placed it on a gray board along with an ABFO ruler, and snapped several digital images.

"By the way, gentlemen, did you know that this odd-looking ruler was designed by a dentist for accurate photography of injuries and physical evidence?"

"As a matter of fact, I did," Chris said.

McPhearson looked mildly irritated.

"My best buddy is a dentist," Chris added. "He's got one in his office. Showed me how it's used. Now I keep a couple in my crime scene kit."

With no comment, McPhearson finished taking photographs, then he dropped the chain into a biohazard evidence bag, sealed it with red Breakaway tape, and handed it to Phil.

"I'm sure your lab people know how to handle this," he said brusquely. The show was obviously over.

"Think they can get prints off it?" Chris asked.

"Due to the acidic environment of the stomach, I doubt your experts will find anything. But let them have a go at it."

"Won't hurt to try," Phil added, looking at Chris.

McPhearson closed the meeting. "Gentlemen, I have much work to do, so if you will excuse me. Before you leave, you need to sign for the evidence transfer."

"Will do," Phil said. "Thanks, Doc."

As Phil and Chris made their way to the door, McPhearson couldn't resist the last word. "You do have an odd case on your hands, gentlemen."

Phil leaned close to Chris and muttered, "No shit."

As soon as the heavy door of the cutting room closed behind Chris and Phil, the Stryker saw resumed its scream.

Chris and Phil signed for the evidence, then nodded goodbye to Deanna. Once outside the building, they gulped mouthfuls of frigid and blessedly clean air. Phil immediately followed it with a fresh piece of gum.

Both men were deep in thought as they drove back to BCA headquarters.

At last, Phil broke the silence. "This is nuts! We have a murdered priest wearing only slippers and a clerical collar while watching kiddie porn—and he somehow swallowed part of a rosary!"

Chris looked at Phil. "I'm beginning to think there's something highly personal about this case. There's no chance in hell someone would voluntarily swallow that."

There was no stop at Culver's.

CHAPTER 8

After Phil dropped him off at his car, Chris had a couple stops to make before he could make his way back home. He was glad he had his own car, since dog hair in a county vehicle would be hard to explain.

Brodie and Del were sitting next to each other on the front stoop waiting when Chris arrived.

"Mr. Peltier, thanks so much for taking care of Brodie," Chris said as he approached the pair. "Hope he wasn't too much trouble."

Brodie snuggled closer to Del and looked up at him.

With a subdued groan, Del struggled to stand up and shake hands. "I was glad to help out. Actually, I wish I could keep him, but I'm too old for that stuff."

As usual, fierce coughing rendered him unable to speak for almost a minute. Chris stroked Brodie, waiting patiently for the spell to stop.

"You saved him from the shelter," Chris added when Del finally caught his breath.

"Well, when you said he could be put down, that was what cinched it for me."

Chris felt a stab of guilt. Manipulating the old man into harboring the dog was not something he was proud of. He hated deception.

"I'd appreciate it if you'd keep this under your hat, Del. What we're doing isn't illegal, but it is a bit of a shortcut." He pulled out his wallet. "Here's fifty for your trouble."

Del shook his head firmly. "Not"—a cough gripped him—"not necessary, sir. If it kept Brodie safe, it was worth it."

Chris shoved the fifty into Del's jacket pocket.

"Thanks to you, Brodie will go to a good home quickly and without any red tape." Chris once again declined to admit it was his own home. "He's been through enough already."

"We *both* have!" Del looked up at the sky but missed sight of a bald eagle soaring over the Forest Lake shoreline. "It sure was weird seeing Father naked like that. It's like I can't unsee it now."

"Certainly a new experience for me too," Chris added. "And once was enough."

"I just can't imagine what was going on in that cabin." Del sighed deeply, following it with a cough. He rubbed the dog's chin. "We'll miss Father Doyle, won't we, Brodie?"

Brodie licked at Del's face.

Del looked up at Chris. "You have any idea why he was murdered, Investigator?"

Chris had heard this same question many times. His response was pat yet sincere. "No idea yet, but we'll find the unsub, I promise you."

"The un...what?"

"Oh, sorry. *Unsub* is police-talk for 'unknown subject of an investigation.' It's a term we use when we don't know who the perp—the suspect—is." He fell back into his standard response now. "But don't worry. We've got a lot of people working on this case. Hopefully we'll have some answers soon."

"I sure hope so," Del replied. "Things like this just don't happen much around here."

"That's good, don't you think?"

"For sure. Finding another dead body would do me in." The old man shuddered a bit, nearly inciting another coughing spell.

"Thanks again for taking care of Brodie, Del. You can be proud. You probably saved his life."

Del smiled.

"And remember, it's our secret." Chris drew an imaginary line across his tightened lips to make the point.

Del gave Chris a thumbs-up and a wink. "Glad to help, Investigator Majek."

Chris opened the back door to his Jeep. With gentle urging, Brodie jumped into the rear seat. Lying down, he rested his head on his forelegs, his tail softly thumping against the vinyl upholstery.

Once he was behind the wheel, Chris hooked his arm over the seat and looked back at Brodie. "Okay, buddy—here's the deal. Once we get home, you and I are in for a challenge. Mrs. Majek doesn't know about you."

With brown eyes and long golden lashes, Brodie looked up at Chris. He seemed to understand the future was still uncertain.

"But honestly, I'm betting that our best luck at winning

her over is to just show up. She's going to be pissed. Really pissed. But you're impossible not to love. You're just so damn cute."

Brodie definitely seemed to understand this. He confirmed it with a little bark.

To make the best impression possible, Chris took Brodie to PetSmart in Forest Lake for grooming. The newest Majek emerged soft and fluffy, with fur and nails trimmed and teeth cleaned. He was ready to win over the family. Or one member of the family in particular.

Chris carefully loaded Brodie, a huge bag of dog food, a bed, a leash, and various dog toys into the Jeep.

Now for the drive home.

The fifteen-minute drive to Scandia seemed like forever. With every passing mile, Chris rehearsed several approaches for presenting Brodie. No matter how he handled the situation, Kimber would not be happy.

They had argued about the "dog thing," as she called it, many times since their neighbors had gotten a dog last summer. He and the kids wanted one; she didn't, because she'd likely be the one caring for it.

And now here Chris was, a block from home, with a dog and all its necessary gear.

He made the final turn into his driveway as slowly as he could, tires crunching on the new snow. The overhead garage door screeched when he pushed the remote. He idled the Jeep into the garage, trying to make as little noise as possible.

Chris left Brodie in the vehicle and headed inside the house. The kids were sitting at the kitchen table doing homework. Which really meant they were each staring down at their phones, as usual.

"Hey, guys—can you come out to the garage?" he asked. "I've got a surprise for you."

The kids didn't move, but they did glance up at him, then at each other.

"A surprise . . . ?" fifteen-year-old Andy repeated.

Seventeen-year-old Laurie just stared, though there was definitely a sparkle in her eyes.

Chris stared back, stone faced. But soon he couldn't contain the grin on his face.

"Oh my gosh, Dad. Did you get us a *dog*?" Laurie said, her eyes getting wider.

Chris's grin grew wider too.

"You did, didn't you? You finally got us a dog!" Laurie now shouted excitedly.

"Take a look in the back seat." Chris pointed to the garage.

Both kids scrambled to their feet and raced into the garage. Brodie, standing on the seat, began scratching at the glass with his paw, his body trembling with excitement.

Instantly, the two teenagers melted into hysterics Chris hadn't seen since, well, the Christmas when Santa gave the kids their phones. Appropriately enough, Andy was holding up his phone now, taking video of Brodie and Laurie, but mostly himself screaming with joy into the screen. Brodie began spinning around on the seat and barking.

"This is Brodie," Chris said. "He'll be a new addition to our family. If Mom approves," he added quietly as he opened the door.

Brodie bounded out, tearing around the garage, nearly knocking Andy over. After several laps of sniffing everything, he settled down, as did the kids.

"I love him!" exclaimed Laurie, patting his back. "His fur is so soft."

Brodie licked her face and barked.

The utility door opened. Having just showered in preparation for their dinner with friends, Kimber stood in the doorway, barefoot and still in her robe.

"What's all the excitement?" she asked. Then she saw the dog, and her eyes widened, then narrowed.

"Mom!" Laurie said, beaming. "Look what Dad brought home! We can keep him, right?"

"Please, Mom?" Andy begged.

Kimber immediately knew Chris had hatched a scheme and positioned the kids as unwitting accomplices. Her glare was as cold as the air outside.

Chris cringed. "Hey, guys—take Brodie to the backyard. I need to talk with Mom." He grabbed the dog by the collar and attached the leash. "Not home yet, Brodie," he whispered. He handed the tether to Laurie, then scooted the kids out of the garage.

"So, Mr. Majek, you've really stepped in it this time." Kimber's voice was loud and razor edged.

"Please, Kimber, the neighbors—"

"I don't care about the neighbors!" Her eyes were on fire.

"Can we have a civil conversation about this?"

"Not when you do this behind my back! And *that*"—she pointed at the sack of dog food and other paraphernalia in the car—"tells me you have every intention of keeping the beast."

"Honey—"

"Furthermore," she continued, "I've been crystal clear about this 'dog thing' since day one. The Speers got a dog because Carrie is a stay-at-home mom. She has time for a dog. Both you and I work, and we know damn well which one of us will have to take care of that thing!" Her anger was rising to a new level. Her breath came in gasps. "Did you even stop to think for a minute how this will change our lives? Especially *mine*? Now I have to take care of him—it—whatever!"

Kimber stormed back inside, banging the door hard enough to rattle the garage walls. A rake fell off a hanger and clattered to the concrete floor.

Chris hurried inside after her. He found her in their bedroom, standing, arms crossed, staring out the window. The yard light illuminated the scene—the kids cavorting with Brodie. Their smiles were a mile wide. There was something sweetly reassuring to see that they were still kids at heart, no matter how old they were getting.

Kimber began to smile—which didn't go unnoticed. Thinking it was okay, Chris tried to put his arms around her.

"Honey—"

"Leave me alone!" she snapped, turning quickly away. "And don't 'honey' me!"

Kimber sat down firmly at her dressing table. "Christopher James Majek, what you did was below the belt. You ambushed me and used our kids as pawns."

She began brushing her hair. At first, her strokes were

rough and angry, but after a wince or two, she slowed down. Chris again noticed and hoped it was a good sign.

"Where did the damn dog come from, anyway?" she asked.

"The owner died suddenly." It wasn't a lie. "Brodie would've had to go to a shelter. Possibly be euthanized." He sat on the end of the bed and rubbed his mustache.

Kimber wasn't an investigator, but she noticed the rub—and knew what it meant. She shook an accusing finger at his mustache.

"You're doing the mustache thing. That means you've either pulled a fast one or you're nervous. Probably both."

Chris pulled his hand away quickly. "I'm sorry. You're right. But I really can't say much more about where he came from. All I can say is that I just had to bring him home."

Kimber's movements with the brush slowed even more. Her eyes softened. "I get that you care about the dog. But couldn't you have discussed it with me first?"

He shook his head. "You'd have said no."

As soon as the words came out, he regretted them.

"So instead, you decided to put me in a position where I'd be the bad guy if I said we can't keep the damn thing?" She slammed her brush down on the table. "Goddammit, that was a dirty trick!"

"You're right," Chris said earnestly. "Yes, I should have discussed it with you first. But I didn't. I apologize." He raised his hands in mock surrender. "Let's not allow this to spoil the evening. We meet Paul and Gayle in an hour."

Chris wasn't sure whether it was due to his apology or merely the mention of their dinner plans, but Kimber's face did relax a bit. "How about we table this for now?" Chris added. "Tomorrow we'll have a family meeting. If you still want Brodie to go, I'll take him to the shelter. And I'll be the one to take the heat from the kids."

It was a bit of a bluff. Chris couldn't dream of taking Brodie to the shelter now. Thankfully, he was fairly confident that the worst was over.

Without a word, Kimber rose from her dressing table and went to the window. She again looked down at her two teenagers playing with Brodie.

"All right," she said slowly. "But we're going to talk about how this is a family dog—with everyone doing their fair share. The kids are old enough now. If they want to keep that thing, they need to take responsibility for it."

Chris nodded swiftly. "Absolutely."

Kimber frowned, but it was suspiciously close to a smile. She went into her walk-in closet and slipped out of her bathrobe to get dressed.

Even after all these years, Chris appreciated her curves, her firm buttocks, her ample breasts. He stepped close, put his hands around her waist, and pulled her to him.

"Maybe I can make it up to you when we get home tonight."

"Maybe. Maybe not. Actually, don't get your hopes up. Don't get anything else up, either!"

She gave him a shove and turned away.

CHAPTER 9

Kimber and Chris headed for Stella's, east of Forest Lake. Arriving shortly before their seven o'clock reservation, they sat in the lounge to wait for their friends Dr. Paul Thomas and Gayle Armstrong.

Chris ordered two glasses of chardonnay. When the waitress left to get their order, Chris clasped Kimber's hand, pulled it up to his lips, and kissed her fingers. "Let me just say, I'm glad all is forgiven now. We're so lucky to have each other. In spite of the 'beast' I brought home today."

Kimber playfully bumped his leg. "You're lucky that beast is so damn cute."

"Are you talking about Brodie—or me?" Chris had a devilish grin.

In response, Kimber smirked and held up her wine-glass for a toast. After a sip, she glanced over her shoulder. Not yet seeing Paul and Gayle, she leaned into Chris.

"I hope things are still going well with them," she said. "Not only because she's my best friend but because I introduced them. I feel responsible!"

"Are you worried it *isn't* going well?" Chris asked, seeing the concern pinching her face.

She gave a small nod. "A bit. Not so long ago, Paul started talking about serious commitment. So she suggested moving in together. But then he suddenly cooled to the idea."

"How long have they been dating?"

"Six months."

"That isn't very long," Chris pointed out gently.

Kimber conceded with a shrug. "I guess not. It's just that she wants things to move along more quickly. She's waited a long time for the right guy."

Before they could continue the conversation, Paul and Gayle arrived. When the ladies exchanged hugs, Kimber noticed that Gayle seemed pensive and pale. Stray wisps flew loose from her usually well-coiffed hair.

Paul, however, was his usual immaculate self, his hair swept back off his forehead with an ample amount of mousse. Random strands of gray added dimension to the style. Though he stood just five feet six, his impeccable style made him seem larger than life.

Kimber and Gayle had been best friends since they were roommates in nursing school in Saint Cloud. Always a bridesmaid but never the bride, Gayle had been in and out of a few relationships over the years. She never wanted a family, but now in middle age, she did want commitment.

The Majeks had known Paul for several years, since they moved to Scandia from Cottage Grove. Looking for a local dentist, they found Paul's practice, and the rest was history. Paul and Chris instantly clicked, and their friendship grew even deeper when they began their annual hunting trips. To Laurie and Andy, he was Uncle Paul.

Paul had been divorced for years, but like Gayle, he had been single as long as the Majeks had known him. Kimber wasn't sure why it took her so long to realize their two closest friends might be interested in each other. Perhaps she had never wanted to face the potential fallout if the relationship crashed and burned. As she studied Gayle's expression and body language, she suddenly wondered if the introduction had been a mistake.

The maître d' escorted them to a table overlooking the closed-for-the-season golf course. Their server arrived. Paul ordered another chardonnay. Gayle asked for a Ketel One martini, extra dry, straight up, slightly shaken, two olives.

"Hey, buddy, have you lost weight?" asked Chris, staring at his friend. The camel-hair sport coat looked large around the shoulders, and the starched Levi's, dry-cleaner pressed, bagged slightly when Paul crossed his legs.

"He sure has," Gayle chimed in. "I've asked him to see the doctor, but—"

"For God's sake, Gayle, give it a rest," Paul snapped. "Dammit, I'm tired of you harping about it!" Then, like the flick of a light switch, his mood brightened. "Say, Kimber—check out Gayle's scarf. Hermès. Bought it yesterday at Nordstrom. A special gift for a special woman."

Gayle gave a sad little flutter of the scarf and turned to look out over the snow-covered golf course.

Sensing the tension, Kimber changed the conversation. "Well, folks, we have big news. Found out a couple of hours ago."

She looked at Chris and grinned slightly. He reached over and squeezed her knee.

"We have an addition to our family," he added.

Gayle sprang to life, unable to disguise her confusion. "Kimmy! You *can't* be pregnant!"

"I almost wish it were that simple," Kimber replied with a laugh.

"Then what?" Gayle pressed.

"We got a dog," Kimber said, realizing it didn't sound so bad when she said it out loud.

"Hope it's a good pheasant dog," said Paul. "Can we take it on our hunting trip?"

Chris shook his head. "Nope, he's just a pet. Golden retriever. Very gentle. He's been through a lot and needed a good home."

Paul paused as he lifted the chardonnay to his lips. He eyed his friend over the glass. "Been through a lot? Where'd you find him?"

Chris again shook his head. "Classified information, pal. No details."

"Before I forget, Uncle Paul," Kimber announced, "Laurie wants to know if the tooth fairy will be visiting after she gets her wisdom teeth pulled next week."

"Sure! Why not? I believe the fairy gives out ten dollars a tooth these days!" Paul added, winking at Chris.

"Not on my salary!" Chris shot back with a grin.

Paul let out a laugh. "Too bad! Well, tell Laurie I'll give the tooth fairy your address anyway." He sat back and smiled. "I just love your kids. Sometimes wish they were mine."

"Really?" Gayle muttered.

"There are days when I wish they were yours, Uncle Paul!" Kimber quipped.

Gayle took a hearty swig from her drink and scowled. "Are the martinis here always this watered down?" she said loudly.

She knew damned well Paul disliked complaining about things in public, especially in the town where he practiced.

"It's probably a standard pour, Gay," he said tersely. "I'll get you another, a little drier."

She swiped a hand in the air. "Never mind."

Kimber scrambled to change the subject once again. "So…the holidays are just around the corner. Do you have any big plans for Christmas?" Kimber looked across the table at Gayle.

Her friend, however, didn't look back at her. Instead, Gayle's eyes bore into Paul.

"Well, do we? Don't we? Why don't you tell our friends your latest plan, Paul?" Gayle stood abruptly, nearly knocking over her chair as she headed for the restroom.

Kimber and Chris stared down at their wineglasses.

"Obviously, we've had an argument—the holiday trip to Hawaii," Paul explained with an eye roll. "I thought we'd worked it out, but apparently not." He sighed. "I think it's better if we just call it a night." He pulled back the sleeve of his coat and looked at the dial on his Rolex Oyster Perpetual Datejust. "You guys go ahead and have dinner without us."

Returning from the restroom, Gayle was a step ahead of him. "I want to go home now, Paul. *My* home." She knotted the scarf tighter around her neck, as if she'd like to strangle herself. "Sorry, guys," she said to Kimber and Chris, her face tight. Trying not to cry. "Just not myself tonight."

Kimber stood and hugged her. "I'll call you later," she whispered.

Gayle's only response was to hug her best friend tightly. She was determined to remain composed.

Paul dropped thirty dollars on the table, and they quickly left.

Chris and Kimber tried to maintain neutral faces, knowing they were being observed. Other diners had noticed the tension at their table—tension that lingered as Paul and Gayle exited the restaurant. Kimber mustered a smile, but it lasted only a few seconds before concern darkened her face.

"What do you suppose all that was about?" Kimber said. "And Gayle's comment about their holiday plans? I know there *was* talk of them taking a trip. Is that off now?" Her eyes hardened. She crumpled her napkin and tossed it on the table. "I *knew* things were off. I swear, I'll never match Paul up with anyone again!"

Chris cringed. "I don't like talking behind his back. He's such a good friend."

"Well, then don't. Leave the bad-mouthing to me!"

On the way back to her Stillwater apartment, Gayle leaned against the car door. She strained her neck to look away from Paul. It was uncomfortable, but she didn't care.

Neither spoke till they crossed Highway 36. Then Gayle finally drew a breath.

"If you think giving me expensive gifts will keep me by your side, in your bed, you're mistaken. You went back on

80

your promise about the trip. Tossing a scarf at me isn't going to cut it." She paused, turning her head partially toward him. "I thought you were serious about us."

Paul didn't respond.

When he pulled the Lexus up to her entrance, she got out and slammed the door as hard as she could. He drove off without waiting to see her enter the building.

Inside her apartment, Gayle wadded up the scarf and stuffed it in the dirt at the base of her ficus plant.

Have I done it again? she thought. *Have I picked another loser?*

A couple of hours later, the phone rang.

"Hi, bestie," Kimber said gently. "You home safely? All alone?"

"Yes and yes," Gayle groused. "Sometimes Paul can be such a shit."

"Want to talk about it?"

Gayle was silent for a moment. "Not yet."

"Okay, I understand. But you and I need some girl time. So how about next weekend? Got any plans?"

"No. Why?"

"It's the guys' annual 'kill the birdies' getaway. The kids will be on an overnight with friends on Friday, so we ladies are free. I'll come to your neck of the woods, and we can hit the Stillwater bar scene."

There was more silence for a bit. "And you'd spend the night at my place?"

"Yep. That was my plan. It'll be like old times."

Kimber could practically hear the gears turning.

"Yeah. Let's do it," Gayle said, determined. "I really

need it—time to talk to you, get things off my chest."

"Great. I'll be there next Friday, eight o'clock, over-night bag in hand! Love you, Gay."

"Love you too, Kim."

Gayle poured her second Ketel One, sighed deeply, and brought the glass to her lips.

CHAPTER 10

Chris arrived at the Doyle cabin. The techs had completed their work, and Chris was meeting Phil to revisit the scene.

Fluttering in the breeze, yellow crime scene tape was still tacked to the front door. Tape also cordoned off the area several feet around the cabin. Sunlight bled through wintry clouds, highlighting the door to the cabin. A flock of Canada geese flew low, squawking noisily. Warm water from the power plant wasn't far away.

Chris ducked under the tape. *What the hell went on here?* he thought. *Dammit, Brodie. I wish you could talk.*

While waiting for Phil, Chris walked the perimeter of the cabin, staying close to the walls, pushing aside branches as he moved. The roof overhang prevented snow and water from accumulating along the crumbling foundation.

At the rear of the cabin, beneath the only window on that side, the ground was depressed. There were no discernible footprints, but the leaves were flattened. If someone had stood there, they would have had a clear view into the den. The thick woods and brush abutting the lake side of the cabin obviated the need for a window shade.

As Chris pressed through the foliage, he scratched the back of his hand on some buckthorn. Dabbing the blood, he noticed barely visible gray fibers clinging to a twig. He removed his pocketknife and snipped the small branch, taking care not to disturb the strands. He searched for more. Finding none, he returned to his car.

While placing the twig in an evidence bag, he heard the slow grind of tires coming down the gravel road.

With bespectacled wide-set black eyes glaring, Phil got out of his car. He took a last bite from a granola bar and a final swig of water from a plastic bottle. He flung the bottle hard on the floor of the vehicle, then slammed the door. He zipped up his black nylon jacket. In large yellow letters, BCA was emblazoned on the back.

His eyes locked on Chris. "Right now, I'd kill for a smoke."

"Not a good idea," Chris replied with a wry smile. "I want to work with you a few more years."

"Seven years and thirty-five days until retirement—but who's counting?" He rubbed his temples. "Since I quit smoking, just about everyone pisses me off. I stopped at the Chisago County courthouse on the way here. The clerks didn't have a goddamned thing done. All I asked was for them to complete a couple of simple forms. Jesus!" He pulled up his collar. "Anyway," he said as he blew out a deep breath, "let's concentrate on the case."

"I'd like to take another look at the room where he was killed," Chris said.

Phil tore off the tape and shoved the door open. They walked down the hall to the den, both noting the stench of decomposing blood.

"They could've turned the heat down when they were

84

done." Chris notched the thermostat down to sixty-five degrees. "It smells like the decomp room at the morgue."

"No shit." Phil held his coat sleeve over his nose and mouth, muffling his voice. "I see my team left evidence markers all over the place."

The yellow plastic A-frame tents were a stark contrast to the carpet soaked with rusty-black dried blood. Silver-black blotches of Sirchie fingerprint powder were visible on nearly every surface.

Chris walked to the window, turned, and faced the desk, visualizing the priest sitting at the computer.

Was someone standing outside, interested in what you were doing?

They moved on to the sparsely furnished kitchen. Grimy caulk surrounded a sink filled with food-crusted dishes. Open food containers from Meals on Wheels littered the countertop. An ashtray piled with cigar butts sat on the white vinyl folding table next to a half-empty coffee cup. Phil raised the window a few inches to let in fresh air, propping it up with a wooden spoon.

Sneering, Chris pushed the ashtray away and chose a folding chair. Using his sleeve, he brushed food scraps and mouse droppings off the table. He then turned the chair around and straddled it, crossing his arms along the back.

Phil remained standing close to the window, so he could enjoy the fresh air. "Funny," he said, "there's no egress on this side of the cabin."

"The place is old. Probably built before inspections were necessary. Maybe the den window or the one here in the kitchen was considered adequate." He bobbed his chin in the direction of the den. "Say, do you know if anyone recovered fibers from behind the cabin?"

Phil shook his head. "No one mentioned fibers."

"Some sleuths you guys are!"

Phil snorted and waved his hand. "Yeah, yeah—*you* never miss anything. So what'd you find that we supposedly missed?"

"Fibers. In the buckthorn behind the back window. Might mean absolutely nothing, but I recovered them. The leaves on the ground were trampled too. My hunch is, someone stood there for a while. They would have had a clear view of him sitting at the computer."

"Buckthorn—that how you got the scratch?" Phil's eyes moved to the angry red scrape on Chris's hand. "Here I thought you'd been attacked by a cat."

Chris laughed.

"Give them to me when we leave. I'll turn 'em over to the fiber lab. Might take forever to get results, though. I'll give 'em to Serena. I can count on her."

"I've met her. She's good."

Phil started to reach into his empty shirt pocket for a cigarette but caught himself. He grimaced, then drew a deep breath.

"Anyway, here's what we know for sure: Father Doyle was no saint, which may give us some insight into motive. Like I told you, the computer's loaded with child porn—downloaded from the DVDs. All teen boys."

"Sick SOB."

"The porn's origin is primarily Asian, based on the language and objects visible in the background. Doyle must've been getting the stuff via snail mail, perhaps from a stateside distributor. We know he didn't get it through electronic file sharing, because he hasn't had an internet connection in years. He did when he first moved here. We found an old invoice. Looks like he used the internet for a couple of months, then defaulted on the contract."

This time, Phil reached for a pack of nicotine gum in his jacket pocket.

"Have you heard of Whisper?" he asked as he struggled to push a piece out of the blister pack.

"Can't say I have."

"It's a relatively new FBI task force," he said, finally getting the gum free. "They scour pornography websites and identify individuals who download and/or share child pornography files. I was hoping they'd get a hit on Doyle's old IP address. Nothing came up. However, thanks to some other angles, we may have Doyle implicated with more than just kiddie porn."

Phil pulled a sheaf of papers from a briefcase and spread them on the table before continuing.

"Yesterday I spoke with Patrick Grayden, an ex-priest who now works as an investigator for Bob Appeny, the attorney who's suing the ass off the Catholic Church in the child abuse cases."

"Grayden used to be a priest at St. Michael's College, right? Where Doyle taught and served?"

"Yep."

Chris nodded to himself. "I've heard about Grayden. Never met him, but I like the man already."

"When I mentioned Doyle's name, Grayden immediately recognized it. He told me that every week, usually Saturdays, he heard confessions at St. Michael's. Many priests came in begging forgiveness for molesting students. Each time, they'd make the necessary promises to change their ways. But then they'd go on to molest again, coming back for another dose of absolution the next Saturday."

"Goddammit!" Chris took a deep breath, pursed his lips, exhaled shakily.

"Grayden said he started recognizing the voices of the repeat offenders—the ones coming in week after week. Of course, the confessants never fully identified themselves. You see, there are screens inside confessional booths, so the priests can't actually see the confessants sitting on the other side."

Chris chewed the inside of his cheek. He didn't need or appreciate the explanation. He'd been raised Catholic. He was pretty sure that fact had come up at least once during his many years working with Phil. But obviously, Phil didn't remember.

"But the seal of confession forbids priests from making a confession public," Chris said, hoping his authoritative tone would jog Phil's memory about his Catholic upbringing.

"That's what Grayden said," Phil said, not catching the drift. "So he couldn't *directly implicate* Doyle. Instead, he *strongly intimated* that Doyle was indeed one of the repeat offenders. He said he always recognized Doyle's voice because it was unusually highly pitched. 'Squeaky and lispy,' he called it."

Chris sighed. "Well, it's hardly proof we can act on."

"But wait—there's more!" Phil said, using one of his favorite expressions, a parody of TV infomercials. "There's a new website called In the Shade of the Evergreen. It lists the names of 'credibly accused' priests from St. Michael's, the ones who have likely assaulted one or more victims." He paused to raise his eyebrows. "And Doyle made the list."

"Bingo!" Chris snapped his fingers. "Now we've got some direction."

"Several victims have come forward to identify Doyle as an offender. Turns out there were suspicions of Doyle's abuse in two parishes near St. Michael's. In each instance, the church paid substantial sums of money to the families involved. Finally, they moved him onto the campus community. He taught speech classes and gave 'private lessons'"—he made finger quotes—"to his favorites. All the while, the college looked the other way."

"Hush money and supervised predation!" Chris hissed.

Phil rummaged for a tissue in his pocket so he could spit out the gum. "The victims coming out against Doyle are much older now. Which means this goes back years—decades."

Chris fell silent as he rubbed his mustache. Then suddenly, the gravity of the situation pushed him back in his chair. "Jesus. I feel so bad for those victims, those kids. I mean, even the college students—they were still just kids."

He instantly flashed to what-ifs about Laurie and Andy ...then just as quickly forced himself to brush aside such dark thoughts.

"Back then," he pressed on, "kids had no one to talk to about this sort of stuff. Nowhere to go. Then again, even if they had spoken up, no one would've believed them anyway. Priests were held in such high esteem."

Phil sat in silence, except for a steady tapping of his fingers on the table. "You have to wonder," he finally said, "how the abused deal with it after all these years."

"Maybe our perp was one of his victims," Chris said.

Phil nodded. "Could be. But I doubt our perp will identify himself as a victim. That would be too obvious. Someone should still check out the ones who did come forward."

Chris nodded in agreement. "I'll have someone handle that."

Almost on cue, both men looked out the window. The cold draft bit at their skin—a welcome distraction. Ice was beginning to form along the lakeshore.

Chris placed a finger on his lips as he thought, then he finally spoke. "In a perverse way, I feel sorry for whoever killed Doyle."

As he pulled his hand away, he was reminded of the scratch from the buckthorn. It still looked angry. He exhaled.

"OK. What else do we have? What did your team find? What about the cigarette butt? If the lab can recover DNA and run it through CODIS, we might get a hit."

Phil popped another piece of gum into his mouth. The urges were coming at him hard today. "DNA *was* recovered from the cigarette," he said as he chewed. "They ran the preliminary results through the database but didn't get a hit. At least not yet."

"Male or female?"

"Male."

Chris gave a faint chuckle. "As I would've guessed."

"So, without a comparative, that's all we know."

"No comparative *yet*," Chris emphasized. "But maybe our perp has been arrested for another crime, and there's just a delay in posting his profile."

"We can hope. Time's our enemy. We've got to get something solid—and soon." Phil stared out the window. "And McPhearson was right about the rosary beads. No DNA or prints. Stomach acid destroyed anything that might have been there."

"Did you get anything on the shell casing?"

"One partial print, barely visible."

"A print on a shell casing? Nice." Chris made a thumbs-up.

"Well, being a larger caliber, there's more surface area."

"That's a lucky break."

"Yup. Doesn't happen often, but it was visible. Been there long enough for the prints to oxidize on the brass."

"Enough to send to IAFIS?" Chris asked.

"Not really. Mostly smudged."

Chris shrugged. "Why not submit it and see what comes up?"

"Our print expert, Ken Zerke, said it looked like a thumbprint. And he mentioned that there appeared to be a scar or injury, sort of shaped like a small V. Anyway, bottom line, he feels there aren't enough individual characteristics to make a database search worthwhile. He'd like a minimum of eight but found only two. And the print on the other side of the cartridge was too smeared to be of any value."

Chris sighed. "How about latent prints here in the cabin?"

"My techs dusted everything. The place was repainted when Doyle moved in, so all the prints are his. Except for the screen door and the paper bag. Those prints belonged to the meals guy." Phil shook his head. "The old man had a tough time understanding why we needed to take his fingerprints."

Thinking of Del immediately made Chris think of Brodie. "How about"—he stopped himself from saying Brodie's name and sounding too familiar—"the dog's vet? The dog looked pretty well cared for. Doyle must have been taking him in for checkups."

"Yep. Our investigator reported Doyle brought the dog in for routine care at a little clinic in Scandia. Always paid cash. Vet said Doyle was real quiet, never talked about personal stuff. Said the priest and the dog seemed pretty close."

Chris flexed his fingers and cracked his knuckles. He had an image of Brodie curled up beside the kids at night after playing in the snow.

Brodie, you're a Majek now.

"Not much to glean from the class-five gravel road either," Phil went on. "Lots of traffic before and after the murder: Doyle's car, newspaper delivery woman, Peltier, Grafton, fire department, our squads, the ME's meat wagon, maybe the perp's."

"Perhaps the unsub left his car on the highway and walked in," Chris offered.

"That's a possibility. Either way, the driveway offers no clue."

Phil massaged his graying temples. Sometimes he needed two pieces of gum to subdue the cravings, but it always left him with a pounding headache.

"We're stymied most of all, it seems to me, by the damned piece of rosary," muttered Chris.

"There's a guy in our department who's a devout Irish Catholic." Phil leaned down and took a breath of fresh air from the gap in the window. "Matthew Hennebry. Studies church history."

"What's he think?"

"First, he gave some background." With that, Phil launched into another encyclopedic rendition. "You see, Catholics pray the rosary as part of their rituals..."

Chris held up his hands, but Phil missed the signal and kept going.

"A rosary has five sections, or decades, of ten beads. Each set of ten is separated by one larger bead. Each decade represents a mystery—"

"Phil, stop," Chris finally interrupted. "For Christ's sake, I grew up Catholic." He got up from the chair. "It's been a long time. I quit right after confirmation. But I remember that stuff. What I mean is, what did Hennebry say that I *didn't* learn in second-grade catechism?"

Faint recollection lit across Phil's face. "Oh, that's right. I think I remember you telling me that." Then he shrugged. "Well, here's a bit of trivia I'll bet you *don't* know. Apparently, in the late 1800s, the Czechs created extremely ornate rosaries. Real works of art. Hennebry thinks this might be one of them. Says it looks like polished red marble."

"Marble?" Chris echoed. "Isn't it odd for a fairly common material to be used in an ornate piece of art?"

Phil wagged a finger. "*Red* marble is unique and valuable. Well, it *was* valuable—until the rosary was cut apart and taken for a ride down Doyle's throat. Also, these beads are faceted, brilliant, nearly flawless."

Outside, a black crow squawked as it flew over the cabin.

Chris closed the kitchen window. As he set the wooden spoon on the counter, he wondered if his old rosary was lying around someplace. Divine intervention would come in handy.

"Oh, I almost forgot," Phil said. "That writing in blood on Doyle's computer screen—it was Latin. '*Prímum mystérium*.' Translation: 'the first mystery.'"

The sun slipped behind gray clouds, the lake blackened, and a gloomy dark descended over the cabin.

Chris spoke next. "You know what scares me?"

"What?"

"There are four more mysteries."

CHAPTER 11

*A*fter atonement, and just before Mass every morning, Father Carlos Rodriguez makes a ceremony of swinging the massive front doors open for the members of his church—as if he alone could reveal the path to their salvation. His rigid routine makes my mission easy.

But this morning, Rodriguez won't be opening the front doors.

It's an hour before sunrise. Wrapped up against the cold, I walk briskly up the concrete steps to the old church. They're slippery beneath my Tyvek booties. I'm panting with excitement. The icy air stings my lungs. A scarf, tight around my chin, is frosted with my breath.

I don gloves, open the heavy doors, and enter the dark vestibule. I stand for a moment, enjoying a respite from the punishing wind. The air in the old church is stale. It tastes like Doyle's cabin, though without the cigar smoke.

I think about Doyle's place, how they probably tore it apart looking for clues. I left them all they'll need, but making sense of it will be the challenge. They'll end up chasing after an event that happened years ago. Not far from here, in fact. They'll never make the connection.

I move to the front of the empty church. The vacant space amplifies the sound of my booties as they slide on the wood floor.

The clock is making a rhythmic ticktock in the silence.

On the altar is the gold chalice the elderly priest uses for Communion. I fill it with wine I find in the sacristy and return it to the altar. I have the cigarette butt. I must remember to flatten it with my heel and leave it in the sacristy when I depart.

Now, fully prepared, I return to the back of the church and wait quietly in the dark.

Footsteps on wooden stairs, followed by a creak of the warped sacristy door, signal Father Rodriguez's arrival. The latch bolt clicks shut behind him as he turns on the lights. Minutes later, properly dressed for devotion in a black cassock and a silver pectoral cross, he plods to the Communion rail. He kneels and bows his head in prayer. He's an evocation of holiness.

He reminds me of my father. He revered priests. One time he punished me for telling him of Father Benedict, who touched my young body. Who'd made me take my pants down, saying, "God would want it so." When I told my father about this, he made me kneel on rock salt until I recanted my story. My knees bled. When I complained of the pain, he said, "It's God's punishment for your lies."

But now I'm excited. Excited about the pleasure I'm about to experience. Good things come to those who wait, and I've waited a long time for this.

As I move down the aisle, Rodriquez hears the whisper of my booties. His head turns. He pushes himself up from the railing, turns to face me, and squints through thick glasses into the dim light.

"Who's there?"

"Just me, Father. Communion will be a little early today."

I notice the arch of his eyebrows too high on his forehead, his hollow cheeks, the tufts of hair sprouting from his leathery ears. He is an ungodly, homely creature.

"Who are you?" he asks. He tries to steady his voice.

"Think of me as an intercessor. Like your Blessed Virgin Mary, I stand here between you and God. But unlike Mary, I'm not an apparition. I'm the real thing."

"What do you want?"

"To help you, Father. To help you atone." I remove the Beretta from my coat and point it at his face.

He gasps, points a crooked, nodular finger at the gun. "But..." His frail body trembles.

"The gun will help you comprehend how serious your situation is."

Fear makes his features even more unsightly. "My situation? I don't understand."

"You will soon, Father." I nod to the Communion rail. "Please kneel again."

He obeys. Tremors ripple through his body.

I walk through the small opening in the chancel rail and up the steps to the altar. I remove the chalice of wine and set it beside Rodriguez. I face him.

He glances over my shoulder at Christ hanging on the wooden cross. His lips mouth words I can't hear.

I pull the hammer back to the second detent for a lighter trigger pull. When it clicks, he flinches. His face tightens, becomes blotched with patches of red. The pectoral cross dances on his chest with every heartbeat.

"Please explain why you're here," he manages.

"To avenge the children."

"The children...?"

"Yes, Father Carlos Rodriguez. The children you betrayed. Let's call it a betrayal by the trusted."

From my pocket, I produce a chain of red beads. "You will swallow this, Father."

He stares at the chain, incredulous. He knows what it is. "You can't be serious."

"I am."

His eyes clamp shut. "This can't be happen—"

"But it is happening, Father. I do this for the children. Do you understand? For the boys."

For several seconds, the priest stares at his bent fingers. The word boys has meaning for him. Now he understands.

"Oh, Lord in Heaven, so many times I've asked God for help."

He shakes so hard the Communion rail wobbles. Wine spills over the brim of the chalice, staining the cloth claret red. There'll be more red very soon.

"The boys..." Rodriguez whimpered. "You must know—I loved them." His eyes plead for mercy. "I'm so sorry. As God is my witness, I'm truly sorry."

My eyes are hard. "Your apology rings hollow, Father. Besides, the time for apology has long passed. Your 'love' has hurt the boys terribly." I push the decade into his hand. "Take this and eat," I command.

Startled, his lips move, but he can only gasp.

"Take this and eat!" I shout. My voice echoes in the small church.

Bent fingers with long yellowed nails grasp the decade and place it on his tongue. He gags.

"Take this and drink." I push the chalice toward him.

His skinny shoulders shudder as he retches. He picks up the vessel and brings it to his mouth. He drinks. The beads are swallowed. He drops the chalice, sending it clattering to the floor. He clutches his throat with twisted fingers, leaning forward, suppressing another retch.

He looks up at me, still on his knees. "I beg you—let me say one last Act of Contrition." The voice has gone from whimper to wheeze.

I can't help but grin. Finally, he's gotten the message. He knows he's about to die. Power surges through my body.

"Father, you may not be an entirely bad person," I begin, not directly answering his question. "But you see, what you've done to the boys has changed them. You set their lives on an irreversible course."

"I needed to be sexual with them!" he blurts, searching my face. "Don't you understand?"

I shake my head. "Such depravity cannot be understood, Father."

"I'm trying to atone! I really am!"

He's slobbering. Spittle forms at the corners of his mouth. Rivulets of tears cascade down his hollow cheeks. Now he's showing the emotion I came to see. Mission accomplished.

Almost.

"You put those boys on their own paths to evil," I continue. "It happened to me—that's how I know. So no. You may not say an Act of Contrition. You may not save yourself from the fires of hell. You will die with mortal sin on your soul."

With that, I grip the Beretta with both hands and squeeze the trigger. The windows rattle when the cartridge detonates.

The copper petals of the Hydra-Shok peel back, allowing the projectile to expand as it spins through the bone over the priest's right eye. The back of his head bursts apart in a rusty, high-velocity mist. His face momentarily distends like the face of a clown, then collapses into an empty rubbery mask.

I'm intoxicated with pleasure. I have an erection. The fear he displayed is reminiscent of my own when I was naked and alone with my parish priest. Rodriguez is lucky. He didn't feel the penetration of the bullet as it spun through his brain. Not like the penetration his victims felt.

It was easier to write on Doyle's computer screen than it is to write on the linen covering the Communion rail. The cloth keeps moving and shifting as I paint my message. The blood soaks in quickly. It takes several dips into the remainder of Rodriguez's skull to complete my inscription. But the message is legible.

That's all that matters.

CHAPTER 12

At 6:30 a.m., Alan Miller was still asleep when his mom knocked gently on his bedroom door. Her knock began his daily routine. Alan liked routine. He needed routine, ever since the ravine claimed his car on high school graduation night and muddled his brain.

Alan rolled his rotund forty-three-year-old body out of bed. He put on a plaid flannel shirt, a pair of too-tight, well-worn Levi's with holes in the knees, and an old pair of high-top leather work boots. He wet his thinning blond hair and brushed it straight back. No part. After a quick face wash, but no toothbrushing or shave, he put on his smudged glasses. He was ready for breakfast.

Every morning, Alan's mother, Gladys, prepared two slices of peanut butter toast with honey, one fried egg over easy, three strips of crisp bacon, and a glass of milk. After breakfast, no matter the weather, she drove Alan to St. Joseph's Catholic Church, where he worked as janitor.

"When will you pick me up?" Alan asked this morning as they neared the church.

Gladys inhaled slowly. As she exhaled, her cheeks puffed. She was frustrated—it was the same question every morning. But she loved Alan and was protective of him.

"Same as always, honey. Nine thirty by the sacristy steps."

"Really? OK." Alan assimilated the information as if it were the first time he'd heard it. "You said nine thirty, right?" he confirmed.

"Yes. At the bottom of the steps." Gladys pulled to the curb. "Here you go. Do a good job." She patted his shoulder. It served as both a gesture of endearment and a nudge toward the door.

Alan clicked his seatbelt loose, grabbed his pair of old Reeboks, and opened the car door. "Nine thirty, right here, Mom?"

"This very spot, honey."

He closed the door, waved goodbye, and watched his mother drive away. He liked it when she called him honey. It reminded him how much he was loved, something he needed.

Gladys watched Alan in her rearview mirror. If the church hadn't hired him after the accident, she didn't know what he would've done—or what she would've done, for that matter. The accident had placed many burdens on them both. But she reminded herself that God must have had a reason; God has reasons for everything.

Gladys smiled. Alan loved the church and liked Father Carlos Rodriguez a great deal. Many priests had come and gone over the years, but Father Rodriguez was Alan's favorite. When Alan found "Rodriguez" hard to pronounce, the priest told Alan to call him Father C.

For a moment, Gladys's smile wilted. She'd heard the rumors about Father C . . .

But in a flash, she cemented the smile back in place. Her faith made it impossible to believe Father C could be guilty of such sin. He was a good man. A man of God. A man who led Mass, changed bread into Body, and absolved sins couldn't be capable of such terrible things. Besides, church teachings strictly forbade such activities.

Gladys pushed the thoughts into the recesses of her mind. The same recesses where she pushed her concerns that Alan had recently become less talkative as well as less attentive to his personal hygiene. She dismissed those as probably nothing more than his brain injury causing mood swings...again.

When his mom's car turned the corner and disappeared from view, Alan trudged up the steps to the sacristy. His tight pants chafed his thighs, and snow grated under his boots. He was quickly out of breath.

When he reached for the doorknob, he became confused. He cocked his head to one side, trying to determine what was different. It took a strong gust of wind for him to realize the sacristy door was not entirely closed. That was something Father C would never do. He always kept the door tightly shut.

Alan stepped inside the sacristy and stomped the snow from his boots. Fluorescent ceiling lights illuminated the small space.

"Father C, are you here?"

As he waited for an answer, he removed his parka and tossed it on a chair.

Silence, other than *ticktock, ticktock.*

As he slipped into his tennis shoes, he noticed Father

C's boots beside the door. The lights were on. The priest had to be there.

Alan squinted through his glasses, which had fogged in the moist air. He wiped them on his shirt sleeve. Then he noticed a flattened cigarette butt on the floor. Father C would never allow smoking in the church.

"Father C? Hello? It's me. Al."

The cabinet where Father C kept his cassock was open. This made Alan more uncomfortable. Was the priest playing a game with him?

He knew Father C played games with young boys. He couldn't forget what he'd recently seen—things that didn't fit into the world as he understood it. But Alan also couldn't forget that it was all his fault. He'd been told never to go into the basement when Father C was with the boys. He planned to apologize to Father today.

Alan rubbed the stubble on his cheeks. Between Father C's games in the basement and now the game he was playing this morning—it was a big change in routine. And Alan didn't like change.

Finally, he decided the priest wasn't there; he had simply forgotten to close the door and turn off the lights. Why Father's boots were still there baffled him.

Alan headed to the closet where he stored his cleaning supplies. He was proud to have an official place in the church that was just his.

When he was first hired, he'd been given a commercial vacuum cleaner. But for reasons the doctors couldn't understand, Alan's hearing had become significantly more acute over the years. Now, the noise of the vacuum bothered him so much he opted for a dustpan and a broom to clean the wooden floors of the church.

With his broom in one hand and dustpan in the other, Alan trudged through the doorway leading to the altar. A weak winter sun trickled through the stained-glass windows, casting eerie multicolored light on a figure slumped over the Communion rail.

Alan dropped his implements, causing an echoing clatter.

His puzzled brain tried to make sense of what he was seeing. He turned away, then back again, as if looking anew might help him make sense of the scene. The clock ticked louder and louder, banging in his ears.

Alan shuffled toward the railing. The identity of the shape became clearer in his mind.

"Father? Father C?" He felt faint; he steadied himself on the rail. "What happened? Did you fall?"

Alan almost tripped over the chalice lying on the floor. Then he saw the blood that had pooled beneath the priest's head.

His brain finally unraveled the horror he'd discovered.

His body not yet in sync with his brain's panic, Alan lumbered down the aisle and through the heavy front doors. Stumbling down the icy steps to the street, he yelled and waved until a passing driver stopped and rolled down his window.

"What's wrong, sir?" Mason Halverson asked. On his way home from the night shift at the BP station, Halverson hoped there wouldn't be a long delay.

"Father—Father C! No! Red!" he babbled incoherently.

"Father C. Boots. Game. Red!"

The words meant little to Halverson, but the fear etched on Alan's face was telling. Understanding something serious had occurred, the driver called 911 while Alan paced through the snow on the sidewalk at the bottom of the steps.

Staying on the line as the dispatcher ordered, the man leaned out his window. "It's cold," he said to Alan. "Why don't you sit in my car? They're sending the emergency responders now." Halverson was now feeling a sense of obligation.

Alan just shook his head. Still babbling unintelligibly, he turned and struggled back up the slippery steps, holding tight to the balustrade. He entered the church and stumbled into a pew in the back.

Worried, Halverson pulled his car to the side of the road and followed Alan into the building.

Alan was kneeling in the pew, crying with his head in his hands. The kneeler creaked as he rocked back and forth. His body shook uncontrollably.

He couldn't apologize to Father C for breaking the rule.

Halverson left Alan at the pew and ventured partway up the aisle—then hastily retreated to his car when he saw Father Rodriguez.

Red.

Within minutes, Deputy Scott Yetterman, a rookie patrol officer, pulled up to the church.

As Yetterman approached his car, Halverson pointed up at the large oak doors. "Looks like something awful happened in there."

Yetterman bounded up the steps, entered the church, and found Alan kneeling and crying in the back pew. Alan turned around at the sound of footsteps. Keeping an eye on Alan, the officer strode quickly to the altar and realized the priest was deceased. While calling off the EMTs, he returned to Alan.

"What's your name, sir?"

Alan was still rocking, unable to speak, face flushed.

"Sir, I need to check you for a weapon." Yetterman's tone conveyed a firm authority belying his rookie status. "Stand up and step out of the pew. Hands on top of your head. Walk backward, slowly, toward me."

Somehow Alan managed to follow the directions. Yetterman patted him down and found no weapon. He instructed Alan to return to the pew and remain there.

"Can you tell me what happened here, sir?" Yetterman then asked.

Alan could only point to the front of the church.

The young officer radioed his captain, who in turn dispatched a detective.

Yetterman studied the scene more carefully now. The priest was slumped over the Communion railing, the back of his head fragmented, mostly missing. Blood puddled on the floor beneath what did remain. Brain matter and bone fragments were scattered over a widening path several feet from the railing, reaching the forwardmost pews. Scalp and hair had been blown into the aisle. Yetterman also observed writing on the railing cloth—which appeared to be in blood—but he couldn't read it.

When the Saint Paul Police detective arrived, he determined the scene was likely a homicide—confirming Yetterman's own deduction. Earlier that month, the state-wide law enforcement brief had reported a similar crime involving a priest in Washington County. Thus, the BCA was contacted.

Forty minutes later, Phil Walker arrived at St. Joseph's Church. He spit a piece of chewed gum into a wadded tissue and stuck it in his coat pocket. This time it was bubble gum. A new experiment. The hope was that perhaps chewing regular gum would provide a sugar hit as well as satisfy the craving for a cigarette.

Jury was still out.

"The water in the aisle—that from your feet?" he asked Yetterman as they stood in the vestibule.

"Yes, sir," the officer responded. "I went up to look at the body before radioing my captain. Also, the gentleman who called nine-one-one said he'd walked near the body. But there was water right up to the deceased and over there"—he nodded toward the sacristy—"when I got here. Someone else with wet feet has been here."

Phil nodded. He liked this kid.

Yetterman was right. Smudged wet footprints led to the body. Phil leaned down and examined the prints more closely. There was no visible tread. Additional smudged prints led to the altar, to the sacristy door, and down the steps, where they had been mostly obliterated by Alan.

When Phil checked out the sacristy, he froze for a second when he saw the cigarette butt on the floor.

It wasn't exactly a surprise, but it filled him with an extra layer of dread.

"The detective from Saint Paul PD took a look and didn't want to mess with the scene," Yetterman explained as Phil returned to the vestibule. "He thought you guys would want to handle it. Seems you had another priest killing not so long ago."

Walker nodded, then looked over at Alan. "Who's he?"

"The church janitor. The one who found the body."

"Check him for weapons?"

"Yes, sir. He's okay. He seems to have cognitive disabilities," he added quietly. "I did my best to explain he was being detained until you could interview him."

"Good call."

"I'm not sure how much he understands," Yetterman admitted. "He's pretty distraught."

Phil watched Alan for a moment. He was no longer crying, but the rocking had intensified.

"I'm wondering if you could bring him down to our office," Phil said. "I'd like to talk to him there. It'll be less confusing for him if you bring him—as someone he's already met."

"Happy to help, sir." Yetterman smiled. "It gives me a little overtime."

"You got scene tape in your car?"

"I do."

Phil wasn't surprised. "Good. Stay with the janitor till the crime scene techs arrive. Then tape off the entire area around the church and the rectory next door. Then bring him"—he nodded at Alan—"down to the BCA. And arrange for someone from his family to meet you down there. I detained the driver and will talk with him, get his contact information. And I'll get one of our agents to canvass the neighborhood."

"The janitor mentioned his mother several times," Yetterman offered.

"Good," Phil said again. "Get her number from him, and have her or someone else from the family meet us at the BCA." He turned and headed up the aisle.

"Sir?"

Phil stopped and faced the young man again. "Yes?"

"One more thing—there's some kind of writing on the cloth." He was clearly eager to share this keen observation, yet he maintained a serious tone. "I think it's in blood. But I can't read it."

Without more than a nod, Phil turned back and resumed walking up the aisle. He was pretty sure he knew what the writing said. Or at least the English translation.

He pulled out a piece of nicotine gum. The real stuff. Bubblegum wasn't gonna cut it.

CHAPTER 13

Phil knew Chris couldn't join him for the interview with the janitor. The investigator was already on his way that morning to South Dakota for his annual hunting trip. Phil chose Room 2-C for the interview. It was one of four rooms discreetly equipped with video- and voice-recording equipment and a two-way mirror.

Phil entered the room a few minutes before Yetterman escorted Alan in. He gestured for Alan to sit on one of the folding chairs next to a gray metal table. Phil then nodded to Yetterman, who left the room.

Phil poured himself a coffee and loaded it with sugar before sitting across from Alan. He faced the window. Phil was thankful the shades had been partially lowered to block light from the low winter sun reaching the second-floor room.

As he positioned a pen and legal pad between them, Phil observed Alan for a moment. The janitor seemed nervous. He was picking at his already well-bitten fingernails. But he was certainly more composed now, compared to at the crime scene. Sending him with Deputy Yetterman seemed to have been a good idea.

Alan looked up from his fingernails. "You're going to ask me some questions now, right?" he asked. "That nice policeman said that's why he brought me here, so you could ask me some questions. He said my mom is on her way too."

"That's correct, Mr. Miller," Phil confirmed. "May I call you Alan? Or Al? Do you go by Al?" His voice was amicable, casual, easy. It was the best approach, given the circumstances.

Alan smiled shyly. "No one calls me Al, but I like it."

Phil smiled back. "Then Al it is. Can I get you a soda? Or maybe you'd like coffee? Something to eat, Al?"

Alan shook his head. "I'm okay."

Phil folded his hands around his coffee cup almost as if in prayer. "Thank you for coming. This has to be difficult for you." He filled his normally nervous eyes with sympathy.

It worked. Alan's words started spilling out. "I can't believe he's dead. Father C was my friend. My best friend."

Phil narrowed his eyes. "Your best friend—how did that come to be?"

"Father C was nice to me. Never yelled, like some of the others did."

"By 'others,' who do you mean?"

"Other priests I worked for."

"Why do you think that was? Why did they yell at you?"

"They'd yell if I didn't do my job right. Some even swore. It made me kind of sad." Alan's shoulders slumped.

"Sorry to hear that." Phil reached across the table and patted the back of Alan's hand.

"But I liked Father C." Alan's face lit up. "I really liked him."

Thick saliva accumulated on Alan's lower lip. Phil

retrieved some paper napkins from the coffee station and handed them to Alan as he returned to the table.

"How long have you worked at the church?" he asked, settling back into his chair.

"Over twenty years. Yeah, twenty-two. Since I got better after the accident."

"Tell me about the accident." Phil took a sip of coffee.

"A car wreck after graduation. It was pretty bad." He pointed to scars on his forearm.

"I'm sorry. Looks like it was serious. Did you ever work anywhere else?" Phil preferred to suddenly change the direction of his interview questions. Different directions often kept suspects off guard.

"A grocery store." Alan swallowed; his throat was suddenly dry.

Phil noticed. And he wanted Alan to know he had noticed. "Sure you don't want something to drink? Water?"

"No, thanks." Alan's eyes dropped to the floor.

"Why'd you leave the grocery store job, Al?" Phil leaned forward. His voice wasn't so easy-breezy now.

Alan couldn't conceal his nervousness. "Um . . . they fired me because I took some candy bars." It was a whisper. "I'm not going to jail for that, am I?"

Phil leaned back in his chair again and fought the twitch of a smile. "No, Al. It's OK. So, back to the church. What did you and Father C talk about as best friends?"

Alan shrugged. "Just stuff."

"Like . . . ?"

"Well, one time he talked about how lonely he was since moving here. He said he missed his church in California, his friends there." Alan swallowed again. "The boys."

The hairs on the back of Phil's neck stood up.

"Why do you say his friends there were boys?"

"Because his friends here are boys—*were* boys." Alan rubbed his forehead as if trying to reset his reality. "Mostly teenage boys from catechism classes. They'd hang out with him down in his office in the church basement."

It was Phil's turn to rub his forehead. Of course, the crime scene suggested this murder was connected to the one in Scandia. Which, in turn, suggested that perhaps Rodriguez had a history of abusing, as did Doyle. But Phil never expected that the forty-three-year-old janitor with cognitive disabilities would be the one to reveal it.

God, he needed a cigarette.

Instead, he spied a paper clip under the table. He reached down, nabbed it, and started bending it in frustration.

"What about girls?" Phil pressed on. "Was he friends with girls too?"

Alan shook his head firmly. "No. Not girls. He only met with them in the church, upstairs, at catechism classes. Never down in the basement."

Phil worked the paper clip. "So, how do you know about Father C's friends in the basement? Were you ever down there when he was with the boys?"

This time, Alan shook his head so hard his entire body shimmied. "No. Never." But then his head suddenly stopped shaking. He couldn't keep up the lie. "Well, except when I broke the rule…"

"What rule?"

114

In the silence that followed, Phil took another sip of coffee. He wished it had more sugar. But he wasn't about to break the pace of the interview.

"I was never to go to the basement when he was with the boys," Alan finally said.

Phil pounced. "Why?"

Alan stared at his hands and didn't speak. He tried to swallow.

Phil waited.

Eventually, Alan spoke. "He told me they played secret games together. I wasn't supposed to see them...but I did. I had to go down to his office to empty the trash can. I didn't know they were down there. I didn't mean to walk in on them."

Alan turned away and looked out the window over the parking lot. He went rigid. An officer was helping his mother out of a squad car.

"It's my mom." Alan turned around, his eyes pleading. "Don't let her in here. Please."

Alan's intensity caught Phil by surprise. "But I thought you'd like having your mom here."

Alan craned his neck to look out the window again. He couldn't see his mom anymore. She was already in the building.

"She—she doesn't know. About Father C. I mean, she'll say I'm lying. She thinks Father C is"—he rubbed his forehead roughly, his words getting jumbled again—"thought he was holy."

"Wasn't he?" Phil raised his eyebrows and looked over his glasses, directly at Alan.

Alan began to cry.

Phil grabbed his cell phone. The last thing he wanted was the mother to derail the interview now. He suspected Alan was about to give a firsthand account of Father Rodriguez abusing teenage boys.

"OK, this can be just between us, Al. I'll have your mom wait outside till we're done. Is that OK?"

Alan nodded, wiping his nose on his sleeve.

Phil made a quick call to Marty. "Keep the mother out there," he said, not waiting for a reply before hanging up.

"So, tell me about the secret games in the basement," Phil urged. "What did you see?"

Alan looked up at Phil in confusion. In his relief about his mother not coming in, he had forgotten that he still had to answer the questions.

"But it's wrong to talk bad about a priest," he said, his forehead pinched with worry.

Phil shook his head gently. "No, it's OK. Talking about things can make us feel better."

Tears again streamed down Alan's unshaven cheeks. He grabbed another napkin and dabbed at the tears. He sat silently for several seconds. His lower lip quivered; the beads of sweat on his forehead began to dribble into his eyes.

"Go on, Al." Phil gave an encouraging nod. "Tell me what you saw in the basement."

"Um . . . I opened the door to the office, and Father C was with two boys. They were looking at pictures in a magazine."

"Can you tell me about the pictures? What were the pictures of?"

Alan's eyes darted around the room as if he were searching for an escape. But he couldn't escape the room any more than he could escape the memory.

"Just pictures of boys..."

"Doing what?"

Alan thrust his hands over his face and muttered something.

"I didn't hear you, Al. What were the boys in the pictures doing?" Phil's voice had grown louder and more forceful.

Alan parted his hands just enough to speak, but he left his eyes covered. "They didn't have any clothes on. They were doing things to each other."

"And Father C—what was he doing?"

Alan half rose from his chair. "I don't want to talk to you anymore. Can I go now?"

Phil pointed a firm finger at Alan. "No! You're going to sit here until you've told me every last detail."

Immediately, Alan sat back down and again covered his face with his hands.

Phil winced. He wasn't sure whether he was taking advantage of Alan's childlike demeanor or whether this was merely what it took to conduct a proper interview with this subject. Either way, he had to get the truth.

"Al, listen to me." He paused. "Look at me."

Phil waited until Alan slowly lowered his hands. The janitor's eyes were pained; the agent's eyes were insistent.

"I *need* to know, Al."

Alan nodded, then took a deep breath. "He was touching himself in a bad place."

"Where?"

"You know … down there." Alan pointed to his groin.

"What about the boys in the basement? Was Father C touching any of them?"

"No. They were just sitting there, watching. But I don't think they liked that game."

Phil let out a deep breath. "So, you opened the door, saw Father C and the boys. Then what happened?"

"Father C got really mad. He yelled at me to get out." Alan's voice began to crack. His words were muted. "I never wanted to disappoint him. I didn't mean to break the rule. I felt bad."

"What did you do then?"

"I ran back upstairs. I tried to just clean, like normal. The Knights of Columbus had been practicing. My mom picked me up later."

"Did you tell your mom or dad what you'd seen?"

"My dad left us a long time ago, right after my accident," Alan said matter-of-factly. Then his eyes widened. "And I didn't dare tell my mom."

Phil didn't need to ask why. "Did Father C ever talk to you about what happened?" he asked instead.

"No. I was going to apologize to him this morning. I guess it's too late now…"

Alan quietly wept.

Phil sat in silent thought. In that first moment when he saw Alan rocking and crying in the back pew, he never fathomed what this interview would reveal. He was glad he'd picked a room with a recorder. He'd need to review this one a few times himself.

"Would you like me to get your mom now?" he asked when Alan's sobs lessened.

Alan nodded. "Yes. But remember your promise—we can't talk about what Father C was doing."

Phil's eyes were sincere. "It's a promise."

After another quick call to Marty, Gladys was at last escorted to the interview room. The woman was distraught.

An officer had come to her door with news that her beloved priest was dead and that her poor son was being interviewed by the police. She had to drop everything and go straight to the BCA—only to be told that she had to sit in a separate room, while Alan was all alone with the interviewer.

They wouldn't even allow her to go in and hug him.

"Alan, honey!" she exclaimed, rushing to him. "I got here as soon as I could, but they wouldn't let me in. Are you OK?"

He nodded, returning her embrace. "I'm OK, Mom."

She could immediately tell he'd been crying. She wheeled on Phil, her eyes accusing. "What's going on here? My son has severe brain trauma. He never should have been left alone to—"

Phil stepped in quickly. "Mrs. Miller, thank you for joining us. I'm Agent Phil Walker." He stretched out his hand. "Al and I have just been talking about his work at the church as a janitor."

Gladys cautiously shook Phil's hand. She wasn't sure she liked this "Al" business, though.

Meanwhile, Alan flashed Phil a thin smile of relief. Their secret was safe.

Continuing the interview, Phil said to Alan, "How long did you say you've been a janitor?"

"Almost twenty-two years," Alan replied proudly. "I do a good job."

Good, he's consistent, Phil thought.

"The church is lucky to have you," he told Alan. He winked.

This made Alan smile even more.

Gladys watched them like a line judge at a tennis match, unsure of what to make of it. She'd been asking over and over whether Alan was considered a suspect. All anyone could tell her was that it was "standard procedure" to interview anyone at a crime scene. It wasn't a yes, but it also wasn't a no.

Here now in the interview room, she could tell Alan seemed comfortable with the agent. Yet he'd also been crying. Well, he was no doubt still in shock about Father Rodriguez. They told her he'd discovered the body. No one would give her any details, but she gathered that it had been a horrific sight.

Phil picked up the pen and pulled the legal pad closer to him. It was mostly for show. "So, Al," he began, "let's talk about what happened this morning. What time did you get to the church?"

"Seven thirty," Gladys answered.

Phil forced a polite smile. "Please, Mrs. Miller—let Al answer the questions."

Both frustrated and sheepish, she looked away.

Phil nodded to Alan. "Al? The time?"

"Yes, it was seven-thirty," he confirmed.

"Is that your usual time?" Phil continued, looking straight at Alan as if they were the only two in the room.

"Yep. The same as always during the week. Saturdays too. I clean after early Mass. Sundays I go in later."

"What door did you go in?"

"The sacristy. The door was open, but it usually isn't," he added.

Phil paused. "By 'open,' do you mean ajar or just unlocked?"

His face clouding, Alan shrugged. "It was . . . just kind of open." He shifted in the chair.

Gladys drew a breath to form words, then she quickly closed her mouth. She looked back down at her purse, nervously fidgeting with the clasp.

Phil realized his mistake. He had to remind himself of Alan's limitations. "Do you mean it was open a little?" He held his fingers an inch or so apart to illustrate. "Or was it closed all the way shut, but it was unlocked?"

"Open a little," Alan replied more confidently this time. "I didn't have to turn the handle. The wind blew the door open."

Finally, a straight answer. Phil punctuated it with a single tap of his pen on the pad.

Gladys gave Alan a supportive nod.

"When you went into the sacristy," Phil said, "what did you see or hear?"

Alan's eyes looked off to his left. "It was real quiet except for the big clock. It ticks real loud. Hurts my ears a lot."

"Did you notice anything unusual, out of the ordinary? Anything that didn't look right?"

121

Alan nodded. "The lights were on. Father C's boots were still there too."

"Can you recall anything else? Think hard."

Now Alan's eyes squinted a little, as if trying to see the scene. "Yeah. There was a cigarette on the floor. I knew Father C wouldn't like that."

"Did you smell smoke?"

Alan tilted his head. "Um … no. Just saw the cigarette."

"Good," Phil said, nodding. "That's a great help." He fell quiet for a moment, readying for the next question.

"Al, can you tell me what you did when you saw Father C?"

Alan glanced back and forth between the agent and his mother. His eyes reddened.

Without a word, Gladys reached over and took his hand in hers.

"I came out of the sacristy, ready to sweep. He was there by the rail. I didn't know … It looked like …"

Gladys let her own tears stream down her cheeks as she squeezed Alan's hand in support.

"I just ran," he finally said. "I ran all the way outside." He turned and faced his mother. "Mom, I know I'm not supposed to run in church. But I couldn't help it—I saw all the blood."

She sniffled and let out a little laugh. "Oh, honey, that's fine. Just fine. God forgives you for that."

Alan beamed with relief.

Phil smiled a little too. "Now Al, I have to ask you one more thing. I want you to think very carefully about your answer."

He paused for effect. His smile disappeared.

Not liking what was coming, Gladys gripped her purse tightly.

"Did you kill Father Carlos Rodriguez?"

Gladys reared forward from her chair. "*How dare—*"

Phil held up his hand. "Mrs. Miller, please."

She lowered herself, shaking.

"Sometimes even good people make mistakes," Phil reminded them both. He looked right at Alan. "Did you kill Father Rodriguez?"

Alan sat up straight, his hair falling over his forehead. He looked directly back at Phil.

"No. He was my very best friend."

Phil nodded, satisfied. "All that's left now is check your hands to see if you've fired a gun recently. It only takes a minute."

Gladys was out of her chair again. "You don't actually think he did this . . . ?"

"I'm scared of guns, Mom," Alan said, more concerned about convincing her than convincing Phil. "They make an awful noise. I've never shot one. Not ever."

Phil waited until Gladys turned her attention back to him. "Mrs. Miller, we don't know who did this. We test everyone. It's just routine." He set the pen down. "Officer Yetterman will take you both to the spectrometry lab, where you can wait," he said, nodding at Gladys. "Then we'll have you on your way in a few minutes. He'll drive you home."

Alan's hands were swabbed. He had not fired a gun.

CHAPTER 14

On the way out of his driveway at five past nine, Paul encountered Roger Anderson plowing the neighborhood roads. After every snowfall, Roger would start by plowing the main road, then he'd go driveway by driveway. Paul brought the Lexus to a stop and lowered his window as Roger pulled over.

"Hey, Doc," Roger hollered from his truck. "When I plowed your road earlier this morning, I noticed tire tracks in your driveway. You should've waited for me to clear it."

Paul laughed. "Yeah, I should have! Had to run into town. I forgot some things for the annual hunting trip this weekend with Majek and a couple other guys."

"Whatcha killin'?"

"Pheasants."

Roger nodded his approval. "Well, you guys have a good time. And drive carefully—another storm's on the way. Sounds like I'll be plowing again tomorrow night."

"Thanks," Paul replied with a wave before slowly pulling out onto the highway.

Paul arrived at Chris's twenty minutes past the agreed time. Chris was dressed and ready for the three-hundred-mile trip to South Dakota, his gear neatly stacked by the garage.

"Not like you to be late, buddy," Chris said as Paul slid out from his Lexus.

"Yeah, I got behind." Paul walked to the rear of his car and opened the liftgate to help load Chris's gear. "Anderson was plowing my road. Got tied up with him for a bit. We'll make it up on the freeway."

Chris carefully positioned his gun case in front of them in the cargo hatch. "Say, have a look at my new shotgun—a Benelli twelve-gauge." He flipped up the latches and lifted the lid to reveal the shotgun nestled in form-fitting foam. "I traded the Remington—wanted to try a pump. Remember how the automatic jammed on me last year?"

"I sure do." Paul studied the Benelli and whistled. "Real nice." He craned to look toward the front door. "Say, where's that new dog of yours? I expected him to come running out to defend his new home."

"Brodie? No. Gentle as a lamb. He's with Laurie and Andy, snow tubing over at Eko Backen. Crazy dog loves playing with the kids. I don't think he's ever played with youngsters. Loves the attention."

"Where'd you say you got him?"

"Never did." Chris smirked. He pressed the button to close the liftgate. "Let's hit the road before it starts snowing again. The forecast is for more of this crap. I'd like to get ahead of it."

The men climbed into the Lexus and headed on their way. Once out on Highway 97, Paul yawned, prompting Chris to give him a long glance.

"Want me to drive?" Chris offered. "We're not even on the freeway yet, and it looks like you're about to conk out."

Paul shook his head. "Nah, I'm fine. Just a bit low on energy. I had three emergency extractions yesterday. Difficult patients. Didn't finish up until early evening. Then I had a tough time getting to sleep."

"You dentists—I swear, you guys are trained to hurt people, and you get paid a lot of money to do it!" Chris mimed a deranged dentist drilling into the tooth of a helpless patient.

"You're just jealous," Paul retorted. "You cops get trained to hurt people, but you *don't* get paid a lot of money!"

They both laughed.

The two friends rode in comfortable silence through southern Minnesota, past endless fields of broken cornstalks jutting through the drifted snow. When they turned west on I-90, Chris cleared his throat.

"By the way, who's taking care of Bella this weekend?"

"No one—she's a *cat*," Paul said emphatically. "Cats don't need much attention. They're easier than dogs, you know. She'll be fine for a couple of days. She's got the run of the house and plenty of food and water to tide her over."

Chris rubbed his mustache. "So . . . Gayle's not going over to check on her?"

"No."

Once again, silence settled between the men, although it wasn't as comfortable this time. Chris decided to push through it.

"All right—what was the deal the other night? She sure was pissed at Stella's. You guys having problems?"

Paul let out a sigh, drawing it out as he emptied his

lungs. "It was my fault. I let her down big-time. I pulled out on a trip we were going to take to Hawaii."

"So why you'd back out? Don't you like traveling with her? I thought you guys had fun on that cruise to Antarctica."

"Every guy on the ship wanted to get to know Gayle, if you know what I mean."

Chris tried to shrug it off. "I bet they did. She's a looker."

"She's *gorgeous*," Paul corrected. "That's why I fell for her. It was an immediate attraction."

He stared straight ahead, both hands on the wheel. Chris waited, never taking his eyes off him.

"There were several lookers on board, actually," Paul continued. "One in particular caught my eye. I found myself trying to figure out how to be alone with her. I don't know why—it's not like I wasn't enjoying my time with Gayle."

He grimaced as a driver in a fast-approaching muscle car started tailgating him. He moved to the right lane.

"And of course, Gayle noticed it all. Apparently, I was too obvious. She said it really embarrassed her."

Once the muscle car burst ahead with a menacing growl, Paul swung back into the left lane.

"She came right out and asked why I can't be satisfied with just one woman," he said.

"What'd you say?"

He shrugged dismissively. "I told her every guy fantasizes about other women." He turned his head toward Chris. "Right?"

Chris slowly shook his head with a wry smile. "Can't help you there, pal. Kimber's more than enough for me."

"Yeah, well, I envy you. You have a great marriage, great kids. Somehow you figured out how to make it work for all these years. For a time, I really thought I could settle down with Gayle. But now I'm not sure. What's wrong with me, man?" He squeezed the steering wheel. "Should've learned my lesson when Sheila divorced me."

Chris raised his eyebrows. He couldn't remember the last time Paul had spoken that name.

"So, what happened there?" Chris pressed. "You never talk about her."

Paul snorted. "I'm not sure why we even got married. I suppose I thought it was time. I found her attractive enough at first, but then I began to find other women more interesting. Sexually, I mean. The less attention I gave Sheila, the more she groused. She didn't buy my 'stress at work' excuses. Then she found out about me and my hygienist—let's just say the relationship had gone beyond professional."

Chris responded point-blank: "Sounds like you really fucked up."

"I know, I know." Paul sighed again. "Truth is, I don't really know what I want in a woman. Maybe I just need more variety than one woman can give me."

"Well, then, I'm flat out of advice, my friend. You're on your own!" Chris reached down to the seat control, reclined back, and pulled his cap over his eyes. "Thankfully, we're on our way to a guys-only hunting trip, far away from any women."

"Amen to that!" Paul replied.

CHAPTER 15

Out on I-90, not far behind Chris and Paul, Ron Grafton reached for his extra-large Diet Pepsi. With a frown, he realized it was empty. Even when he shook the ice around, he still only sucked up air. He'd have to get another one in Mitchell, South Dakota, before heading to Cabela's to meet up with that Matt guy. Maybe another bag of potato chips too.

Ron had been more than a bit surprised that they'd be a quartet, not a trio, this year. Since the very beginning, only Chris, Paul, and Ron had taken part in this annual tradition. No one had even considered extending other invites—even though they each knew several guys dying for the chance.

Yet for some unknown reason, now they'd be joined by Matt Kaufmann. A virtual stranger.

The only explanation Chris had offered was that it was a favor for Matt's wife, the receptionist at the BCA. Ron had met her once. Strawberry blonde, front teeth fighting for space, lots of gums, and not exactly drop-dead gorgeous—though that didn't stop her from putting on a show for every man in her vicinity.

Ron shook his head in confusion. Chris would never stray an inch from Kimber, so Ron knew this wasn't a hanky-panky-type favor. More likely, this was some sort of charity case. Chris could be a pushover for that sometimes.

Ron let out a sigh as he exited the freeway for Mitchell. In a short phone call a day ago, he and Matt had agreed to meet at Cabela's, buy licenses and ammunition, then caravan to the ranch. Matt told Ron to look for a Boss Ford F-150 with oversized tires and red flames airbrushed on the rear fenders.

Ron pulled into the busy parking lot, spotted the truck, and pulled his Honda CR-V next to it. Matt and Ron got out of their vehicles, exchanged handshakes, then headed into Cabela's. Not many words were spoken, other than Ron's few attempts to start a conversation.

While in line to get their licenses, Matt looked at the young woman checking his ID. "You don't exactly give this shit away, do you?" he snapped. He hefted three boxes of 12-gauge shells to make his point.

She looked back down at his ID and ignored his comment. Ron unconsciously took a step backward, trying to distance himself from Matt.

Soon they were back in their vehicles, heading for the Circle J Ranch. After a twenty-minute drive on I-90, they exited at Plankinton, bounced down a rutted country road, and parked in front of the lodge. Chris and Paul had arrived just minutes earlier.

Marv, the owner—rugged, six feet, and younger than his years—came out of the old farmhouse to greet them. The strong west wind slammed the door shut behind him.

"Welcome back," Marv said, stretching out his hand to Chris. "Your sixth year with Judy and me, isn't it?"

"Sure is," Chris said. "First time we came, you'd just built the new lodge. We were the first to stay in it."

"That's right," Paul added. "You hadn't finished the deck yet." He glanced around and noticed several horses gathered around a hay feeder in a fenced-in pen. "Hey, what's with the horses? I don't remember them from last year."

"They're rescued mustangs," Marv said. "Got 'em from the Bureau of Land Management. Want to adopt one?"

Paul held his hands up and shook his head. "No way. Those things scare me to death!"

"Yeah, well, dentists scare me to death!" Marv slapped Paul on the back.

Matt feigned a laugh.

"I see we also have Ron Grafton again," Marv said, once again stretching out his weathered hand. "And who's the newcomer?"

"Matthew Kaufmann. A friend of mine," Chris quickly explained, even though this was the first time he'd ever laid eyes on Matt.

Matt wasn't a tall man, but he was in reasonably good shape. He had a military-like buzz cut, large hands calloused from work as a mechanic, hard eyes, and a thick neck. He nodded to Marv but didn't shake hands.

Marv gestured to the F-150. "That's quite a truck you've got there. You like it?"

Matt crossed his arms with a rough shrug. "It's OK. Your shitty road almost knocked the mirrors off."

Silence followed. Marv looked visibly shocked. Ron and Paul both glanced over at Chris, who was doing his

133

best to maintain a pleasant face, as if all were well.

Thankfully, Judy, Marv's wife, diminutive but spirited, came out of the lodge to break the awkward moment. She was wiping her hands on a towel.

"Just finished cleaning the place. Kitchen's ready for your magic, Majek!" She giggled at her own humor.

"Thanks, Judy."

Chris was the camp cook, a title his culinary skills warranted. Tonight, they'd make a quick supper out of the food Kimber had packed for them: sandwiches, homemade pickles, slaw and potato salad, a huge bag of chips. Tomorrow, Chris would go all out with prime rib, baked potatoes, and all the sides to celebrate what he hoped would be a successful hunt.

"It's cold out here," Judy said, rubbing her hands together. "Why don't y'all go in the lodge and get settled."

Marv nodded. "As always," he said in his baritone voice, "we'll have the safety meeting before heading out tomorrow. If you have any questions, we'll be at the house. Just give us a holler."

Marv and Judy headed back to the farmhouse, arms around each other, Judy leaning her head against her husband's shoulder.

"Married that long and still in love," Paul said, opening the liftgate of his Lexus. "Those two have been together fifty years and counting."

"Not everybody is that lucky," Ron said with the somber wisdom of a widower.

Matt snorted. "I sure as hell can't imagine fuckin' the same woman for fifty years."

Silence returned, as did the glances from Paul and Ron. Once again, Chris couldn't meet their eyes. He didn't wear a pleasant expression this time. He was starting to curse himself for letting Marty persuade him to invite Matt.

With tension still lingering in the air, they hauled their gear into the lodge. A granite-tiled foyer led to a great room adorned with deer and elk mounts on the wall, stuffed pheasants in flight on tabletops, and a winter weasel perched on a gnarly oak branch, guarding the well-stocked bar. Two gray suede leather sofas and three recliners sat in a semicircle, all directed toward the fireplace. Ring stains on the wooden end tables told of many cocktails.

"Looks like they spared no expense furnishing the place," Matt commented.

With that, Chris relaxed a bit. It was the first decent thing to come from Matt's mouth. Maybe they had just gotten off on the wrong foot. Perhaps Matt was tired and cranky after the long drive, but he was settling in now.

To engage Matt even more, Chris gave a nod toward the floor-to-ceiling fireplace. "Marv built that himself. It's all fieldstone from the land we'll be hunting tomorrow. And the oak floor you're standing on came from trees he harvested and dried in his kiln. Just wait until you see the kitchen."

Matt's blank face indicated that he had suddenly lost interest, but Chris pressed on.

"Bedrooms are upstairs. You'll love the king-size beds."

He pointed to the loft dominating the other end of the great room. On the knotty pine wall adjacent to the staircase hung a rug that once belonged to a bear.

"Take your pick of rooms, everyone," Chris instructed, settling into the unofficial role of lodge leader. "Let's all get settled, then we'll meet down here for cocktails before I set out our dinner."

"Fuck that," Matt said as he tore into a case of Coors he'd hauled in. "I'm not waiting." He grabbed a can, gathered up his gear, and headed upstairs.

The other three men just stared after him.

"Actually," Paul said, his voice thin and tense, "I think I'll skip dinner tonight, guys. I'm gonna hit the sack. It's a big day tomorrow, and I'm really bushed." Without waiting for a reply, he headed upstairs.

Chris frowned. Paul had never gone to bed this early. He usually enjoyed the first night at the lodge—sitting by the fire, swapping stories over cocktails before finally retiring. Then again, Paul had seemed tired all day. And quite frankly, Matt's behavior would push anyone away, tired or not.

By early evening, Chris, Ron, and Matt reconvened for drinks in the great room. Chris and Ron were sipping single malt scotch. The empty cans on the kitchen counter indicated Matt was already on his third beer.

"How's work going for you, Matt?" Chris asked. "Marty tells me you're at 3M. Whaddya do there?"

"Mechanic. It's boring. But gets me away from Marty for a while. That's the good part." He rolled his eyes as he took a swig.

No wonder she flirts every chance she gets, thought Chris. *She sure picked a loser.*

"How long you two been married?" Ron asked.

"Three years. But it seems like goddamn forever, know what I mean?"

Ron narrowed his eyes. Chris could tell it was getting harder and harder for the deputy to disguise his dislike of Matt.

"Second time for you both, right?" Chris quickly interjected before Ron could speak.

Matt wiped his mouth on his sleeve. "Yeah. I tried to get my first marriage annulled. Thought we had a chance, since we'd failed to carry out orders."

"Orders?" Ron looked confused.

"You know—Holy Roman edict. Go forth and multiply. Have kids even if you can't afford 'em. Pray, pay, and obey! Especially pay." In disgust, Matt crushed his empty beer can.

"What do those things cost, those annulments?" Ron asked.

"Upward of a thousand dollars," Matt said, shaking his head in disgust. "What a fucking racket. So we took the simple way out—lived apart for a year. That satisfied Ontario's grounds for divorce."

Matt let out a belch, then made his way to the kitchen for another beer. He tossed the empty can on the counter with a clatter.

"The recycling bin is right next to the stove, you know!" Ron called out, annoyed. "Put your empties in there!"

"I'm going outside for a cigar," he said, leaving the cans on the counter.

Ron and Chris could hear the telltale crack of the beer can being opened before Matt slammed the door behind him.

"Jesus, Chris—what'd you get us into, inviting that guy?" Ron asked point blank.

Chris cringed. "I know. I know. I had no idea. Marty said he was a great guy..."

"And you *believed* her?" He let out a terse laugh. "Well, maybe he is a 'great guy' to her. She's not exactly a catch."

"I think she's kind of attractive," Chris retorted, more out of loyalty to Marty than out of honesty. "But gorgeous or not, she doesn't deserve to be married to that prick."

"Well, she better start saving up for a divorce attorney," Ron deadpanned.

They were both laughing a half hour later when Matt returned from the porch, a stubbed Cohiba Robusto bobbing between his tobacco-stained lips. He glanced back and forth between them, an eyebrow raised.

"Sounds like I missed a joke, eh?"

"Nah, just work stuff," Chris said.

Ron smirked as he took a sip of his scotch.

Matt nodded to Chris. "Marty says you're working on the priest murder in Scandia, right? What's the deal with that? Got a suspect yet?"

"I can't discuss unsolved cases," Chris said, firmly but politely. "Just leave the investigation to us." The edge in his voice was unmistakable.

"Yeah," Ron said, not so politely. "Go with what you read in the papers and hear on TV."

"That's fuckin' bullshit," Matt snarled.

With that cue, Chris popped to his feet. "Let's eat, huh?" he said.

Chris began to set out the food Kimber had prepared. The men filled their plates and ate at the kitchen table in silence. Chris thought of Paul already in bed. He always loved Kimber's pickles. She had packed them especially for him.

As Matt helped himself to another sandwich, Ron helped Chris clean up. Ron roughly threw Matt's beer cans into the recycling bin one by one, hoping the newcomer would get the point. Matt just continued to eat.

"You know what—I'll see you in the morning," Ron finally said to Chris, shaking his head.

"Oh, OK. Night," Chris replied.

Chris, too, was more than ready for the evening to end, but he felt uneasy about leaving Matt on his own, so he puttered around, looking busy, while Matt finished eating.

"Wanna join me for a cigar?"

Chris looked over at Matt in surprise. It seemed like a genuine invitation.

"I'm not a cigar man myself, but I'll come sit with you," Chris replied.

The pair donned jackets and headed out to the porch steps. Wind rattled the branches of the maple trees. Lights on the semitrucks pierced the darkness as they coursed down I-90.

Matt shivered and pulled his jacket tighter to his body. "Damn cold out here." He cupped his hands around his lighter as he lit another cigar.

Chris nodded. "Yeah. It'll be cold again tomorrow, but the clouds are supposed to clear. The sun will be shining, so it won't feel so bad. Hunting should be good."

"Sure as hell hope so," Matt said, taking a puff, "considering what this cost us." With his free hand, he reached for his beer. It was empty. "Shit. I shoulda brought another."

All Chris could do was sigh. "Hey, just a little word from the wise: you should call it a night. You need to stay sharp for tomorrow. Guns and hangovers are a bad combination."

Matt leered at him, his eyes glossy. "Don't worry about me. I got no problem with guns."

He took a last puff, then snuffed the cigar on the step. He pushed himself to his feet, stumbled a second, then headed inside.

Chris slowly rose to his feet and followed after him, subtly but successfully herding him toward the staircase.

"You know that guy deserved to be killed—that priest," Matt said suddenly, without turning around to face Chris. "I read in the paper that he had been accused of abusing kids." His words slurred together quietly. "All those perverts deserve to be killed ... Fuckin' scum."

As Matt disappeared into his room, Chris stood frozen at the bottom of the stairs. Since the moment Matt had stepped out of his truck, he had been nothing but cocky, rude, arrogant—a total asshole. But these words were different. They were angry, yes, but Chris could sense pain behind them. He thought back to his conversation with Phil Walker as they contemplated what life must be like for

140

adults who had been abused at the hands of priests. For all Chris knew, Matt was one of them.

Chris made a mental note to check out Matt's alibi for the night of Doyle's murder.

CHAPTER 16

T he drive to Stillwater was taking longer than Kimber had planned. An early freeze-thaw cycle had caused chunks of rock to tumble onto the road from the sandstone cliffs, and she was behind someone driving as slowly as possible to avoid hitting them.

With no opportunity to pass on the winding road, she settled back and thought about Paul. *What is it about this guy? He's got a great woman who loves him. They seemed to share the same interests. Got along great at first. But suddenly something's changed. I wonder if he's intentionally causing this relationship to fail.*

Kimber crossed Highway 36, then turned right onto Pickett Avenue and into the parking lot of Oak Bluff Apartments. Standing out from the surrounding structures, Gayle's apartment building was an upscale ten-story property. Dried vines still adorned with Christmas lights clung to the brick facade.

Stepping around patches of slushy snow, Kimber made her way along the winding cobblestone walkway to the foyer and rang the buzzer for "307, Armstrong, G." When the security lock clicked, she pushed open the door and trudged up three flights of stairs to the apartment.

By the time Gayle greeted her at the door, Kimber was out of breath.

"The elevator is there for a reason, you know," Gayle said.

"Yeah, but I need the exercise," Kimber replied, handing Gayle her leather coat. "Nurses on my floor are always bringing cookies and candy, especially over the holidays. I can't resist the stuff, and it ends up on my hips!" She patted her sides as if for proof.

Gayle laughed as she draped the coat over a bar stool by her kitchen island. "What are you talking about, Little Miss Perfect? In that dress, you'll be getting a lot of attention tonight!"

Kimber shrugged, unconvinced. "If you say so."

Gayle pointed to an open bottle of chardonnay sitting on the counter. "How about a glass of wine before we hit the town? We'll take an Uber so we don't have to worry about drinking."

"Sure. Why not?"

As Gayle poured the wine, Kimber strolled about the apartment, admiring the orchids on a teak bench by the windowsill and the newly painted pastel walls. She settled into an overstuffed easy chair as Gayle handed her a wineglass.

"Let's make it a fun weekend!" Kimber said, tilting her glass toward Gayle.

Their glassed clinked.

As Kimber glanced around again, she realized something was off in the otherwise perfect room. Then it dawned on her. "No Christmas tree this year? No decorations?"

There was a pause as Gayle frowned.

"We put up a tree at Paul's house, but I could tell his heart wasn't in it. And . . . well . . . Christmas sucked this year anyway. That fight we had at Stella's the other night—we were supposed to go to Maui for Christmas, but Paul cancelled the trip at the last minute. Said he was too busy. Just another one of his 'It's all about me' maneuvers lately. I was really disappointed. Had a tour of the Haiku orchid plantation arranged. And I was really excited about Christmas on the beach."

Kimber cringed. In contrast, Christmas at the Majek household had been, well, magical. Good food, good cheer, and good times together as a family—including Brodie, who ended up with more presents than anyone else. Kimber knew that Gayle wanted that same feeling of togetherness and love, and she had thought she'd found it in Paul.

Kimber tried to find a bright side. "Well, did you at least exchange gifts or celebrate in a special way here at home?"

"I haven't heard a word from him since Stella's, and there's his gift," Gayle replied flatly. She pointed with her eyes toward the potted ficus plant, then took a long drink.

Kimber followed Gayle's glance and discovered the wadded-up Hermès scarf stuffed in the dirt. "What the hell did you do? Isn't that the scarf he gave you? It must have cost him a fortune!"

Gayle nodded. "Oh, I *know* it did. But there's more to that story."

"Let's hear it." Kimber's eyebrows raised in anticipation of a juicy tale.

Gayle chewed at her fingernail. "When he seemed to

be losing interest in me, I started snooping around in his dresser drawers—"

Kimber's eyebrows shot up even more.

Gayle spoke quickly before Kimber could interject. "I know, I know. I shouldn't have done it. But I couldn't help myself. He's been acting so strangely lately. Everything just started going downhill a few weeks ago, out of nowhere. I guess I just wanted 'answers,' so I went looking." She bit at her fingernails again. "Anyway, I found a whole bunch of scarves and jewelry and other expensive women's gifts in his drawer."

Kimber shook her head in confusion. "Do you think they're for another woman?"

"No. I think it's just a stash he keeps handy so he's ready to dish something out to the lucky lady of the hour. Incidentally, there was a receipt with the scarf he gave me. Turns out he bought it a couple years ago."

"But he told us he'd bought it for you at Nordstrom the day before . . . ?" Kimber couldn't help but form it as a question.

Gayle took another drink. Her face grimaced as if she had swallowed a bitter pill.

"I nearly died when I opened it," she said. "And then I nearly died again as I sat there and listened to his lie about how he'd picked it out just for me. He gives me material things to keep me around, but he won't give me *himself*. I feel like a whore." Her eyes filmed over.

Kimber could feel her gut tighten. "I'm so sorry." She pointed her thumb at herself. "This is my fault for thinking the two of you would be a good match."

Gayle's expression softened. "No," she said, gently but firmly. "There's no way you could have known it'd turn out this way. I mean, when Paul and I first started dating, we *were* a good match. It felt real." She stared into her glass for a moment, then looked up and sighed. "It felt normal. It felt good. He seemed serious about me. I thought he might be the one. But suddenly, he's losing interest. I sense it. Do you know that when we were on that Antarctica cruise, he was seriously hitting on another woman the entire time? He didn't even care that I was upset. And it's just gotten worse since then."

She sighed, dabbed her eyes, and waved her hands as if literally clearing the air.

"Enough about that," she said, determined. "Let's table it for now and concentrate on having a fun evening."

"All right." Kimber nodded in approval. "Where ya wanna go?"

"Freight House would be good. There's a nice bar there, and we can find a quiet place to chat. If we're really hungry, we can go to Marx—or we can just stay at the Freight House and do appetizers."

Kimber raised her nearly full glass for another toast, then noticed Gayle's glass was empty. "Downtown, here we come," she said, tilting her glass toward Gayle anyway.

Ten minutes later, Gayle and Kimber were gazing out the window as their Uber driver slowly squeezed through Stillwater traffic, passing the ice castle lit up in red, blue, and yellow lights. The colors glowed through the frozen blocks.

"Have you been through the castle yet?" Kimber asked Gayle. "Chris and I went last week. It's quite a project: ice slides for kids, coffee, cider, hot chocolate. The one in Saint Paul is even bigger, they say."

"Paul and I were supposed to go, but . . ." She didn't complete the sentence.

Kimber wanted to kick herself for bringing up yet another painful memory. Instead, she reached over, took her friend's hand, and squeezed it gently. They fell into an uncomfortable silence, punctuated by shrieks from excited children riding down the slides.

The Freight House was abuzz with activity. As the women walked in, men noticed—Kimber in her wrap dress, Gayle in leggings and below-the-knee boots.

A live band was playing, making the bar noisier than Gayle had expected. "I'm sorry," she shouted, leaning toward Kimber's ear. "I didn't know they'd have music tonight. I hope we can find a quiet place to sit."

They waited for a table in the corner, where the music was tempered. When the server arrived, Gayle ordered prosecco.

"I need something bubbly to start with," she explained to both the server and Kimber. "Then chardonnay later. And maybe even a cosmo." She was definitely in the mood to drink.

The server looked expectantly at Kimber.

"I'll just have prosecco," she said succinctly, indicating she didn't have such grand plans for tying one on.

When the drinks arrived, Gayle took a long sip and gazed across the room at a couple with their arms around each other, laughing and kissing. She nodded toward them.

"Seems every other couple is happy and madly in love. Except me." She turned back to Kimber with searching eyes. "You ever feel that way about your relationship with Chris?"

"Sure, a long time ago," she admitted. "But not anymore."

"What did you do about it?"

"We went to counseling. It helped a lot. Turned out, it wasn't about what I thought he was doing 'wrong' or vice versa. It was about the things I needed to address about myself and the things he needed to address about himself. Maybe it'd help you guys too?" she suggested gently.

Gayle let out a sharp laugh. "Paul says counseling is bullshit." She raised her glass and spoke from behind it before taking a drink. "I just think he doesn't want to let me in. Lately, he's been keeping everything from me, it seems. Like, what's going on with his health?"

"He *has* lost some weight," Kimber agreed. "Even Chris noticed it at Stella's."

"I keep asking about it, and he gets madder and madder each time—you know how men think we nurses know too much."

"It's because we do!" Kimber laughed.

Gayle tried to laugh, but it sounded more like a sigh. "I don't know. Maybe it's just me. Maybe he'd be willing to talk about all this stuff with another guy. Like Chris." She held out her hand toward Kimber. "Has Chris ever said anything to you about Paul? About me?"

Kimber snorted. "Chris didn't even know you guys were having issues until the dinner at Stella's. Totally clueless."

"Well, then, does he know anything about Paul that might give me some insight? Maybe about his childhood?"

Kimber had to think. "I sort of remember Chris saying that Paul's dad was rough on him—controlling, abusive, a bit of a bully. There was a younger brother too, but he died . . . somehow . . ." She trailed off. "I don't know anything more. You know guys—they don't like to get into details."

Gayle pouted. "That's more than I've ever heard! Why can't Paul talk to me about these things? Whenever I ask him about his family, he just changes the subject." She tapped a fingernail on the table. "I'd like to talk to his ex-wife. Find out why they divorced."

"Oh yeah. I'd forgotten he'd been married before. I never knew her. She was history long before Chris and I met him."

Both women were quiet as they sipped their drinks. In the background, the band played a rendition of the Rolling Stones' "You Can't Always Get What You Want."

Finally, Kimber sighed. "Gayle, my best friend—you're a smart, attractive woman. You deserve better than this. The right man's out there. You just haven't met him yet."

"Trouble is, it's Paul I want." Gayle gripped the stem of her wineglass. "I care for him so goddamn much my heart breaks when I think it might not work out."

Just as tears welled in Gayle's eyes and began to spill, a server arrived with two fresh glasses of prosecco.

"Compliments of the guys over there," she explained, nodding toward the end of the bar.

Two smartly dressed men wearing sport coats raised their glasses and began strolling over.

"Heads up. Looks like we're getting company," whispered Kimber, elbowing Gayle. "Kind of fun. Reminds me of our college days!"

Gayle quickly dabbed her eyes and put on an attempt at a smile.

"Hi, ladies. I'm Rick, and this is Ben."

"Nice to meet you. I'm Kimber, and this is Gayle," Kimber said, gesturing.

Then Rick noticed Kimber's wedding ring. "Oh, sorry," he said sheepishly. "I didn't realize you were married."

She laughed. "That's okay. We're just having a girls' night out."

"Actually, we're moving on for dinner soon," Gayle added somewhat tersely. "But thanks for the drinks."

Kimber tried not to react to hearing they were leaving soon, even if it was news to her.

"Maybe you've got time for just one dance before you go?" said Ben, his kind eyes looking brightly toward Gayle.

Kimber looked at Gayle too. "I don't know about you, but I'm in. Just because I'm married doesn't mean I can't dance."

A genuine smile slowly spread across Gayle's mouth. "Hell, why not? Let's dance."

Kimber grabbed Rick's arm with one hand and Gayle's with the other. "C'mon!" she said, motioning to Ben as well.

Not one but two dances later, the ladies thanked Ben and Rick, then gathered their belongings to head over to Marx. As they neared the door, Ben rushed over and slipped his business card into Gayle's hand.

"If you'd like to meet up for a drink sometime, give me a call or text me." He smiled at her and gave her hand a gentle squeeze. "Seriously, I'd like to see you again."

Kimber could all but see a warm flush move through Gayle's body. They linked arms and giggled a bit as they headed across the street.

Marx, sans band, was more conducive to conversation. They chose a booth at the back of the dining room and ordered salad, linguine with shrimp, and a bottle of Oak Creek chardonnay.

Gayle sighed. "OK, I have to admit, it felt good to be noticed." She peeked at Ben's card. "Ben Porter, VP, Merrill Lynch, Saint Paul."

Kimber let out an impressed whistle. "Well, hang on to that, girl. You sure were smiling out on the dance floor."

Gayle fidgeted with her napkins. "So why did it feel like I was cheating on Paul?"

"There's nothing wrong with a little dance," Kimber argued. "Look at me—I'm married, and I didn't feel like I was cheating on Chris. You, you're not even engaged!"

That did it. Gayle burst into tears. "Exactly," she said, trying to quiet her sobs. "We're not engaged! But we almost were." She caught her breath, but her voice still trembled. "Remember when Paul flew me to New York for a romantic weekend a while back? We were walking down Fifth Avenue, and he actually stopped outside Tiffany's to look at the window display. He said, 'Next time we're in New York, we'll come back here, buy you the biggest diamond I can afford, and tie the knot.' I even thought he might propose in Maui, but then *this* happened—whatever *this* is."

She buried her face in her hands and cried. Tears streaking her makeup, she looked through her fingers at her friend.

"What changed? What did I do?" she asked, pleading. "What didn't I do?"

Kimber wanted nothing more than to give her friend an answer that would end her confusion and misery. But she couldn't. Instead, all she could do was be there for her through the pain.

"I'm so sorry, Gayle," she whispered.

Just then, a handsome young waiter arranged their supper on the table. Gayle wiped her tears and picked at the food. As hungry as she had been moments earlier, Kimber, too, found herself barely able to eat.

The Uber ride back to the apartment was silent, save for the rhythmic thump of the wiper blades and the whoosh of the tires on the slushy pavement. Gayle laid her head against the window and quietly wept. Kimber, at a loss for words, closed her eyes and said a small prayer for Gayle.

They rode up the elevator to the third floor, both unsteady on their feet, thanks to alcohol but more to emotional exhaustion. Without a word, they each headed into a bedroom to change into their nightclothes.

Minutes later, Kimber tapped on Gayle's door.

"Come in."

Gayle was in bed, her head propped up on pillows, hands folded across her stomach. She was staring into space. Kimber sat on the edge of the bed.

"I wish there was a magic wand that could make things better, Gayle. I really do."

"I know you do."

Gayle's eyes were once again puddling with tears. Kimber nestled down beside her. Gayle snuggled her head on Kimber's chest, crying uncontrollably. Kimber held her tight, stroking her hair.

When Gayle finally fell asleep, Kimber lay still for a while. Atop the dresser next to the bed was a framed photograph of Paul. He was standing on his deck above the Saint Croix, wrapped in a wool coat, hands in his pockets, smiling into the camera, without a care in the world.

Paul Thomas, you sure had me fooled.

CHAPTER 17

As the sun crested the horizon and chased away the stars, Chris stepped outside into the cold December air. The dogs began barking, and the horses, a light dusting of snow on their backs, ran to the edge of the corral. The soft early light fringed their black manes with a golden glow. He chuckled to himself when the sun reflected off Dr. Paul Thomas's car, illuminating the vanity plate reading FLOSSEM.

Soon the lodge was astir as the other three came to life. Chris prepared coffee and omelets.

Matt was moving slowly, his feet shuffling on the oak floor. "Somebody shoulda told me not to drink the last couple of beers," he groaned.

Chris raised his eyebrows and poured Matt a cup of coffee. "Cream? Sugar?" he asked.

"No, just black," Matt replied. "It better be strong."

"Maybe you should just eat the grounds," Ron offered flatly, his hands tightening around his own coffee cup.

Chris gave Ron a look as he began putting plates on the table. Tolerating Matt was difficult enough without Ron stirring the pot even more. And they had a long day of hunting ahead of them.

"How about you, Doc? Coffee?" Chris asked as Paul came into the kitchen.

A grimace came over Paul's face. "No. It's hard on my system." He waved a hand over his stomach. "And no omelet for me. Just toast."

"Sure thing," Chris answered. He studied Paul carefully. For someone who went to bed before supper, he didn't look rested.

After breakfast, the men walked over to the garage. They took seats at an old picnic table for the mandatory safety meeting Marv and Judy required all groups to attend before being allowed to hunt. The foursome sat close together in the unheated building.

In addition to discussing gun safety, Marv stressed that only roosters could be shot. "*Never* shoot the hens." His deep, rich baritone voice rattled the windows of the small structure. He removed his glasses and scanned each man, one by one. "You guys get it? *Never*! Start shootin' hens, and the game warden will be all over my ranch." He was silent for a moment for emphasis.

His directive commanded everyone's attention. Even Chris and Ron, who had taken plenty of orders from stern authority figures, sat up a little straighter and nodded their compliance.

"Because you guys are a small group," Marv continued, "we'll hunt some of the narrow fields. You'll be close together. So be safe. Look out for one another."

Ron immediately turned to Matt, somewhat accusingly. Matt scowled back. "Fuck off," he muttered.

Chris wanted to give them both a talking-to, but he didn't dare interrupt Marv.

After the meeting, the group climbed into a reconditioned school bus and stowed their shotguns in a crude wooden rack. Judy would drive them to the fields Marv had chosen for the hunt. Behind the bus, Marv would follow in a rusted Ford pickup carrying two Labrador retrievers in wire kennels.

The bus bounced and pitched as it crossed the fields on the bumpy narrow dirt lane. Chris couldn't recall the ride being so rough in past years, but Judy was putting the pedal to the metal this morning. She looked in the rearview mirror and smirked as she watched her passengers holding tightly on to the grab bars while bouncing on the seats.

Everyone knew she was specifically punishing Matt, whose eyes were still red and whose rude comments from the night before were still fresh. Chris wondered if perhaps he, Ron, and Paul were being subjected to the same punishment simply for having brought Matt along on the trip.

The narrow path twisted through the fields, passing a sign Marv had made to discourage illegal hunting: AREA 51—NO TRESPASSING! VIOLATORS WILL VANISH WITHOUT A TRACE. The sign was prominently displayed on a fence post.

At the first field, each hunter disembarked the bus and was assigned a field position. Ron and Matt couldn't hide their frowns as they were designated to walk through the sorghum and tall corn together, the toughest part of the hunt. Paul and Chris would be wingmen, walking along the sides.

Marv released the dogs. They ran wildly through the field until he calmed them down.

"All right now," Marv said with a wave. "Good luck, fellas." He drove the pickup to the far end of the field, where he would be the spotter. Judy stayed behind and would pick up the men once the field had been hunted.

"Shall we, gentlemen?" Chris said, gesturing to the field stretching out in front of them.

"No time like the present," Paul replied.

"Your fat ass better keep up," Matt said to Ron under his breath as they took their first steps into the thick sorghum.

The group hunted through the morning. By most accounts, it was a grand success. Birds were plentiful, and the dogs worked well. Everyone got their limit—everyone but Paul. Typically a sure shot, he'd missed several birds. And the one he did shoot was a hen.

When Marv saw the hen, his face flushed crimson.

"I'm sorry, Marv," Chris said, stepping up and covering for Paul. "It was a complete accident. What would you like us to do?"

Marv frowned a long time. "Nothing," he said in a huff. "I'll handle it." He turned and walked back to his truck, taking the hen with him.

Chris glanced at Paul, but Paul wouldn't return the look.

In past years, a successful morning of filled limits would have been followed with photo ops in the field, high fives, and congratulatory banter. Instead, the men boarded the bus in silence. Judy didn't smile on the way back to the lodge, though the ride was just as bumpy. Maybe even more so.

Back at the garage, the men began unloading the shells from their shotguns. Marv let the dogs out for some water. They were a bit subdued, as if they, too, sensed the tension.

Chris studied his new Benelli. He knew he could unload by using the pump action to release the rounds from the magazine. He chose instead to manually remove them from the ejection port. It was safer.

Just then, a shot exploded only feet away. Dirt flew as Matt's gun accidentally fired into the ground. Everyone crouched defensively—as if that would have made any difference, had Matt's barrel been pointed at them.

Chris locked in on Matt with laser focus. For a split second, Matt's face registered horror and regret as he stared down at the shotgun in his hands. It was an expression of someone shocked by the power of a gun and how close it had come to killing someone.

"Jesus Christ!" Marv bellowed. "You could have killed one of us or the dogs!"

He shook his head in disgust as he stormed to his truck. He called the dogs to their kennels, slammed the doors, and then wheeled around, finger pointing at each of the men.

"First the hen, now this. Another incident like this tomorrow, and you guys are done!"

Chris winced as Marv's eyes, so full of disappointment, met his for a brief moment. Marv held his point on Matt a while longer.

"And you—I haven't liked your attitude from the beginning. If you can't take safety seriously, you can leave right now!"

Matt looked away but refused to respond.

Marv stomped into the farmhouse. Judy stood there long enough to give a disapproving stare to the group before following her husband.

"Goddammit!" Ron hissed at Matt as soon as the door closed behind Judy. "That scared the shit out of us!"

"Scared me too," Matt said with a shrug. "Whatever."

"Listen here." Ron's voice was rising now. "The three of us have been going on this trip for years. But now we may never get asked back, thanks to you."

"Me? What about Dr. Dentist over here?" Matt fired back, hiking a thumb at Paul. "He couldn't hit the broad side of a barn today. The only thing he did hit was that hen. That's *illegal*. If they kick your asses out, that's why. Not me."

"Yeah," Ron said, turning his sights on Paul now. "What the hell happened there?"

"I don't know." Paul stared at his shotgun propped up next to the picnic table. "Damned bird startled me, bursting out of the snow like that. I just shot."

"Chris and I yelled 'Hen!'" Ron pressed. "But you still shot. Twice. What were you thinking? The difference between the roosters and the hens is obvious—the colors, the long tail, the white collar."

Paul said nothing. His foot started bouncing.

"Even the fuckin' dogs know the difference!" Matt shouted.

Seeing Paul's pinched face, Chris had to intervene. "Hey, knock it off, guys—that's enough."

He wasn't sure why, but Paul wasn't himself. Perhaps the fallout from his fight with Gayle was affecting him more than he let on.

"Let's go back to the lodge and have a little lunch, all right?" Chris said. He rubbed his face and sighed. "And maybe we could all use a nap."

By the evening, tensions seemed to abate—likely due to Chris's fantastic prime rib dinner. The group was spread around the great room, enjoying after-dinner drinks. Chris was happy to see Paul join them this time, though he was still quiet.

A bottle of Chivas Regal Gold Signature rested on an end table for Chris and Ron. Matt was nearing the end of his case of Coors, having gotten yet another early start. Paul wasn't drinking.

"That prime rib was out of this world," Ron commented. He lounged on the sofa, his stockinged feet up on the coffee table.

"Really? Even better than at Meyer's?" Chris joked. The restaurant had a reputation for excellent prime rib.

"Well, your prime rib may be better," Ron said, "but you can't beat Meyer's for 'customer service.'" He winked, knowing that Chris also knew Brenda.

"This is true," Chris replied, tipping his drink.

"Say, Doc," Ron said, turning to Paul. "I keep meaning to tell you about my niece. She's thinking of dentistry."

"Good for her. That's great!"

"Where'd you do your pre-dent?"

"I went to St. Thomas," Paul answered, smiling.

"Why didn't you go to St. Michael's?" Ron asked. "My niece says they have a stronger science program."

Paul's smile immediately disappeared. A pause hovered in the room before he spoke. "My younger brother went to St. Michael's. Dad chose that school for him before he even graduated high school. Said he wanted us to have 'different experiences.' Anyway, I had a scholarship to St. Thomas, so it made more sense for me to go there." Paul looked away.

For a moment, no one said anything.

As Paul's closest friend, Chris understood the reason for the painful silence. He subtly gestured a signal for Ron to let it go. Knowing Paul only through the hunting trips, Ron didn't quite understand what had just transpired, though he respected it. He nodded back at Chris.

Of course, Matt was entirely clueless. "What?" he said. "I don't get it."

Paul's head was still turned away, looking at the fireplace.

Chris cleared his throat. "Paul's younger brother passed away in college."

It was a pat response. He himself knew very little about the situation, so there wasn't much more to add. All Chris knew was that Paul and Nick had been close—best friends as well as brothers. When he died, a part of Paul died as well. He was still grieving all these years later. Having a difficult relationship with his father only compounded the situation.

162

Ron quickly changed the subject. "How about those Rice Krispie bars Kimber made? I could have eaten the whole tray."

"You look like you *did* eat the whole tray," Matt muttered. He crushed his empty beer can and tossed it on the coffee table. "You know what? I'm gonna switch to scotch. Pass the bottle."

"No," Ron said sharply, as if scolding a child. "You are not mixing scotch with beer. It's a stupid combination. You'll be sick tomorrow, for Christ's sake." He sat up straight, hoisting his belly high. "And quite frankly, I think you've had enough. You were drunk off your ass last night, you nearly killed us all today, and now you're drunk off your ass again."

Chris raised his hands in an attempt for peace. It was ignored.

Matt's eyes flashed with contempt. "You know what? As much as I *appreciate* being invited on this little trip of yours, I didn't come for a fucking lecture on my drinking. I get enough of that shit from Marty."

"If it weren't for Marty"—Ron was practically shouting now—"you wouldn't be here. I don't know why Chris gave in to her and let you come."

Chris outwardly cringed now. "Ron, that's—"

But before Chris could finish, Paul abruptly stood, silencing everyone. He was still looking away. His face was white. He held his arms tightly down at his sides.

"I am going to bed." His words were clipped. He tilted his head slightly toward Chris. "And I will be going home first thing in the morning."

Still silent, the other three men watched as Paul strode past them, walking quickly up the stairs. Then both Ron and Matt turned to Chris, their expressions a mix of confusion, concern, and expectation.

A tired ache spread through Chris's entire body. He was done. Enough.

"You know what, guys?" he began, pressing both hands into his lap. "Let's chalk this one up as a loss and all head home in the morning. Agreed?" Without waiting for their replies, he pushed himself to his feet.

It was the end of the evening. And the end of the hunting trip.

CHAPTER 18

My work with Doyle and Rodriguez is making the front page of both newspapers. The reporters leave out certain details, such as the rosary decades the priests received in their last rites. Typical of the police to hold back secrets. Not unlike the church.

The rosary was a gift from an aunt many years ago. It came in an engraved ivory box, a bas-relief of Christ on the cross adorned the top. When I lifted the cover and saw the bright red beads, I feigned appreciation. As perhaps the most pious member of a very religious family, my aunt hoped the rosary would bring me closer to God. She didn't know I was already lost to the church.

Today, the rosary would be quite valuable, had I not cut it apart into the decades. I have three decades left.

But killing is not on my mind today. My destination is a condominium in Bloomington. There's a corner penthouse on the fourteenth floor. It offers panoramic views of the Minnesota River, Fort Snelling, and the Saint Paul skyline. The parking is underground, but I wear my dark glasses and baseball cap, just in case. Overconfidence can be costly. But I'm smarter than that.

The elevator opens on the top floor, and I walk down the hall to 1410. I knock. The peephole darkens as Alexa looks out. The door opens.

Alexa nods at my feet, a subtle reminder to take off my shoes. Everything in the apartment is kept clean, including Alexa.

The penthouse is exquisitely decorated. A red Tabriz Persian carpet covers most of the hardwood floor, leaving a border of beautiful white oak. The coffee table is modern—stainless steel and glass. The sofa is soft white leather. Alexa's own art adorns the walls: watercolors of flowers and distant European places. French landscapes are the dominant theme.

I move to the window and watch a passenger jet on final approach to the Minneapolis–Saint Paul International Airport. It reminds me of the days when I could sit on Post Road and watch airplanes land. Not anymore. Not since 9/11.

Alexa is a moniker, not a real name. I know that. My real name has been revealed, however. It was a requirement that I be fully vetted before we could do business. A risk I was prepared to take.

"What is it you wish for today?" Alexa asks. "You wanted extra time. That's unusual."

Brown eyes with long eyelashes stare at me seductively. Alexa's skin is flawless. Soft, carnal, bestial, lightly dusted with smoky perfume.

I explain that I'd like to talk afterward. Alexa reminds me the price for conversation is the same as the price for pleasure. I remove a thick envelope from my pocket and place it on the coffee table. Paid in full. In advance. Alexa picks it up and carefully thumbs through the contents before setting it aside.

"And I brought you a gift," I say. "Something that reminds me of you. Found it in Chicago." I hand Alexa a Neiman Marcus bag, which gets blandly set aside on a countertop of hammered copper.

"Thank you, Paul. But just to remind you, the price is the same."

I nod my understanding.

As I follow Alexa into the bedroom, I admire the smooth, gliding movement of the slim body I'm about to enjoy. I'm aroused, getting hard. I love the straight black hair that flows to Alexa's round, delicious backside.

The room is lavishly furnished with mirrors. A variety of lotions and lubricants are neatly arranged on a shelf above the bed, within easy reach. Bright sunshine streams through the floor-to-ceiling windows. No need for curtains fourteen stories above the world.

"Your test results, please," Alexa asks.

It's required that every client get an STI test within five days prior to an encounter. STI—that's the new name for it. It used to be STD and just VD, back in the day.

My papers are in order, and I hand them over. Alexa also carefully examines my body. I'm deemed safe.

We kiss. I relish Alexa's deep, moist kisses. Soft lips traverse my body, down my stomach, gently sucking the head of my penis, licking the shaft. Delicate fingers caress my balls. Alexa is well lubricated. For the first hour, we focus on my needs, then Alexa's.

Afterward, showered and dressed, we return to the living room and sit beside each other on the white sofa. I'm nursing vodka on ice. Alexa nods discreetly toward the clock. I know my time is running out.

I mention the valuable red marble rosary my aunt gave me long ago. In my hand are the remaining decades. The pieces swing with my gesticulations as I explain how my aunt could *never have guessed how this rosary would become communion for those who labor in the name of the Lord.*

None of this means anything to Alexa. I know I should stop. Leave now. Before I reveal something I shouldn't.

But I can't stop. My voice gets louder, a noisy clamor. I blather on, pontificating about whether killing a sexual predator is murder or an essential service. Blood pounds through my ears. My face is hot. I'm in a long, dark tunnel.

My lover grows confused, afraid. My manic intensity makes no sense to Alexa, because I withhold details that would give it meaning. Alexa slowly slides away from me.

My head begins to spin. I stand and pace the floor.

Fear scuffles across Alexa's brow. His beautiful creamy cheeks, barely smudged by facial hair, bloom a rosy red. He stands abruptly. Informs me my time is up. His beautiful eyes darken further. I must leave. I must never come back, he demands.

I plead to stay longer, to explain. I beg.

He mentions those who will do me harm if I return. His voice is lower now, reflecting his masculinity. No more fake falsetto. No soft lisp. He reminds me that he knows who I am, where I can be found. He tells me to go. The warmth in his eyes is replaced with cold blackness.

I don't remember the elevator ride to the parking garage. I find myself walking unsteadily to my car. I'm trembling. Fumbling for the key fob in my pocket, I accidentally activate the alarm. The staccato blare of the horn further rattles my galvanized nerves. I look around the enclosure to see if anyone's noticed. Satisfied I'm alone, I unlock the vehicle and get in.

My car isolates me from the world outside. For several minutes, I sit quietly in the heated garage, waiting for my breathing to normalize. My mouth is dry, and my shirt is soaked with sweat. The trembling slowly subsides.

For a moment, I think of calling Gayle. I won't, though. I can't.

It's time to go home.

PART II

MEA CULPA

The consecrated person, chosen by God to guide souls to salvation, lets himself be subjugated by his own human frailty, or by his own illness, thus becoming a tool of Satan. In the abuses, we see the hand of evil that does not spare even the innocence of children.

—POPE FRANCIS, FEBRUARY 24, 2019

CHAPTER 19

After tossing and turning most of the night, Chris cut his losses and got an early start Monday morning. He was on the road already at seven, heading for the BCA. He knew Phil would be there. As he turned onto County Road 4, his shortcut to the interstate, his cell phone buzzed. Phil's name lit up on the screen.

"You heard, right?" Phil's voice was tense and staccato.

"Yeah," Chris replied. "Kimber told me the second I walked in the door. Another dead priest." He sighed. "You should have called me. We get zero reception out at the lodge, but I could have gotten the message on my way back home."

Phil let out a breath. "Why? What could you have done? I didn't want to ruin your trip."

Chris didn't have the heart to admit that the hunting trip had ruined itself.

"Anyway, it happened early Friday morning," Phil continued. "Time of death was determined to be around seven o'clock, give or take an hour, according to Doc. We should talk soon."

"I'm already on my way. You're still gonna be at the office for a while, right?"

"Yep. See you soon."

As Chris hung up, he realized he himself had just become Matt's alibi. Matt had called Chris around seven Friday morning, confirming the meeting time with Ron at Cabela's. He knew Matt was calling from home, because he could hear Marty calling out "Tell Chris hi from me!" in the background—which Matt had blatantly ignored.

Just thinking of Marty made Chris tighten his hands on the steering wheel. He wasn't sure what she did or didn't know about the weekend's events. For that matter, Chris wasn't sure what he was prepared to say in return. How do you tell someone she's married to an asshole? As if she didn't know already…

When he arrived at the BCA, Chris steeled himself to come face-to-face with Marty and tell her the truth. Instead, he came face-to-face with a substitute receptionist. At first, he was relieved. But then a little worry crept in.

Hope Marty's OK. Matt seems the type who might hurt her.

Phil was out on the portico, smoking a cigarette and holding a Starbucks coffee. He stabbed the hand with the cigarette at Chris.

"Don't say a damned thing about the smoking, all right? It was the only way I could cope with this crap over the weekend. Already got enough shit from my wife."

"It's OK," Chris said, holding up his hands.

"We're dealing with a shitstorm here." Motioning to the door, he said, "Let's go inside." He flicked his cigarette onto the concrete, ground it out with his heel, and kicked it into the snow. "Goddamn," he muttered.

Phil settled at his desk, a portrait of fallen agent Paul Rydning staring over his left shoulder. Rydning had been killed while arresting a bank robbery suspect in the Selby-Dale district of Saint Paul. Another officer had searched the suspect for weapons. The knife in the suspect's waistband went undetected. Rydning had been one of Phil's closest friends at the agency.

On the window ledge sat a potted ivy, its leaves long dried and fallen, far beyond salvation. It mirrored the tragedy.

Chris tossed his coat over the back of a chair. "Give me the basics. I know what they're saying on the news, but what do *you* have so far?"

Phil leaned forward. "Father Carlos Rodriguez, parish priest at St. Joseph's. Previously, he'd been at St. Vincent's, a small rural parish outside of San Diego. Transferred at the suggestion of the bishop out there. There was suspicion he was tagging boys. Turns out, those suspicions were probably right, 'cause the St. Joseph's janitor says he walked in on Rodriguez playing 'secret games'"—he made air quotes—"with some boys in the church basement not too long ago."

Chris cringed. "What's the similarity to the Scandia murder?"

"A lot." Phil let out a breath. "For starters, there was another message left at the scene. '*Secúndum mystérium* in blood on the Communion railing cloth."

"The second mystery," replied Chris. "Please tell me there were no rosary beads …"

Phil began fiddling with a paper clip. "Wish I could."

Chris groaned, squeezed his eyes tight, and grimaced.

"McPhearson did the autopsy. Again, he found no sign

that the beads had been forced into the vic's mouth. He sent the beads to our intake immediately after he found them. The cut on the chain matches perfectly with the section from Doyle's gut, and the beads are identical."

"So, part of the same rosary."

"You got it."

Chris leaned back in his seat. Five mysteries. Five decades of the rosary. Two dead priests—so far.

"You think we're dealing with a serial killer?" he asked.

Phil nodded slowly. "Seems to be headed in that direction. One more dead priest, and it's a certainty."

"So, not only do we have two crimes to solve, but now we're in preventative mode."

"Dead on, Investigator."

Chris watched in silence for a moment as Phil tossed the mangled paper clip in the wastebasket, then immediately grabbed a fresh one.

"Office Services will run out of paper clips if you keep this up," Chris finally said.

Phil responded with a snort.

"OK, what about the weapon?" Chris continued.

Phil set the paper clip down so he could shuffle through some papers. "The firing pin indentation has already been run through Drugfire, and so have the ejector marks on the casing. And guess what?"

"Same gun?"

"Dead on, again." He picked up the paper clip again, only to toss it in the wastebasket. "We got an immediate confirmation. The only thing we know for sure is that it's not a Glock. A Glock firing pin creates a rectangular indentation. The indentations on these cartridges were round."

"Did you recover the projectile?"

"From the floor."

"Not too distorted for comparison?" Chris asked hopefully.

"Nope, it was good. A forty-caliber jacketed hollow point, just like the one that blew up Doyle's head."

Sighing, Phil flipped through more pages of the crime scene report.

"After the round passed through Rodriguez's head, its trajectory was downward, toward the pews closest to the rail. The techs found the bullet embedded in the flooring. Markings on the bearing surface also matched those from Doyle's—more proof of the same gun in both homicides."

Phil paused, his fingers busily bending and twisting another paper clip.

Chris stared at him expectantly. "Is that it?"

Phil was ready. "But wait—there's more!"

Chris should have known better than to walk right into that one. "All right—surprise me again!" He waved his hands in the air, feigning surprise.

"Another fingerprint on the shell casing. Not very good, but the V-shaped laceration—or scar or whatever the hell it is—showed up again." He used the clip to tap his desk. "You know, I'm wondering if the killer wants us to find that print. It's almost like it was intentionally placed there."

"Has Ken Zerke looked at it yet?"

Phil nodded. "He said the prints are similar on both

cartridges. This print appeared to have two characteristics near the scar. Not enough to query IAFIS. Just not enough area on the cartridge."

"So we still can't tell whether this guy's in the system?"

"Nope." Phil let the word pop.

Chris scratched his head. "Did you check the ViCAP database?"

"Yep." Again, he popped the word. "No luck."

"So this guy isn't in any database, anywhere?" Chris asked, incredulous. "Are you saying he went from fine upstanding citizen to serial killer overnight?"

"Maybe," Phil said with a shrug and wry smile. "Look—the distinct similarities between the two cases suggest a signature. If this guy had killed before, he likely would have used the same signature. Which means we likely would have found a connection in the database by now."

He tapped the desk again.

"Bottom line is, I think we're dealing with a first-timer. Given that both priests were child molesters—or at least *accused* molesters—I bet our perp is an abuse victim looking for revenge."

Immediately, Chris thought of Matt. Chris didn't know whether Matt had been abused. But he did know that Matt was full of pain and vitriol. Was the killer someone like him? To what lengths would—could—a victim go?

When Chris came out of his thoughts, he found Phil looking at him, his mouth poised and open, just waiting to speak.

"So," Chris said, "what's your next surprise?"

"Another cigarette butt left at the scene."

Chris nodded. "Of course." He leaned forward. "DNA?"

"Lab's on it as we speak. Bet it'll be the same profile as Scandia." Phil had given up on paper clips and was now twirling a pencil.

"Oh, by the way—got any information on those fibers your techs missed but yours truly noticed?" Chris grinned.

Phil tightened his lips and stared at Chris through his thick glasses. "Serena analyzed them," he said. "She gave me quite a lecture about sheep. She's smart, that one." He shuffled papers around. "The fibers are merino wool, the highest quality."

"Merino wool?" Chris echoed. "Well, guess *I'm* the perp! My closet is full of that stuff! Got a new merino wool sweater from my in-laws last Christmas, in fact."

Phil pointed his pencil at Chris. "Good. Then you know that merino wool is commonly used in coats, sweaters, mittens, socks, and the like. It's sold in stores worldwide. In other words, the fiber *you* found doesn't give *us* a lot to go on. For all we know, it's not even from our perp. Those fibers could've been stuck in the buckthorn since God knows when, from God knows who."

Chris considered Phil's information, then shook his head. "Yeah, but I just have a hunch those fibers are relevant. I'm convinced the killer stood at Doyle's window that night. Those fibers are from our perp. I just know it."

With that, Phil let out a long sigh. He shook a cigarette from his pack and laid it on his desk. "Been a long day—and it's not even nine yet."

"I hear ya," Chris replied. "Let's get back to this tomorrow."

Both men stood. Phil was grabbing his cigarette and Chris was grabbing his coat when the phone rang. Phil held up a finger, gesturing Chris to wait.

Phil answered, hunching to hold the receiver between ear and shoulder. He rolled the cigarette in his fingers as he listened. Chris tried to pick up any key information, but all Phil said on his end was a nebulous "Got it," "OK," and "Thanks."

Phil hung up, then slowly looked at Chris. His eyes were surprisingly wide. He smiled.

"You're never gonna believe it—CODIS kicked out a match on our DNA from the cigarette. The perp's been identified."

Chris had to steady himself by grasping the back of the chair. "Holy shit. Who is it?"

Phil's smile morphed into a smirk. "The same guy who killed Doyle!"

"Asshole," Chris muttered as he pushed himself away from the chair and turned to leave.

They were both chuckling as he headed out the door.

Chapter 20

*T*he snow is coming down with furious intensity, as if determined to impede my progress. The wipers are laboring to keep up, pushing thick slush to the edges of my windshield. My headlights are dimmed by the accumulation of snow, but my tires keep a tight grip on the icy road. Good thing I'm familiar with this eastern Saint Paul neighborhood. I've been through the area often at this time of morning to make sure no one would be out. I've got work to do.

The rectory is where I'm headed. Next to it is a playground. It's a large field isolating the rectory from other houses. This makes my job less risky. An elderly couple lives across the street, not likely to be awake at this hour.

The building has been standing for too many years—an old wooden two-story house with dormers protruding from two sides. White lathe-sculpted timber columns support the sloping roof of the screened three-season porch.

The housekeeper is a gray-haired Hispanic woman, small and bent. She was getting out of her car when I drove by just before six thirty the other morning. Her name is Edna. I learned that from the church bulletin. She has a routine and is dedicated to her work and to the Catholic Church. I'll be considerate of her when I complete my task. She doesn't deserve to endure the frightening aftermath. I'll leave as little as possible to clean up.

This morning I'm going to defrock Father Roosevelt Simon, who came to Saint Paul from Wayland, Massachusetts, a Boston suburb. He was a black priest in an overwhelmingly white community.

Apparently, Father Simon enjoyed playing "tickling" games with members of his boys' choir there. Suspicious parents reported this to the archbishop, resulting in one less pedophile in Boston, one more in Saint Paul.

I pull up in front of the rectory and open my car door. No dome light illuminates. I removed the bulb before leaving home. As I step out, snow slips from my roof onto the armrest. I glance around to ensure I'm alone. I push the door shut, holding the handle back so it doesn't make any noise.

As I walk to the house, I'm glad I slipped galoshes over my tennis shoes. My galoshes leave imprints in the new snow, but they'll fill quickly. The wind will help.

The blowing snow adheres to the windowless screens, creating U-shaped arches along the bottoms. The screen door has no lock. I cover my fingers with the cuff of my jacket and grasp the cast-iron latch. The old hinges emit a faint squeal when I pull the door open.

The door to the rectory itself is locked. Simon keeps things secure. Through the thick window in the top half of the heavy oak door, I can see a blue glow from the microwave clock in the kitchen.

There's no doorbell, so I knock several times. This time, I am Death knocking at the door.

A dim yellow light suddenly lights up a stairwell at the back of the house. I can see Father Simon descend the stairs and waddle to the door. Perhaps he's imagining a confessant deep in despair, needing immediate absolution. If he's really lucky, a young visitor, a boy he can fuck.

I can see he's breathing heavily from the simple act of moving his massive weight. His heart is pumping mightily, providing oxygen to the miles of vessels in his immense body. Soon that will stop.

Father Simon wears a purple terry-cloth bathrobe held tight to his body by a matching belt tied in a loose knot. The robe stops short of his feet, exposing swollen ankles. Leather slippers, stretched tight, match his brown skin.

He reaches into his pocket for a pair of wire bifocals and sets them upon his broad nose. The priest studies me closely through the glass in the door. He opens the door partway and asks what my business is so early in the morning. He glances at the microwave clock. It's just past two in the morning.

I explain I'm a lost soul, needing redemption for a terrible sin. Can he help me?

He's sympathetic and gestures me inside. Silently, I credit him for this compassion, but the balance still isn't in his favor.

Father Simon asks if he might change into more presentable garb. I say yes. He asks me to please remove my snowy galoshes in the meantime. Again, I say yes. He turns on a table lamp before leaving to change clothes.

While he's gone, I remove my galoshes, then slip booties over my tennis shoes. The soles of the booties quickly become wet from the rug upon which I've placed my boots.

He returns, dressed in a black-collared shirt, black pants, and a clerical collar. I ask for a glass of water. He fills a crystal goblet from the kitchen and puts it down next to me. He lowers himself into a recliner and motions for me to take the seat across *from him. The straight-backed wooden chair is uncomfortable, but I won't be sitting long.*

The priest looks at the glass, then at me, not understanding why I've not taken a drink. He doesn't understand that it's he who will drink from the cup.

That is when he notices my booties. He grows more concerned, ill at ease. His fingers tug at his clerical collar. He twists his neck as though the collar is too tight.

He seems to care about the dilemma that has brought me to his door at two in the morning, yet I still haven't disclosed. He prods nervously, asking what's troubling me.

I tell him what is troubling me is priests who fantasize about fucking young boys.

Simon closes his eyes and nods. He breathes more rapidly. When he opens his eyes, they seem to grow darker behind the bifocals. He's beginning to sweat. His ebony hands grip the arms of his chair tightly. His fingers blanch. The vein in the middle of his forehead pulses rapidly. Again, he stares at my feet. He tries to stand.

I pull the Beretta from my coat and direct him to remain seated. The feet of my chair squeal on the wooden floor as I slide closer.

The sound startles him. His eyes flit about the room, seeking an escape.

But I'm in control. I feel the beginning of an erection.

He asks why I have the gun, what I want with him.

I disregard his questions. I've heard them before. And I think he already knows the answers.

Instead, I ask why he left his last church.

For a moment, he pretends to be confused, but he soon breaks into penitent tears. Admits his problem with teenage boys. Tells me he's happiest with them. Says he's seeking help.

Not soon enough, I tell him.

I remove his Communion from my pocket and dangle it in front of him. In a soft voice, I tell him to swallow this. Please.

Like the others, he balks. But when the Beretta muzzle nears his chest, he chooses to cooperate. It takes him a little longer than it did the other two. I suspect he prefers foods that are fattier. After three swallows of water, the beads slide into his stomach. He looks at me, eyes blinking rapidly.

I say it's time.

He doesn't understand. Time for what?

To join the others.

Wrinkles form around the pulsing vein. He still doesn't understand.

I explain that I mean time to join other perverts such as himself. I ask if he remembers Archbishop Bernard Law from Boston. Of course he does. He's the church leader who engineered the transfer of scum like Simon.

But Law is dead, Simon argues, panicked. Died last year.

I'm aware of this. I tell Simon that Law is in hell, waiting for him. I ask whether Simon believes in hell. I remind him of the catechism. I also remind him that he's about to die in a state of mortal sin. He's doomed to the eternal fire because he won't be able to say the Act of Contrition before he dies.

"Please, don't…" are his last words.

For the sake of his housekeeper, I push the muzzle tightly against his chest, just above the left pocket, and squeeze the trigger. The projectile jumps from my Beretta and penetrates his black shirt and the T-shirt beneath. Although I can't see it, I know the bullet stretches his skin, plunges through his rib cage, shatters his heart, and comes to rest against his spine. Expanding gases pulverize his left lung and burst his aorta.

Father Roosevelt Simon jerks convulsively for several seconds, leans forward, settles back, and takes a shallow breath. His huge hands clutch the goblet, then relax. The goblet tips onto his lap. The spectacles remain on his face, eyes behind them seeing nothing.

Father Simon has been defrocked. He's joined his abhorrent brothers in the inferno of hell.

I smile. Satisfied.

A painting of the Last Supper hangs on the wall behind where he rests. I laugh at the irony. He's just had his last supper.

I put on my gloves, remove the painting, and set it on the floor. With his blood, I scribe my message onto the vacant space on the wall. I leave the cigarette. And this time, I leave an extra surprise to baffle them further.

As I stand there, I'm suddenly confronted with regret: because of my lack of self-control, Alexa's love is lost to me. I can no longer reward myself for a job well done with his particular kind of attention.

It's time to leave. I gather my wet galoshes. My snowy footprints on the unheated porch have not yet frozen. I shuffle in my booties to obliterate the details. At the screen door, I slip back into my galoshes and head out into the snow.

CHAPTER 21

Seventy-year-old Edna Martinez worked at the rectory Monday through Friday, six thirty in the morning until one o'clock in the afternoon. She did light housekeeping and prepared Father Simon's substantial breakfast and lunch. He preferred Southern foods with rich sauces and gravies—which, given Edna's heritage, was a challenge for her.

Father Simon was almost always sitting in his recliner, reading the morning newspaper and waiting anxiously for a cup of coffee, when she arrived. Edna never managed to persuade him to switch on the Keurig, put in a pod, and brew his own.

It was still snowing when she arrived at the rectory that morning. Several inches had already fallen, and according to reports from the Minneapolis airport, more snow and more wind were in the forecast.

When Edna parked, she noticed indistinct depressions in the snow—there appeared to be footprints leading to the porch steps. It was odd. The newspaper was rarely delivered on time during a snowstorm. The footprints were set wider apart than her own stride, but she forced herself to step in them, allowing for an easier trek through the snow.

Edna crossed through the porch, noting frozen puddles on the floor, but no newspaper. When she inserted her key in the lock, the key twisted easily. This was also curious. Father Simon always kept the heavy door to the house locked, even during the day.

She entered the hallway and set her purse on the small wooden table. As she had been instructed on her first day of work, she removed her boots and stepped into the well-worn tennis shoes she carried in her bag.

Out of the corner of her eye Edna could see Father Simon sitting in his recliner. The light from the table lamp reflected off the spectacles perched on his nose.

"Good morning, Father," she called as she pulled back her thinning gray hair and tied it into a bun.

He didn't respond.

Moving closer, Edna saw that the front of his black shirt was shiny and wet. A small hole over his heart punctured the fabric. A red tinge was visible on the white T-shirt underneath. A goblet was tipped in his lap. His closed lips appeared welded by a dark, rusty seam.

"Oh, *Dios mío!*"

Edna raced out to the porch, the rubber soles of her tennis shoes slipping on the icy wood floor. Her panting sent small billows of fog into the cold air. The streetlights were still burning; the area was vacant of people. No cars passing by. She skidded across the porch, back into the house, grabbed her purse, ran to the kitchen, and called 911 on her cell phone.

Staying on the line, as the dispatcher instructed, Edna slumped into a chair at the kitchen table. The phone shook in her hands. This wasn't the first time she'd called the police about Father Simon.

From the kitchen, Edna had a clear view of the living room. She forced her eyes to move about the room even while avoiding looking at the body in the recliner.

On the end table next to his recliner was a saucer. From her vantage point she could see it held a cigarette butt and a chewed wad of gum. She stared so intently at the plate that her eyes began to puddle. Neither the butt nor the gum made any sense. Father Simon didn't smoke or chew gum. At least not that she knew. But he had surprised her in other ways.

Forcing her troubled eyes away, she noticed the picture of the Last Supper had been removed from the wall. A rusty-red message was crudely scrawled in its place. *Tértium mystérium.* Edna had studied Latin at the Catholic school in Juárez.

"*The third mystery,*" she whispered to herself.

Dispatch was busy with numerous weather-related calls, and driving was slow along neighborhood streets. Therefore, it took nearly twenty minutes before Officer Lisa Nimczek arrived at the rectory. Edna met her at the door, pointed at Father Simon, and walked hastily to the kitchen.

Nimczek removed her boots, leaving them out on the porch. She stepped inside and moved immediately to the man in the recliner. She was careful to avoid stepping in the watery smudges on the floor.

No carotid pulse. Skin cool to the touch. Obvious chest

wound. Resuscitation efforts would not be necessary.

Observing the area, Nimczek studied the amorphous wet footprints trailing to and from the front entry. No sign of actual shoe tread, other than the housekeeper's tennis shoes. Whoever else had been here had taken precautions.

Nimczek called the dispatcher, who in turn contacted an investigator. Aware of the recent priest homicides in the metropolitan area, the investigator in turn notified the BCA.

When she finished her call, Nimczek saw Edna hunched over at the kitchen table, trembling uncontrollably, tears making their way down the creases in her aged cheeks.

Knowing the housekeeper would undergo a thorough debriefing when the investigators arrived, Nimczek did not want to rattle the poor woman further. She chose to pursue a gentler conversation.

"You must be Edna Martinez, who called in this . . . ah . . . *situation*."

Edna nodded.

Nimczek realized more prompts were needed. "How are you?" she asked with a sympathetic tilt of the head.

Edna searched for words. "Scared. Confused," she finally replied. She reached in her pocket for a tissue, dried her eyes, and retrieved her glasses from a faux-leather pouch.

"I understand. There are just a few questions I have to ask before the investigators arrive."

Edna nodded again. Nimczek gave her a moment to take a breath and compose herself before beginning.

"When did you arrive here this morning?"

"My usual time, right at six thirty."

"Did you see anyone when you got here? Was anyone else in the house?

"No, there wasn't anybody here. Well, except for . . ." Edna nodded toward Father Simon's body. "But I think someone had been up the walkway before me."

Nimczek's pen hovered over her notebook. "How do you know?"

"There were places in the snow where someone had already stepped. I stepped in them too. And there was water on the floor here." She pointed. "There still is—you can see."

Nimczek was the one to nod this time. "I do. Yes. It's important we don't step in it." She scribbled a few more notes, then gave a small smile. "Thank you. The investigators will want to ask you more questions when they arrive. In the meantime, is there another room where you'd be more . . . comfortable?" In a wordless gesture of understanding, she angled herself away from the body.

Relieved, Edna led the officer to a small sitting room adjacent to the kitchen. The still-trembling woman settled in a worn red velvet wingback chair that showed its age. She folded her hands in her lap.

Nimczek preferred to stand, leaning slightly against the matching chair across from Edna. They looked at each other for a moment, exchanging tight smiles. Then Edna looked back down at her hands, which she now was clenching tightly. As if a cliché, the only sound was the *ticktock* of the pendulum clock hanging on the far wall.

Nimczek didn't want to pepper the woman with any

more questions, so she opted to return to friendly conversation.

"I'm sure you're shocked by this," Nimczek posited, clearing her throat.

"*Shocked*, yes…" Edna looked away as though avoiding an image she didn't want to see.

There was something in Edna's behavior that made Nimczek pause. She looked at Edna expectantly, her head tilted this time in puzzlement.

Edna glanced at her, then looked away again. She opened her mouth but struggled to speak. "Shocked, yes. But sad…no." Her cheeks flushed.

Nimczek did her best to keep her expression steady. "How so?"

"I am not a cold-hearted woman, Officer. But I do not feel so bad. Father Simon is—was—an unholy man." She paused, looking at the clock, then back at Nimczek. "I clean the entire house, except his office. He always keeps it locked. A few days ago, he forgot to lock the door." Her eyes darted again, and her voice dropped. "I know it was wrong to snoop. But I found…a picture. In the printer." She pulled another tissue out of her pocket, removed her glasses, and wiped her eyes.

"What was the picture of?" Nimczek asked. Even more effort was needed now to keep a steady face.

"A boy."

"How old?"

Edna grimaced. "Young. Naked. Maybe a teen. And he was"—now she needed to search for an English word to suit her purpose—"*excited*. You know what I'm trying to say?"

Nimczek cringed. "Yes, I think so."

"There was a book next to the computer. It had all kinds of awful pictures too." Edna squeezed the tissue in her hands. "It was right next to a Bible and readings for Mass."

Nimczek watched in silence as Edna shook her head. Shock was giving way to anger and disgust.

"Did you tell anyone about this?" Nimczek asked.

"I called the police."

"When was that?"

"It was about a week ago. I made them promise not to tell Father Simon it was me who'd called. And then . . . this happened."

She nodded her head toward the doorway that led to the kitchen and living room. Toward the cold body still propped in the recliner.

CHAPTER 22

My sex drive and my vengeance have become inextricably connected. With each murder I commit, a rage inside me burns hot, but with no way to release it. There's a compulsion now to move more quickly. To kill more predators who have harmed children.

It brings back memories I've kept buried for years. Many years.

Uncle George was a firefighter. He was my hero. He stayed at our house a lot. I was only seven. He did things to me that I wasn't sure were wrong but I thought they might be. He touched my private parts with his hands and his mouth. After a while, he asked me to do the same things to his body.

What was odd was that he never did these things when my mother was around. It was confusing but mysterious in ways that felt good. He called me his little firefighter. He said if I kept our secret, I could ride in his fire truck someday.

That day never came. I never rode in the truck. Uncle George hanged himself.

When I was nine, a teenage babysitter watched us every day after school. Somedays she'd send Nick to his room. To close his door and play with his toys.

The babysitter's name was Sandra. She was obsessed with cleanliness. She told me it was necessary for her to wipe my penis each time I peed. I was reluctant, but she insisted she had to do it for me. She often asked, "Are you sure you don't have to pee?"

One day she asked if I'd ever seen a girl naked. Of course I hadn't. Not a girl.

She pulled her pants down and got on her hands and knees. She told me to push my finger inside her. I worried my ragged fingernails would hurt her, so I used my little finger. I didn't understand my feelings. I was confused because Sandra was a girl. These were feelings I'd only had with Uncle George.

Then there was Father Benedict. I was ten when he began to groom me. It started during catechism class. He'd compliment me on my memorized answers. At recess, he'd say I was the best ballplayer, the fastest runner. Then he began to hold me over after class when the other kids had gone home. He'd offer me candy, put his arm around me, and tell me I was handsome. He'd tell me I was his favorite.

Then one day, he said he had something to show me.

In the parish house.

In his room.

Just the two of us.

I remember it as if it were yesterday.

"Do you like movies?" he asked me.

"Yeah, I do, Father."

"Well, I have a movie that's a little different. We'll see if you like it," he said, loading a movie reel into a projector. "It's called Men Will Be Boys."

We sat side by side. We watched boys. About my age. A little older. They were all naked. They touched one another as Uncle George and I had.

Then an older man entered the scene. He was naked too. He started to touch the boys, and they touched him.

"Does that look fun to you?" Father asked.

I hesitated. "I don't know, Father."

The room suddenly seemed hot. I was anxious and confused. Did he know about my secret with Uncle George? How could he?

"Why don't we give it a try?" Father Benedict said. "You can touch me."

He unzipped his pants and exposed his erect penis. "You'll be like this someday too," he said. He took my hand, placed it on his penis, and began to rub slowly.

I was scared, but at the same time, I felt special. Again. The emotions were as familiar as they were unsettling.

I was Father Benedict's favorite. I'd always wanted to be my father's favorite, but for some reason, it never came to be.

I was Father Benedict's favorite until my thirteenth birthday, when he was transferred to another parish. I never saw him again. He never came to see me.

Guess I wasn't really that special after all.

CHAPTER 23

Phil's pager was vibrating on his bedside table. He squinted at the clock. The digital numbers had just flipped to 7:25. He'd been consulting on a missing person case until the early hours and had planned to sleep in and go to the office around ten. Phil returned the call, then dressed as quickly as he could.

"Retirement can't come soon enough," he muttered to himself.

Within minutes, Phil was on the road. The snow had abated, but the relentless wind was creating drifts in the newly plowed streets. Grabbing his cell, Phil attempted to reach Chris. But he was told the investigator was in the southern part of the county, working a double shift on a DUI saturation patrol.

"Crap!" Phil said aloud.

Instinctively, he reached into his pocket for his pack of cigarettes. Instead, he found only nicotine gum. It was a coat he hadn't worn in a while—obviously not since he'd fallen off the wagon. Worse yet, only one piece of gum was left.

"Shit!" he said this time.

When he arrived at the rectory, Phil took a glimpse of himself in the rearview mirror. The left side of his face still bore creases from his pillow. The hair on his temples had been hastily combed. He decided the best course of action was to carry himself as if nothing were amiss.

Inside, Phil was met by an officer.

"Good morning, Officer"—he leaned closer to read the name badge—"Nimczek." He wiped his hand on his pants leg and extended a handshake. "Agent Phil Walker, BCA."

"Nice to meet you, sir," she replied. "I understand you've had your share of priest killings lately."

He didn't respond, but the grim look on his face was answer enough.

"The housekeeper—she's the one who found the body?" he asked.

"Yes. Mrs. Martinez. Edna."

"Did Mrs. Martinez mention seeing anybody in the neighborhood when she got here?"

"No. She did say there were footprints leading to the porch, but they were mostly filled in with snow. She said she walked in them. She also noticed wet footprints on the wood floor from the porch to where Father Simon was, um, sitting. Apparently, that was unusual. According to her, the priest insisted everyone take their shoes off just inside the front door."

Phil looked down at the floor. It was nearly dry, but he could envision snowy shoes or boots dripping and leaving slush in their wake.

"Hmm. I guess someone didn't get the memo."

The scene was remarkably similar to the previous murders: forty-caliber shell casing, cigarette butt, featureless footprints, and a message scrawled in blood. The goblet was disconcerting, given what the ME would likely find in the priest's stomach.

It was obvious now that these scenes were staged. Each cigarette butt and shell casing had been deliberately left behind. As to *why*—that continued to elude Phil and his team. They were chasing an echo.

This time, however, there was a new twist: chewing gum next to the cigarette. The perp was upping the game, adding even more "evidence" that would no doubt lead to maddeningly inexplicable dead ends.

Phil briefly reached for the gum, but then he decided to save it.

"Let me go chat with Mrs. Martinez," Phil said to Nimczek.

Nimczek led Phil to the sitting room, where Edna was still perched in the wingback chair. Next to her, on the end table, a Christmas cactus was in full bloom. Expressionless, she was staring at the pink flower.

Phil caught her attention, smiled politely, and chose the matching chair for himself. He moved it a bit closer to her, then pulled out a legal pad.

"Hello, Mrs. Martinez. I'm Agent Phil Walker from the BCA."

She was barely able to respond. "I can't believe this," she finally said.

"This is hard for you. I understand." He gave her a sympathetic smile. "I'd like to ask you a few questions, if that's all right," he said softly. "Some of these questions you've been asked already, but I need to confirm things."

She nodded, understanding.

"What time did you arrive here this morning?"

"Right at six thirty."

Edna's hands were shaking. Phil recognized the worn knuckles and chafed skin of a lifetime of manual labor. She spoke with an accent. Quite possibly she was an illegal immigrant, which would explain why she was nervous about being questioned by law enforcement. Phil needed her to feel comfortable in order to keep the information flowing, so he made a mental note to keep her immigration status out of the conversation.

"When you arrived, did you see any other cars nearby? Anyone driving away?"

"No. There were hardly any cars out this morning. None near this house. It was early and was snowing a lot."

"Did you see anyone walking?"

"No. For sure, no one out walking."

"I know Officer Nimczek asked you about this, and I am sorry to make you repeat it, but you mentioned footprints. Can you tell me more about those?"

"Yes, in the snow. They were starting to fill in, but I could still see them from the streetlight—they made shadows. I walked in them because the snow was not so deep there. They were far apart for me. I had to stretch a bit."

With a quick tilt of his head, Phil gauged Edna's height. Even with her sitting, he could tell she was of shorter stature. If she could manage to step in the perp's footprints with only a bit of a stretch, perhaps the perp was of shorter-than-average stature himself. Or who knows—perhaps the perp had deliberately shortened his stride as yet another misdirection.

"And you also told Officer Nimczek about water on the floor." He paused and waited for a response.

"Yes. I was very surprised. Because of the wood floor, Father Simon never lets anyone in with shoes on."

"Anything else that was different or unusual?" He raised an eyebrow in silent inquiry.

"The cigarette and chewing gum on a plate," she said. "Father Simon didn't smoke or chew gum, at least not that I know. But he surprised me other ways. You know, the pictures..." Her eyes returned to the Christmas cactus.

Phil nodded. Officer Nimczek had filled him in about Edna's previous discovery in the priest's office. The officer also told him that thanks to her tip, the FBI's Whisper task force was getting involved. Dating back to Father Simon's stint in Boston, they had identified him as a person of interest for consuming child pornography and sharing pornographic video files over the internet.

Phil grimaced when he realized this part of the case was an echo too. Kiddie porn. Alleged sexual abuse. Someone was seeking revenge for sins against the innocent.

Phil remembered the single piece of gum in his pocket, wondering if it was time to break into it. Letting out an exhale, he decided to push on.

"When you parked in front of the rectory, you said you didn't see any other cars. But could you tell if a car had been there recently? Were there any car tracks in the snow?"

Edna seemed to be re-creating the scene in her mind's eye. After a moment, she shook her head. "I don't remember seeing any. But it was windy, and the snow was blowing."

"Did you like Father Simon?" Phil asked point-blank without any segue.

"I don't like what he does with that computer." Her lips curled in disgust.

"Mrs. Martinez, are you married?"

"Yes. My husband is Enrico." Without realizing it, she touched the simple gold band on her finger.

"Did you tell him what you found in Father Simon's office?"

"Yes," she said with a small shrug. "I had to tell Enrico. I didn't know what to do."

"What did he say when you told him?"

Her eyes got big. "He was very, very angry. It was his idea to call the police. He wanted to do it himself, but I told him I needed to make the call."

Phil's pen hovered as he looked at her. Several questions came to his mind. He picked the simplest one first. "Why's that? Why did you need to make the call?"

"Because I was the one who saw those terrible pictures. I told the police to keep me out of it. I didn't want them to tell Father Simon I had called."

Without missing a beat, Phil launched the more complicated question. "You said Enrico was very angry. Did he say what should happen to Father Simon?"

"He said—" She looked through the doorway, toward the living room.

"Mrs. Martinez." Phil cleared his throat. "Please."

She twirled her wedding band, then looked up at Phil, meeting his eyes. "He said priests like him"—she nodded toward the doorway—"should die and burn in hell."

Phil held her stare. "Do you think your husband killed Father Simon?"

She raised her chin. "I know he wanted Father Simon to die," she said frankly. "But no, he could not do something like this. It would make him no better than Father Simon."

"Where was your husband last night? This morning?"

"At the packing plant. Hormel. In Austin. He works nights. He called to tell me he was staying longer to pick up extra hours. Some nights he does that." She looked away and rubbed her weathered forehead.

Phil had a gut feeling she was telling the truth, but he could tell something bothered her. He made a note to have someone follow up on Enrico Martinez just to be sure.

"And what about you, Edna?" he asked. "Did you want Father Simon to die? Did you want someone to kill him for what he'd done?"

Her eyes never wavered this time. "No. Never."

"Why?" he asked, leaning forward with curiosity.

Her eyes raised to the crucifix hanging above a short bookcase. "Because such things are for God to decide." She paused. "And he is not happy," she added with a whisper.

The pendulum clock made the only sound for a few moments. Then Phil sat back in his chair and closed his notepad.

"Mrs. Martinez, I think that is all for now. Thank you for your time. We may have more questions later. If so, we'll be in touch."

Edna's shoulders visibly dropped in relief. She let out a cleansing breath.

Phil glanced out the window. "I see the plow has finally come through the secondary streets. Can you drive yourself home, or would you like one of our officers to drive you?"

"I'll be okay. Thank you." She gave him a small smile.

Phil smiled back, then started to stand. As he did, Edna briefly held out her hands—a timid gesture for him to stop. He froze with his six-foot frame awkwardly bent over.

"May I ask you question?" she asked, now wringing her hands.

Phil lowered himself back into the chair. "Of course—I hope I can answer it."

Edna pointed toward the door. "The writing on the wall where the picture of the Last Supper used to be—I know what it means. 'The third mystery.' Why would someone write that?"

Walker shrugged, not wanting to admit it was both an echo and an omen.

CHAPTER 24

Aside from having to maneuver around a few slow-moving state vehicles and workers picking up orange cones and barrels on the roadside, Chris's drive to the BCA headquarters was effortless. Road construction on the interstate had come to an end, only to resume somewhere else in the spring.

The parking lot was nearly full. The BCA was hosting a seminar on evidence collection, so police cars from dozens of cities filled the lots surrounding the building. Chris miraculously found a close spot on the street, locked his car, zipped up his jacket, and walked briskly to the entrance.

Every step seemed heavier than the one before it. A third priest had been murdered, yet they still had next to no leads on the perp.

Chris was so lost in troubling thoughts that he didn't even remember who would greet him at the reception desk.

"Investigator Majek?" Marty asked in a small voice the second he stepped through the door. "Got a sec?" She looked dispirited, low key, not her usual flirty self.

Chris's muscles tensed, not knowing quite what to expect. "Sure. You OK?"

"Yeah, I'm OK. I just want to apologize." She looked down at her desk, then up at the ceiling, trying to will away tears. "I know Matt was an ass during the hunting trip—and that's from hearing only his side of the story. I can hardly imagine what it was like from your side." She fussed with her necklace. "I never should have asked you to invite him."

Chris shook his head. "Hey, Matt's behavior is nothing *you* need to apologize for. All right?" He forced himself to smile.

He waited expectantly until she looked back up at him and nodded. Glancing over his shoulder, Chris made sure no one was in earshot before continuing.

"What about you? You have to put up with him every day. Are *you* OK?" he asked. His muted voice was sincere with empathy.

Marty was silent for a moment, then her voice trembled. "I'm getting so fed up," she finally admitted. "He drinks a lot. He stays out late—I don't know where he goes. He's missing work." She turned her palms up as if she didn't know what else to say—or do. Then she let out a sigh and gave a wry smile. "Anyway, I'm just sorry you had to experience him in all his glory."

Chris reached over and gave her hand a quick squeeze. "Again, no apologies needed. And just remember—you don't deserve to be treated that way."

Her smile faltered as she again fought back tears. "Thank you," she mouthed.

Just then, someone stepped into the office, waiting to speak to Marty next. Both Marty and Chris composed themselves.

"So, your boss in his office?" he asked in a louder voice.

"Yes, he's expecting you." She gave him a wink as he walked away.

Phil was leaning back in his chair, feet on the desk. Chris detected the sour smell of recently smoked cigarettes lingering on Phil's clothing. Keeping mum, Chris headed to the credenza to pour himself coffee.

"Any trouble parking?" Phil asked. "Just about every cop in the state's here today."

"I finally found a spot out on Prosperity Avenue."

"That close, huh? Lucky."

Both men were quiet for a moment, allowing a segue from small talk to the point at hand. Chris pulled a chair close to Phil's desk and sat down. The crime scene report was on the desk.

"So," Chris began, tapping the report, "fill me in on the latest." He looked at Phil with anticipation.

"Well, even the FBI showed up for this one."

"You're kidding! Why?" He took a sip of coffee.

"Turns out they've been watching our latest victim. Remember the Whisper task force we talked about at Doyle's cabin?"

"Yeah."

"Simon has been on their radar since his days in Boston. And then just last week, the housekeeper contacted the police, saying she saw kiddie porn in his office. Printouts. Books. That garbage was sitting right next to his readings for Mass." He shook his head with disgust. "When the feds came in, they found even more than what the housekeeper had found. The closet was full of magazines."

"Jesus." Chris grimaced. "Well, I guess the feds have one less sicko to watch now."

"Yes and no. Father Simon may be off their list, but apparently he had been sharing files over the internet. That'll lead them to some of the other creeps doing this shit."

"I'm surprised so few get caught," Chris said. "I mean, I thought everything you do on the internet stays around forever. I can't buy a gift online without Kimber or the kids immediately figuring it out, no matter how much I try to cover my tracks."

"You ever heard of onion routing?"

Chris shook his head.

"It's the practice of wrapping files and instructions for routing in several layers of encryption. Makes it difficult to trace internet activity for kiddie porn and other illegal activities. Another way around detection is to use what's called single point anonymizers. They obscure a computer's local identifying information."

Chris puffed his cheeks, then let out a big exhale. The look on his face indicated he had no clue what Phil was talking about. "That stuff's beyond me, Phil."

"It's beyond most people—which is why no one finds these guys."

"So, that's the feds. What about us? Give me the details." Chris reached out with his hand, beckoning with his fingers.

"Our vic's full name was Roosevelt Javaris Simon. Sixty-seven years old. Grew up in Clarksdale, Mississippi. Ordained when he turned thirty. Served small parishes up and down the East Coast, then has been in Saint Paul ever since."

"Another 'move 'em around under the radar' situation?" Chris asked.

"Actually, the first suggestion of abuse was from the parish in Boston. Anyway, other than his being black, the case is similar to the other two priests'." Phil leaned forward, pulled his feet down from the desk, and stared at Chris. "Even His Excellency Doc McPhearson isn't surprised to find rosary beads in their stomachs anymore."

"And the DNA on the cigarette is identical to the others?"

"Preliminary estimate is positive, but…"

An interested look crossed Chris's face. "But…what?"

"We noticed something about the cigarette this time. Something we missed before—I'm embarrassed to admit it."

Chris gave a roguish smile. "Gee, you forgot to say, 'But wait—there's more!'"

"There *is* more," Phil replied. "It's been there the whole time, right under our noses." He stood, moved around the desk, and sat on the edge, facing Chris. "The first two cigarette butts were crushed flat, so I didn't notice it. But the techs in the biological lab saw that the butt left at the Simon murder scene wasn't crushed. It was left on a saucer. Stubbed."

Chris stared up at Phil over the cup. "You're losing me."

"It's all about the filters." With some chagrin, Phil reached into his shirt pocket, removed a pack, and shook out a cigarette. "See the filter?" He passed the cigarette across the desk.

Chris's face took on a quizzical look. "What about it?"

"A cigarette that's been smoked will have brown stains on the filter. Right there." Phil pointed with a pencil. "Because the cigarette wasn't crushed flat this time, we noticed that the filter didn't have that stain. Looking more closely at the other two, we see they didn't have the stain either. But they've all been lit."

Chris raised an eyebrow. "Where're you going with this?"

"You ever hear of cheiloscopy?" Phil returned to his chair and leaned back. "It's the study of lip prints on objects like cigars, cigarette butts, glassware, tissues, and the like."

"Oh yeah." Chris lit up. "We studied it in one of our forensic lab courses. But the class was called 'Lip Traces,' not 'Chei-whatever.' It's similar to fingerprints—unique to each individual, right?"

"Exactly." Phil plucked the cigarette back from Chris. He shook it like a pointer. "But there are no lip prints on the butts left at the murder scenes. No fingerprints on the filter sleeves either. Or the paper. And that means..."

"They've never been smoked. They've been planted." Chris slammed his hand on Phil's desk. "Goddamn this bastard."

Phil tucked the cigarette back in his pocket. "But wait—there's more!"

Chris had to laugh. "Let's have it. You're on a roll."

"The perp gave us something new this time. A wad of gum was left in the saucer next to the butt."

Chris piped up. "Lemme guess—once again, the DNA

212

is not the priest's nor anyone's in the database."

"Right. But here's a new wrinkle: based on the preliminary results, it's not the same as the DNA on the butts, and it's female."

Chris ran his hands over his face. "So now we have an additional suspect?"

Phil's expression showed his skepticism. "I'm not so sure. We'll keep checking the profile to see if anything comes of it, but I'm thinking it's just another attempt to sidetrack us—another ruse."

Both men sat in silence. Through a cloud of thoughts, Chris suddenly noticed a cluster of undeformed paper clips sitting in a small bowl on the desk. It wasn't good that Phil had started smoking again, but at least it saved on office supplies.

Phil was the first to speak. "We're never gonna match that DNA in the criminal database—you know that, right?"

Chris slowly nodded his head in agreement.

"Same with the fingerprint," Phil continued. "I'm certain those prints were intentionally placed on the cartridges. In two cases, the print characteristics with the laceration are smeared. Only the scar is obvious and consistent. Our perp wants us to notice it." He covered his mouth with his forearm and coughed into his sleeve. "My guess is that whoever's doing this has more already prepared."

"Well, what about the gum?" Chris asked. "Any dental information we can glean?"

"I showed it to Dr. Ann Norgren, the forensic dentist for the Ramsey County Medical Examiner. She said there's evidence of teeth from both arches, but that's about all she could determine. Too much distortion to see any individual tooth characteristics. Not to mention we have no exemplars to compare to anyway."

"Anything else?" Chris asked, his voice sounding tired.

"Yes." Phil paused for effect. "I've been saving this last pearl."

"Pearl?"

"Trust me—you're gonna love this. We found fibers stuck on the outside door handle of Simon's porch. Serena analyzed them. And guess what?"

"Phil, get to the point. Please." Chris pleaded with his hands.

A smirk crossed Phil's face. "They're identical to the ones you found behind Doyle's cabin."

"Ha!" Chris smacked his hands together and broke out in a broad smile. He cocked his head and gave Phil a sly look. "I *told* you those fibers would turn out to be important."

"Yeah, well, just because the fibers are the same type of wool doesn't prove they came from the same article of clothing." Phil sighed. "But it *is* more likely," he reluctantly added.

Chris leaned forward and picked up the crime scene report to page through it. "I see mention of the housekeeper's husband, Enrico. Anybody check on him?"

Phil nodded. "Yep. One of the detectives in Austin did. Both Mr. and Mrs. Martinez are in the United States illegally. Scared the shit out of him when the law showed up. He thought it was ICE. Was sure he and his wife would be on their way back to Mexico."

"I can imagine."

"Once he realized it wasn't an immigration issue, he was more forthcoming about his whereabouts the night of the murder…" He trailed off dramatically.

"And?" Chris stared, expecting breakthrough information.

"As Edna said, Enrico was in Austin the night of the murder. Turns out, though, he wasn't at the plant putting in extra hours, as she thought. Instead of putting in extra hours, he was putting it in a mistress there in town. He spent that night with her. Says he's with her every night he tells Edna he's 'working late.' Begged the detective not to tell her."

Chris bit his lip. "So the guy's getting a little nooky in Austin while his wife busts her ass taking care of a pedophile priest. Great husband! Asshole!"

Pent-up frustration pushed Chris to his feet. He paced for a moment, then returned his cup to the credenza.

"Damn," he said. "Another dead end. I was hoping this would lead somewhere."

"I was too," Phil replied. "What about on your end? Did you follow up on the individuals who filed complaints about Doyle on the In the Shade of the Evergreen site?"

Chris returned to his chair and gestured with three fingers. "Located three of the four. The other's deceased. For the three, all their alibis checked out. And all three gave the same story: abused during private speech lessons in Doyle's basement office."

"Did they give you any leads? Did they know anyone else who had been molested but didn't report it?" Phil asked.

"No. Actually, each of them said they thought they had been the only one. They never realized Doyle was doing it to others. Nobody talked about that stuff back then. And there's one more thing."

"What?"

Chris looked Phil square in the eyes. "None of them were sorry Doyle had been murdered."

From behind his thick frames, Phil didn't blink. "Doesn't surprise me." He absently straightened his desk calendar. "The interval between these murders is decreasing."

"I've noticed," Chris answered.

"He's getting relaxed. It's getting too easy for him. He's getting more and more confident. He's losing control of his urges. My gut says this monster's got more work to do."

"Well, we know there are two more mysteries."

"And that scares me, Chris." Phil looked off in the distance for a moment, then nodded as if making up his mind. "I'm going to contact the Behavioral Analysis Unit at the FBI. They have experts who might be able to help us figure this guy out."

CHAPTER 25

Two days later, Phil and Chris gathered in the conference room at BCA headquarters, waiting for their Polycom meeting to begin. They were waiting to speak with Dr. Merrill Sleeman of the Behavioral Analysis Unit in Quantico, Virginia. As a criminal behavior analyst with expertise regarding serial killers, Sleeman was eager to discuss the case. In prep for the meeting, Phil had emailed him the crime scene reports of the three homicides.

At the scheduled time, the screen flickered and Sleeman appeared. A handsome older man, he was dressed casually in jeans and a striped blue button-down oxford shirt. He looked more like a retired professor than an FBI agent.

Phil and Chris, both in coats and ties, immediately exchanged uncomfortable looks, feeling overdressed for the occasion.

"Greetings, gentlemen—it's good to meet you," Sleeman began. He had an air that put them at ease.

"Likewise. Agent Phil Walker here with the Minnesota Bureau of Criminal Apprehension."

"And Investigator Chris Majek from the Washington County Sheriff's Office," Chris added. "Dr. Sleeman, you spoke at the regional sheriffs' conference in Minneapolis last year."

"I did, yes!"

"It's good to see you again."

All three men had been standing during introductions. Sleeman now retired himself behind a table covered with organized stacks of printouts. Following suit, Chris and Paul took their seats as well. They leaned forward, elbows on the table.

"I've looked at the crime scene reports," Sleeman said, pulling some papers closer. "This perp is keeping you busy."

"Sure is," Phil replied. "This is new territory for us. I'm hoping you can maybe give us some insight about who—or what—we're dealing with. You ever hear of a case like this?"

"Not exactly. No serial killers of priests specifically. But there are similar cases, which we'll review. Let's start with Gary Ridgway and Ted Bundy."

He paused to allow time for Chris and Phil to reach for their legal pads.

"Both Ridgway and Bundy murdered very specific people," Sleeman continued. "Ridgway—known as the Green River Killer—claims to have killed as many as eighty women, though he was convicted of only forty-nine. Prostitutes and runaways in their midteens to late thirties were his targets. And Bundy was responsible for at least thirty killings. His preference was brunettes who parted their hair in the middle."

Jesus Christ, Chris thought as he wrote these numbers—eighty, forty-nine, thirty. *How many more priests will die before we catch this guy?*

"Like Ridgway and Bundy," Sleeman said, "your perp has very specific targets. It's more than just priests—it's priests with a history of sexual exploitation of children. The specificity of these murders leads us to make some assumptions."

"Such as?" Phil asked expectantly. His dark eyebrows lifted.

"First, let me stress that these are only assumptions—generalities based on our knowledge of previous serial killers and statistical probabilities. As for your unsub, we can assume he—" Sleeman stopped to give a wry smile. "Ah, even this is an assumption, that this is a *he*. It's the most likely scenario."

"We assume so too," Chris said. "On average, only one in six serial killers are female right?"

"That's correct!" Sleeman affirmed with a wide smile now.

Chris couldn't help but sit up a little taller in his chair. Now Sleeman was truly acting the part of the professor. And unlike Doc McPhearson, Sleeman encouraged his students to participate, not just listen to braggadocio.

Sleeman resumed. "Along these lines of demographics, my suspicion would be that he's white. Again, a matter of probabilities. There are relatively few serial killers of color, although decades ago, many serial killers were black. Another assumption is that he is in his fifties or older."

A small chill went up Chris's neck. White. Male. Fifties. It was the first time he found himself identifying with the killer.

He edged up to the microphone. "Why do you say that?"

"Because of the organization. These aren't spur-of-the-moment crimes or random actions. They're well thought out. Methodical. Meticulous. He's fully aware of what he's doing. He's studied his prey. He's planned to execute these crimes under the best possible circumstances."

Sleeman pointed to a sheaf of reports to make his point.

"In each case, the victim was alone. The unsub studied the priests' behavior enough to ensure he could approach them unseen. He knew exactly where they'd be and when. And look at the staged evidence he's leaving behind. It wouldn't surprise me if he'd planned this for years."

"Isn't that true of any serial killer?" Phil asked.

Sleeman raised a finger. "Not necessarily. Some serial killers do little to no planning. Their crimes are random, spur of the moment, impulsive. David Berkowitz, known as Son of Sam, randomly killed six people and nearly killed several others in fairly populated areas of New York. He taunted the police with letters that promised future kills. The thrill for him was the spree, killing in public to cause fear and mock the police. There was recently a case in Tampa as well, with someone killing random people right on the street, some in broad daylight."

"I remember reading about that," Phil said. "The Seminole Heights serial killer, right?"

"Yes! That's the one."

Phil gave Chris a side glance and a wink. Apparently, he was looking to score some points as well.

"More relevant to your situation," Sleeman continued,

"is Dennis Rader, the BTK Killer—an acronym for 'Bind, Torture, Kill.' He murdered ten people, including an entire family, in Wichita. His killings were methodical and about power and control, although he generally chose older victims who were easier to control. He left brazen clues for the police, which eventually led to his arrest."

"So, what's motivating *our* killer?" Phil asked, pushing himself back in his chair.

"Well, Agent Walker—"

"Please, call me Phil."

Sleeman gave him a pleasant smile. "To answer your question, Phil, let me explain the four categories of serial killers. Keep in mind they're not mutually exclusive, as there can be overlap. And again, these are generalities. I think your unsub falls mainly into one category but overlaps others."

As if on cue, Chris and Phil both flipped to a fresh page in their legal pads.

"First, we have the category of killers who, like Rader, want power and control. Rader enjoyed controlling and torturing his victims. Second, there are the killers who simply have a mission. For example, to kill teenage boys of large stature, perhaps because of bullying the killer experienced as a child."

Phil and Chris scribbled as Sleeman continued.

"Next, we've got the hedonistic killer. Ted Bundy's a prime example of this type. He killed purely for self-gratification, but he was very specific about his victims. He had to be sexually attracted to them. You might recall, he went back to his dump sites and had intercourse with his victims or masturbated on them as a way to further defile them."

"Jesus!" Chris shuddered.

"There's that sexual component," Phil added.

"Of course," Sleeman said. "But it was about more than just sex to Bundy. Careful planning and clever deception were paramount to him." He shifted in his chair. "Moving on—last but not least, there's the visionary killer. He's motivated by voices perceived to be coming from God or some other source considered a deity. The unsub feels compelled to follow these perceived directives."

Phil reached for his cup of coffee, cradled it in his hands. "So, four categories. You said our guy falls mainly into one, with some overlap in another."

Sleeman nodded. "Indeed. You're dealing primarily with a mission killer, with overlap into the power-and-control arena."

Both Chris and Phil looked down at their notes.

"Can you explain further?" Chris asked, still reading.

"Sure. The fact that the victims are all priests who have committed or allegedly committed sexual abuse leads me to think your unsub had one or more negative experiences at a young age. Possibly many. Highly likely Catholic. Or a lapsed Catholic."

"In particular, do you think he was a victim of sexual abuse from a priest himself?" asked Chris. "We've been toying with that idea from the beginning."

Sleeman nodded in a deliberate manner. "Yes. Very likely. Possibly he's killed one of his abusers. He was probably raised in a very devout, very strict family. If he had been abused, he likely felt it was impossible to tell his family for fear of retribution. In addition, it is possible he was abused by others as well—family, acquaintances. As an adult, he may be confused about his own sexuality."

"Do you think we can find him among those who've reported abuse—like on the In the Shade of the Evergreen website?" Phil wondered.

"I've looked at that site." Sleeman shook his head no. "I doubt that. He knows better than to put his name on a website like that. It's the first place anyone would look for a suspect. He's too smart for that."

"That's maybe the only thing we do know," Phil quipped. "Like Bundy, our unsub's clever at deceiving us."

"You're right, and from what I've read in these crime scene reports"—Sleeman pointed to the papers on his table—"he feels the deception is part of the 'fun,' if I may use such an expression. He's clearly intelligent and organized. In my opinion, you're dealing with a very clever killer."

"So," Phil said, drawing the word out slowly. "We're looking for a clever white male in his fifties, former Catholic." His voice was laced with sarcasm but also hopelessness. "I mean, my neighbor fits that description. So does Chris here."

Sleeman gave an understanding nod. "You're absolutely right. If and when you do find him, you'll be surprised. He will very likely be a well-educated professional, respected in the community. Perhaps married, possibly has children. On the outside, to the rest of society, he appears perfectly normal. He fits in. Even his closest friends and family will have been deceived."

Chris looked back down at his notes, tapping his pen lightly. "So, I get how he's in the mission killer category. But you said he overlaps in the power-and-control category too. Like the BTK Killer. The only thing is, we're not seeing signs of torture of the priests. No injury, trauma, or mutilation, other than the obvious gunshots."

Sleeman gave Chris a smile for his observation. "Good point. There's no physical torture. But my suspicion is there was psychological torture before the killer brought about physical death."

The Polycom screen briefly flickered, then stabilized.

"Evidence suggests these priests were not shot suddenly, without warning," Sleeman said. "The fact that one of the priests—the one who was naked—urinated on himself indicates he was under extreme stress, knowing he was about to die at the hands of this man standing in front of him. That alone would provide a great deal of satisfaction for your killer. Perhaps he tortured them with his knowledge of their abuses. And forcing them to ingest rosary beads—that is quite likely some form of spiritual torture."

"'Take this, all of you, and eat of it,'" Chris said out loud, suddenly making the connection.

Sleeman gave Chris a thumbs-up. "Yes. Exactly! Some twisted form of last rites. We can guess, too, that the rosary beads are very personal to him. It's his message, not so much to law enforcement but to the Catholic Church."

Sleeman looked down at the papers surrounding him, as if absorbing their essence by osmosis.

"The rage he's endured all these years is just now bubbling to the surface. It usually takes a long time—decades—

for all the factors that cause this behavior to come together. At a critical time in his social development, everything coalesced to put him on this path. You might say his past was his path to the present. He is troubled, and his motives are unique to him."

Both Chris and Paul fell silent, feeling the weight of that statement. Just before Chris began to speak, the doctor looked off camera. An unexpected interruption. He listened, nodded, gave the gesture for five minutes, then turned back.

"My apologies, gentlemen—I have another appointment in just a few minutes. Any last questions?

"Yes," Chris said. It was the question he had meant to ask before. "Do you think the current state of affairs in the Catholic Church could be an impetus for these killings—along with the unsub's own personal motives?"

"Yes, I do. This has been boiling for some time—for the unsub himself and for the church as a whole. The more victims and cover-ups the world learns about, the more his rage grows. And now it's grown beyond his control. Each new revelation of clergy abuse gives him more reason to kill."

"And the revelations will just keep on coming," added Chris.

"Sadly, yes." Sleeman affirmed emphatically. He tapped his fingers on the table. "A priest from the Vatican just yesterday was indicted for downloading and distributing child pornography. And not long ago, a priest close to you, in Madison, Wisconsin. These revelations give your unsub additional motivation.

"Well, thank you so much for your time, Dr. Sleeman," Phil said. "This has been incredibly helpful. We'll let you get to your appointment."

"Happy to help," he replied. "Keep me posted."

As the monitor went dark, Chris and Phil leaned back in their chairs. For a moment, they stared at each other.

"Additional motivation?" Chris repeated.

"Just what he needs," Phil said. "Just what he needs."

CHAPTER 26

*S*leep was elusive last night. An owl, probably a great horned, had captured a small animal down by the river. The animal's shrieks pierced through my bedroom window. The squeals reminded me of the cat I tortured when I was a teen. Set fire to it with gasoline.

I had to go to the office early to recement a temporary crown. I must have been a bit groggy because I knocked over a bottle of eugenol.

But now I'm alert. I'm heading for St. Margaret's Nursing Home in Avon. The midmorning sun is brilliant. The sky is bright blue with a few wispy clouds. The roads are clear of snow.

I'm wearing a disguise because today I will exact punishment in daylight. It will be my first kill with others nearby, where someone will see me. I'm dressed in dark blue bib overalls, and next to me is a toolbox I'll carry. The dark brown fake mustache looks good on me. I wear a cap low over my eyes and sunglasses with bright red plastic frames. The glasses, especially, will help the receptionist remember me. The plumber. The wrong me.

Father James Crowley, OSB, is eighty-seven years old. One way or the other, with or without my help, he's about to die. He is in the final throes of dementia. But I want to get to him before he dies a natural death.

227

Crowley molested preteen boys and girls at a cabin on John-son Lake. He's one of the few who didn't specialize in boys. His one criterion: the child had to be twelve or younger. I learned this from In the Shade of the Evergreen. Like Doyle, Crowley and other priests from St. Michael's College are named on that site. They are credibly accused, with tales of their misdeeds that are all too familiar to me.

Inside the nursing home, a young woman sits at the re-ception desk. I know she's been filling in over the holidays. Her name tag says she is Madison J. She barely glances up from her phone as I approach. I want to tell her how silly that neon orange streak looks in her hair, but I don't. There's no point.

I tell her I'm Arnie Patterson. From Patterson's Plumbing. I say that the night nurse called about a faucet leak in room 11.

She writes nothing down. Asks for no ID. Looks for no notes from the night nurse to confirm my story. She simply points down the hall to the room. This is easier than I expected.

I thank her. Her head droops, and she instantly goes back to texting. Inane gossip with girlfriends, no doubt. iPhonaddicts, I call them.

Hanging on the door to room 11 is a crucifix encircled by a plastic Christmas wreath of simulated holly with the usual fake red berries. I can hear the television blaring. Contestants vying for prizes on a game show. Anything for money—or whatever shit is behind door number 3.

I knock.

There's no answer.

I enter and close the door behind me. As I walk to the bed, I slip my hands into my vinyl gloves.

Father Crowley's fast asleep. His mouth is half-open. There

228

are spaces, yellow-brown roots, and swollen gums where teeth used to be. His room smells of death. The skin on his neck is nearly transparent; the thin tissue pulses with each heartbeat. Mucus crusts beneath his nose and in the commissure of his lips. His few remaining white hairs have been neatly combed back.

I pull back the comforter and carefully unbutton his flannel pajama top.

He stirs as if awakening from a dream, then succumbs again to sleep. Slowly, his frail chest rises and falls. His breathing is shallow.

Soon it will cease.

This one has to be a quiet kill. No forty-caliber Hydra-Shok. An MTech USMC Marine Corps "Iron Mike" from Walmart is my weapon of choice this time. I open the spring-assisted blade. The words "The Few. The Proud." are stamped above the serrations on the black blade. I appreciate the irony.

I clamp my left hand tightly over Crowley's nose and mouth. His rheumy eyes open wide. His pupils dilate with fear. His frail hands, mottled with the purple discoloration of the aged, reach up and hopelessly try to pull my hand away. I lean over, my mouth next to his ear.

"This is for the children," I whisper.

I know he understands despite his dementia.

I slowly, very slowly, push the sharp blade between the ribs over his heart. It slides easily into his chest. I hear the crackle as it makes its way through the brittle cartilage.

He emits a muffled groan.

The hilt reaches the thin skin. I press firmly and move the grip back and forth. The blade is short, but the wound is deep enough. I don't want death to release him too quickly. I want

229

him to suffer. Like the children at the lake.

Soon his feeble hands slide away. I keep my hand over his mouth a moment longer to stifle the death rattle. He is still. His eyes are half-open, pupils still dilated, now forever fixed. I release my hand, remove the knife, and lay it beside him. His lips are already losing color, turning pallid gray.

There's surprisingly little blood, but enough for my message. With a Q-tip from the little table next to his bed, I scribe my missive on his hairless white chest and down onto his pale abdomen.

Next, I deposit the beads.

And leave a flattened cigarette on the floor.

I fold his hands on top of the comforter, which I've pulled up to his chin. It's thick enough so the small amount of blood won't soak through. He looks as though he's sleeping peacefully.

But I know his soul is screaming in hell.

It will be at least an hour before my deed is discovered. By then, Arnie the plumber will be far, far away.

CHAPTER 27

Emma Bergstrom, employed at St. Margaret's since Thanksgiving a year ago, had begun her shift. She was short and rotund. Her stringy black hair was swept back and tied with a piece of pink ribbon. The thick lenses in her glasses enlarged her eyes and made her appear flummoxed, even when she wasn't.

It was a morning of routine rounds. Before lunch, Emma would rouse the residents, many of whom would be sleeping. She'd check vitals, help with toilet duties, and ready the residents for the noon meal.

Emma could hear the television in Crowley's room from across the hallway. This was not uncommon. In her short time at the nursing home, Father Crowley had come to be one of her favorites. He caused little difficulty, and despite his dementia, he usually remembered her name. And he always said, while looking at her through cataract-clouded eyes, "God bless you, my beautiful little child."

Father Crowley was one of the "sleepers"—very hard of hearing and difficult to wake. She expected this morning to be no different. As a courtesy, she knocked firmly on his door before she entered. She was not surprised to find him still in bed.

His eyes, still partially open, were inert.

Emma jostled his arm. He felt cool to the touch. She immediately felt for a carotid pulse. There was none. She would have to move him to the floor and start CPR.

As she pulled off the thick bedding, she froze, then screamed. A knife lay next to a wound on Crowley's chest. The blade seemed to point to the red-black scrawling down his torso.

Her scream brought receptionist Madison Jasper running to room 11. She found Emma gasping, her hair even more disarrayed than usual, mascara-stained tears streaming down her cheeks, staring at the wound in Father Crowley's chest. Madison looked at Emma, then at Father Crowley. She stiffened. Her mouth moved and a scream formed, but it welded itself in her throat.

"Call nine-one-one immediately!" Emma ordered.

Madison shook herself loose and ran to the front desk to make the call.

When the EMTs arrived, they tried to resuscitate Father Crowley, only to quickly determine he was beyond their help. EMT Tim Aker contacted the Avon Police Department.

When Officer Olin Langguth came through the front door, Madison, still unable to speak clearly, motioned him down the hall to Crowley's room.

Langguth was a no-nonsense police officer. Superficial conversations were, in his opinion, unnecessary and a waste of time. His piercing blue eyes, muscular stature, and stern countenance made that clear. Langguth took a quick look at Crowley, had a brief conversation with Aker, then returned to the reception desk.

"Your name?" His voice commanded attention.

"Madison Jasper," she said, pointing a trembling finger at her name tag.

He began writing in his note pad. "Middle name?"

"Ann."

He lifted his pen from the page. "Ann with an *e*, or just A-N-N?"

"No *e*."

"Jasper just as it sounds?"

"*Yes*," she replied with the slightest hint of annoyance.

He looked up from his notepad. "Ms. Jasper, is there a manager or supervisor on-site?" He glanced around and behind her, hoping someone with authority would appear with his beckon.

She shook her head. "No. Mrs. Simmons is off today for a funeral."

"Well, call her and have her get hold of me as soon as she can." He handed Madison his card.

Looking around again, Langguth noticed that several residents and employees had gathered in the hallway, wondering what was happening. Their faces were tight with concern and confusion.

"No one enters or leaves this facility without my permission," he told Madison quietly. "This place is locked down until I tell you otherwise. I'll call in another officer to secure the entrance. But until then, it's your job. You have any problems, just holler." He rapped his knuckles on her desk and began to walk away.

She raised her hands in frustration "But—but we have family who visit our residents."

Langguth came to a halt, spun around, and pointed at her. "Apparently," he said softly but sternly, "you didn't hear me." He gave her a commanding stare. "This entire place is a crime scene until I determine otherwise. No one comes in. No one goes out." His words were staccato.

The crowd in the hallway looked at each other, knowing there had been a tense exchange they weren't privy to.

"In addition," Langguth said, "I want a list of everyone who entered the building since you came on duty."

Madison crossed her arms and sighed. "Only two. One lady came to visit her grandmother in room 3. The other was a plumber."

"A plumber?"

Immediately, Langguth stepped closer and loomed over her desk. It made Madison slide backward, sending the chair rolling several inches away from the desk.

Langguth locked eyes with her. "Tell me more about the plumber."

She shrugged. "He was here this morning. To fix something in Father Crowley's room."

"What was his name? The name of his company?"

Madison's shoulders inched up even more and froze. What began as a shrug was now a defensive crouch. "Um, I think he said his name was Arnie. Yeah, it was Arnie...Patterson. From Patterson's Plumbing." She broke her eyes away. "I have an uncle Arnie. That's why I remember."

He leaned in even farther now. "Did you sign him in? Ask for ID?" He stabbed his finger at a notepad on Madison's desk. These were more accusations than questions.

"No. I mean, he was a *plumber*."

"Oh, Jesus." Langguth groaned. He couldn't believe the lack of security. "Isn't every visitor—I mean *every* visitor—supposed to sign in?"

Madison's eyes welled with tears. "Yes, but I *told* you, he was a plumber. He technically wasn't a 'visitor.' He was here to fix a leak. He had a toolbox. I didn't know I had to sign him in or make him prove who he was." Her face was red with frustration. "I'm just a temp over the holidays!" she snapped. Anger was now dominating her voice.

Langguth scratched his forehead in aggravation. "Fine. What time did you get here, and when did the plumber arrive?"

She wiped at her tears and sniffled. "My shift started at seven. The plumber came in around ten."

Langguth was writing in his notepad again. He looked directly at Madison. "He came around ten? *Around*?"

"That's what I said!"

Madison was downright angry now. She had had enough trauma for one day. She'd never seen a dead person before—let alone one with a huge, gaping hole in his chest. That old man had been *murdered*. Maybe by someone pretending to be a plumber—someone she let right in. And now she was supposed to just sit here and take this guy's "bad cop" bullshit?

"What time did he leave?"

"I—don't—know." Her voice was severe.

His eyes flared, but she spoke before he could chastise her yet again.

"He must have left when I was away from my desk. I don't just sit here every minute! They give me other things to do, you know."

"Can you give me some idea what he looked like?" Langguth pressed.

She lifted her chin. "Small guy. Couple inches shorter than you. Thinner than you too."

Touché, asshole, she added to herself.

Langguth's eyes narrowed a fraction of an inch.

Madison continued. "He had a mustache, a Minnesota Twins cap, and red sunglasses. He was wearing bib overalls—blue, I think." She thought for a minute. "And he smelled kind of funny."

Langguth bolted upright at this. "Funny? How?"

"I don't know. It was just weird. Yet familiar. Can't put my finger on it…" She looked down and off to the right, in deep thought.

Langguth summoned as much patience as he could muster. It wasn't much. The skin beneath his eye twitched.

"Maybe it was kinda … clovey?" She considered that answer, then nodded to herself. "Yeah, that's it. Cloves." A small smile of satisfaction began to form on her lips, but then she looked at Langguth. It immediately turned into a scowl.

Without a word, Langguth wrapped the desk with his knuckles once again, then headed around the corner. Madison waited until he was completely out of sight before collapsing into the chair behind her. With trembling hands, she reached for her phone—to call her mother.

After pausing in the hallway to call the Bemidji BCA

office, Langguth continued on to Crowley's room. Emma was still there, slouched in a chair. The TV was still blaring. It was a talk show with a discussion that would have been heated at any volume.

Langguth glanced around the room. "Someone been smoking in here?" Once again, it really wasn't a question but an accusation.

Emma sat forward. "Smoking's strictly prohibited," she snapped. "We use oxygen here."

He pointed to the floor. "There's a cigarette butt."

"What?" Emma stood and headed over to pick up the butt.

"No—leave it!" he practically shouted. "Don't touch anything!"

Startled by the officer's brusque demeanor, Emma jumped back and raised her hands in surrender. "Jeez—OK!" Legitimately flummoxed, her eyes filled the full circumference of her frames. "Well, then, I don't know how that got here. There was no smoke smell when I found Father Crowley. I would've noticed." She squared herself defiantly.

Langguth clenched his teeth. First the young girl at the reception desk, and now this nurse. These women had information he was supposed to coax from them, not force out of them. Perhaps he was coming on too strong. He begrudgingly dialed it back. He pulled out his notepad and very deliberately relaxed his jaw.

"So," he began, "please walk me through what you know about this situation." A nice open-ended prompt. Less demanding.

Emma exhaled and relaxed herself a bit as well. "I checked on Father Crowley at eight thirty this morning, and he was fine. Sleeping, of course. Snoring. The TV was going."

"Always this loud?"

She nodded. "He was very hard of hearing. Most of our residents don't hear well—or at all." She glanced at her watch. "At eleven thirty, then, I came by to get him ready for lunch. That's when I found him like . . ." She nodded toward the body as if to finish her sentence.

"How long has he been a resident at St. Margaret's?"

Emma cocked her head and thought for a moment. "A little more than a year. He arrived just after I started here."

"Any idea who's been visiting him since he arrived?"

Emma shrugged. "We don't pay much attention to who comes to visit. We're kinda laid back here. Small town. Everybody knows everybody. He has a younger sister— retired nun—who comes once in a while. Name is Sister Mary Ruth. Haven't seen her in a long time, though."

"Know anyone who might want to do this to him?" His look was intense, pressing for information.

She shook her head. "I can't imagine anyone wanting to kill him. I mean, he's a priest. He has dementia. He's innocent—like a child." She stared at his lifeless body. "Who would hurt a child?"

CHAPTER 28

Agent Tom Muller and a team of techs from the Bemidji BCA office arrived at St. Margaret's Nursing Home around four thirty. Tom began with a briefing from Officer Langguth, then spoke with the receptionist and the nurse. The techs were still processing the scene in room 11 when Tom stepped outside to his car to call the Saint Paul BCA headquarters.

He knew shit would hit the fan when the team in St. Paul learned about this one.

Phil was in the cafeteria when Marty patched the call through to him. He was in no mood to be bothered. Lately the priest homicides had been getting to him, and his demeanor was not pleasant.

"This is Walker," he answered, in a gruff voice.

"Phil—this is Agent Tom Muller."

Phil's mood brightened. He had met Tom at a seminar. Seemed like a good guy.

"Hey, Tom." Phil paused to brush crumbs off his sleeve. "How are things up on the frozen tundra? You calling from a fish house?"

Both men chuckled.

"I wish," Tom replied. He sighed. "Until this morning, things were going along just fine up here. But then we got

239

a case I think you're gonna be interested in."

Phil's gut tightened. He reached for his pack of cigarettes. He couldn't light up there in the cafeteria, but he needed to touch the pack anyway to feel the future satisfaction.

Tom didn't mince words. "We got a murdered priest in a nursing home in Avon. Our team is still processing, but I wanted to give you the heads-up."

"Aw, Jesus." Phil closed his eyes and rubbed his head. "Shot?"

"Nope. Stabbed. Knife was left at the scene."

Phil opened one eye. A knife—that was new. It was probably the only new detail, though.

"I bet you found a cigarette butt, right?" he asked, already sure of the answer.

There was a pause. "Yeah. On the floor." Another pause. "How'd you know?"

"ESP," Phil cracked. "Nah. It's just that we've had three priest murders down here, with a cigarette butt left behind at every one of 'em. This has got to be the same guy."

Tom whistled. "I knew you had a slew of priest murders down there, but I shoulda read up on the details."

"Yep," Phil said, "the crime scene details have been consistent from case to case, with minor exceptions. The one thing that has been very consistent is that the murdered priests have all been credibly accused of child molestation. Are you hearing any word along those lines with this guy?"

"Not a word, no," Tom answered. "This guy was in his late eighties, retired for many years, and, according to the nurse, in the final stages of dementia. If he was an abuser, musta been a long time ago."

Phil's gut tightened another notch, just thinking about the horrible details his team would surely dig up about the latest victim. This perp was on a mission. The likelihood of priest number four not having the same sins on his hands as the other three was slim to none.

"Anyway," Tom said, "I hope you can get prints off the knife. Maybe DNA from the butt too."

Phil was sure they wouldn't get either. "Anything else?"

"Well, this is a long shot, but the receptionist at the nursing home may have seen the killer."

Phil bolted upright and grabbed a pen and legal pad.

"He convinced the girl he was a plumber. Gave her a name: Arnie Patterson from Patterson's Plumbing."

Phil furiously scribbled. "Name's gotta be fake, but go on."

"The girl said he was a little guy—about five-six and thin," Tom continued. "We think he was in disguise— bib overalls, hat down over his eyes, sunglasses with red frames, mustache."

"Figures. Simple disguise. What kind of hat?"

"Baseball, red, with Minnesota Twins logo. Dime a dozen." Tom paused to let Phil catch up with his notetaking.

"Anything else?"

"This might not mean much, but she said he smelled like cloves."

"Cloves!" Phil rolled his eyes. "Great. We'll get a clove-sniffing dog and go around smelling guys in bib over- alls!" Phil made snuffling sounds into the phone.

Tom laughed. "Hey, all I can do is relate what she told us! You can't make this stuff up."

Phil tossed his pen aside. "Sorry for the sarcasm. It's just that we're on overload down here. Priest cases are coming fast and furious—never mind the usual crap we have to deal with."

"One last thing," Tom added.

Phil scrambled to retrieve the pen. "Christ, give it to me."

"There was some sort of writing on the victim's chest. Detectives said it looked like it was done with the victim's own blood. We can't really read it. Might be Latin?"

Phil picked up the pen and tossed it again—farther this time. He kicked back and put his feet on an adjacent chair. The fourth mystery. He figured there'd be more beads too. Perp probably forced them down before he stabbed the old man.

Psychological torture. That Sleeman knew his shit.

"The knife went with the body," Tom said. "The butt will be delivered by our staff today. Midwest Medical Examiner's Office in Anoka County has the contract for autopsies from this area. I'd like to think they'll give priority to the postmortem."

Phil knew Valerie Raon at Midwest. She was sharp. But wait until she found the beads.

"Anything else, Tom?" Phil said, suddenly feeling exhausted.

"Nope. That's all we've got right now."

"All right. Keep me posted."

"Roger that."

Ending the call, Phil lowered his feet. They felt like lead.

He looked at his notes. The perp sure seemed to be enjoying himself. Four murders. The same old, same old with the cigarette butts and the messages in blood. But some new twists too. Knife instead of gun. Crime committed in daylight at a public place. First time the perp had allowed himself to be seen. He was getting bolder.

"Happy fucking New Year," he muttered to no one.

He grabbed another coffee and headed for his office. After donning his coat, he went out to the portico. He called Chris, holding his cell phone to his ear while he smoked. He raised his collar and turned his back to the biting wind.

"Hey, Phil," Chris answered. "What's up?"

"Dead priest number four, that's what."

CHAPTER 29

The call from the Midwest Medical Examiner's Office came sooner than Phil expected.

"Agent Walker, this is Dr. Valerie Raon from Midwest. You got a minute to talk?"

"Of course, Doc." Phil put aside the cold case folder he had been reviewing, an unsolved abduction at a Manning Avenue gas station several years ago. "This about the Avon homicide?"

"Yes. Agent Muller from the Bemidji BCA office said I should keep you in the loop on this one. Told me they processed the scene but that you guys are doing the lab work."

"Correct." Phil slid his chair back and opened the middle drawer of his desk. He retrieved a couple of Rolaids, popped them into his mouth, and began chewing. "Go ahead, Doctor. What do you have?"

There was a slight pause. "Sorry—did I catch you at a bad time?" she asked.

"No. Why?" His teeth crunched on the Rolaids.

"Sounds like you're eating. Lunch? I can call back."

Phil let out a laugh. "No. Just some antacids."

"Actually," she replied, "those aren't good for you. They neutralize too much stomach acid. My dentist says they're bad for your teeth too. Neutralize your saliva."

"I know," Phil said out loud. *Jesus, you sound like my mother*, he added to himself. "Anyway, whatcha got?"

Valerie drew a breath. "The deceased was killed with a short-blade knife, which our technician delivered to your facility."

"Yep. Evidence Intake already has it. Our print guy, Zerke, gave it priority in the lab." He decided not to voice his doubt about any prints being found.

"As you might know," Valerie continued, "we always do full-body x-rays before an autopsy in the case of a suspicious death. The chest picture showed something in the thoracic cavity. Baffled us at first. Turns out it was a string of beads."

Still holding the phone, Phil lowered his arms onto the desk and rested his head in them. He knew where this was going, but he let her finish.

"Ten faceted red stones on a chain. Looks to me like part of a rosary. It appears that after the priest was killed, the beads were pushed into the wound."

"Pushed in, not swallowed, huh? That's new," Phil said mostly to himself.

Valerie wasn't quite sure how to respond. "Yes. Pushed in," she repeated. "So, my understanding is that you've had two other—"

"Three," he corrected. "This makes four."

"Anyway, if I may continue . . ."

Phil didn't miss the edge in her voice. She didn't like being interrupted, especially not to be corrected.

"You've had other murders"—she conspicuously omitted any reference to a number—"similar to this one, so I'm sure your team will want to examine this string of beads for comparisons. One of my staff will deliver them once they've been photographed."

Phil rubbed his chin. "OK, thanks, Doc." Of course, he knew they would prove identical to those from the three previous murders.

"There's another thing," she said.

"And that is . . . ?"

"Writing in blood on the victim's chest. It was in Latin: *Quartum mystérium*, which translates into—"

Phil didn't interrupt her this time. Instead, he quietly mouthed the translation along with her.

"The fourth mystery."

"Anything else?" He put the phone on speaker, walked to the credenza, and poured a coffee. Only one pack of sugar nowadays.

"No defensive wounds. Didn't look like there was a struggle. Of course, he was elderly. I doubt he could've put up a fight," she added. "Slight petechiae around his eyes, which—"

"So he was suffocated?" Phil blurted.

"No." Her voice was crisp. "As I was saying, the petechiae was minimal, which means his breathing was compromised in some way. Perhaps there was a hand or pillow blocking his airway, for instance. But suffocation was not the cause of death. The bleeding in the chest cavity indicates he died from the chest wound."

"Anything interesting about the wound?" asked Phil. He walked behind his desk and looked out the window, took a sip if coffee.

"Yes. The perpetrator, he or she—"

"He!" Phil said emphatically, turning now from the window and facing the speaker on his desk.

Valerie huffed. "May I *please* finish?"

"Yes, I'm sorry. Go on." He gestured apologetically, as though she was standing next to him.

The doctor continued, emphasizing the pronoun: "*He* only stabbed the victim once. This is not indicative of a rage killing, where we'd expect multiple stab wounds and perhaps blunt-force injuries. In this case, the killer stabbed once and moved the blade around inside the chest cavity. The cross-guard mark on the victim's chest was obvious. The heart was nicked three times, though not deeply cut. It was a short blade, so no doubt the victim suffered. At least for a while."

Suffered! Just what the asshole wanted. Phil nodded in silence for a moment.

The doctor was silent as well.

"Anything else?" he finally said. He grabbed his coat. He was ready for a smoke.

"No. That's all we have at this point."

"Okay. Thanks, Doc. Call us if you find anything else we should know about."

"Will do. Have a good day," she said politely. She was glad to be done with this conversation.

Phil reached for his smokes as he retreated to the portico.

So the perp pushed in the knife, then moved it around. He couldn't use a gun in a public place in broad daylight.

But he still wanted his victim to feel the pain.

CHAPTER 30

I'm enjoying this. It feels good. It really does.

 The best part is not the moment of the actual death. It's the fear that grips the evil bastards when they realize they're about to die. Their pupils dilate. Their bodies shake. It's my special torture.

 Doyle pissed himself. I really got off on that. When he begged to say the Act of Contrition, he knew his end was near.

 Torturing him, lording over him—it was personal. Very personal. He was the only one who thought he knew me, though he didn't. I killed Doyle for a certain someone as well as for myself. His sins killed a part of me.

 And Carlos Rodriguez. Such a hypocrite, making a flamboyant display of holiness every morning when he swung the church doors open for those waiting to be delivered from sin. Did he feel the flames of hell licking at his feet as he descended? I hope so.

 Roosevelt Simon, the glutton. As much as I wanted to shatter his brain with my Beretta, I couldn't leave that mess for his housekeeper. She didn't deserve that.

 The news says there was evidence in his home that links him to other pedophiles. I'm certain that his predatory associates are nervous. Very nervous. As they should be. As long as I can, I am coming.

And then there's Father Crowley. Demented. Fragile. But still evil. His life was soon to end of its own accord, but I couldn't let that happen. I needed to be the master of his fate.

Through it all, the police have no idea who I am. Idiots. By now they must be aware that I'm too shrewd for them. My clues lead them down nothing but dead ends.

And I've already selected the next evil soul to send to perdition.

They probably think I'm a monster. A psychopath. No remorse. That's not entirely true. I'm remorseful for the pain I've caused the families and friends of my victims. I know what it's like to grieve, to lose a loved one, to have your heart broken.

But someone has to avenge the children. The youth. The innocents.

One special innocent in particular.

So no, I am not a monster. I feel. My greatest sympathy is for those who have no one to tell, no one to share their horrible secret with. The innocents who are punished when they do tell. The pain they live with is unspeakable. It lasts a lifetime.

I know. I'm one of the innocents.

Some of the innocents die with their secrets.

That I know for sure.

CHAPTER 31

Gayle turned off the headlights as she approached Paul's driveway. She slowly rolled up the slight incline and parked by the double garage. The back seat held her overnight bag, just in case. She longed for things to be the way they'd been months ago: cocktails by the fire, music on the stereo, lovemaking and cuddling far into the night.

Gayle sat for several minutes, contemplating the risk of dropping in unexpectedly like this. She knew Paul wouldn't like it. She'd be walking in the door with one major strike already against her. But it was a risk she had to take.

From her car she could see Paul's living room. The window blinds were partially drawn, but the lights were on inside. Paul called his home an "untouched man pit," meaning it was untouched by the bent of a woman. She could see him slouched in his recliner, staring at the TV.

When reaching for her key to turn off the ignition, Gayle noticed her thumb was bleeding. She'd bitten the nail down to the quick during the drive from Stillwater. Wiping the blood on a fast-food napkin she found at the bottom of her center console, she stepped out of the car and slowly made her way up the steps to Paul's house.

Gayle paused on the concrete porch, hesitant to ring

the bell. Would she regret this? Her finger trembling, she finally pressed the doorbell. Fearing Paul might not open the door if he saw her through the tall side window, she edged out of view.

Paul's figure appeared, peering through the window. Not seeing anyone, he opened the door. When he saw Gayle, he tensed and forced his sneer to morph into a stiff, uncomfortable smile.

"Well. This is a surprise." He tightened the string on his sweatpants. "I was watching TV. Didn't hear you drive up."

"May I come in?" she asked, keeping her voice level.

"I suppose we can sit in the living room." His voice was flat. His tongue felt like lead.

As she followed him into the living room, Paul turned off the television and resumed his position on the recliner. A glass of vodka and a near-empty bottle of Tito's sat on the end table next to him.

Gayle tossed her coat on a chair, then perched on the leather ottoman. She faced Paul, but he stared blankly at the burning logs in the river rock fireplace. The flames reflected off his glasses. His eyes were sunken, his cheeks drawn. He looked even worse than he had the last time she'd seen him—that horrible night at Stella's.

She wanted to ask him about his health, but she deferred. She was determined to complete the task she'd come to accomplish.

"You weren't expecting me, I know," she began, nervously fidgeting with the hem of her blouse. "But we have to talk. About us. About the issues we've never resolved."

Expressionless, Paul never took his eyes off the embers glowing behind the sooty glass doors of the fireplace.

She swallowed hard, almost unable to speak. She tucked her raw thumb under her tightly clenched fingers.

"Paul, we're supposed to be in Hawaii right now. Just us, alone, loving each other, having fun. Instead, I feel like I'm at an amusement park, riding a rollercoaster. For weeks now, it's been 'Come here, honey,' then 'Go away, honey.' When we make love—which has been less and less often, by the way—you send me home right after. You manipulate me to get me close, but once you're satisfied, you dismiss me. I don't know where I stand anymore with you. You're tearing my heart out." She pounded a clenched fist to her breast.

He shrugged.

Words failed her now. Forcing back tears, she glanced around his "man pit." The orange-and-brown afghan his mother had crocheted hung over the back of the leather sofa. Bella, his cat, was curled up on it, eyes nearly shut, but she was still alert. On the distressed-wood mantel, she saw several photographs of himself on hunting trips. But not one picture of the two of them. No snapshots from their excursions to New York or Antarctica, or even from their first overnight weekend in the rustic cabin up in the Boundary Waters...where he told her he loved her. Where she gave herself to him.

Paul rose, placed another log on the fire, went to the kitchen, and refilled his glass with ice. When he returned, he added vodka to his glass and sat on the hearth. The new log burst into flames behind him. He took a sizable drink, then set the glass down with a clink on the hearth.

"You know I hate these talks," he said.

It was her turn to shrug. "I don't care. I need to know where I stand with you."

She moved the ottoman closer to him and grasped both his hands. She tried to smile.

"Don't you remember how we talked about moving in together? About buying a ring the next time we were in New York?"

She squeezed his hands and looked into his eyes, searching.

"Paul, I love you."

He chewed the inside of his lip. "I . . . care about you too."

She sat back, dropping his hands. "*Care*? You *care* about me?" Her voice began to crack.

"You know what I mean." He looked away.

She shook her head firmly. "No. I don't know what you mean. So, tell me, Paul. What *do* you mean?"

He turned his head and stared toward the kitchen. The fire cast shadows across his face, emphasizing the deep shadows beneath his sunken eyes. "I get scared sometimes."

Once again, she reached for his hands. "Of what? Scared I might leave you? Scared I might want more than you can give me?" Her voice had softened, but her grip was so tight that her thumb began to bleed again.

Paul looked directly at her. "You don't know why my marriage to Sheila failed."

"You're right. I don't. So *tell* me." She pleaded with her eyes.

"I pushed her away. Cheated on her."

"Is that what you're scared of—of being with just one woman? Am I not enough for you? Is that it?" As nonjudgmental as she knew she needed to be in that moment, she couldn't keep the bite out of her tone.

Paul was increasingly uncomfortable. "No, of course not."

He sighed and closed eyes. When he reopened them, they were hard in a way Gayle had never seen before.

"When I was with Sheila, I became more like my father."

"What do you mean? What was he like?" she pressed. "He died years ago, right?"

"He was an asshole." His voice was almost inaudible.

"What does *that* mean?"

"He was emotionally dead."

One of the embers popped as if to fill the silence.

"I get that way sometimes too," Paul continued, his voice distant. "Maybe I'm afraid of emotional intimacy. That's what scares me to death—you and I being together all the time, making our relationship permanent. I just don't know how to love."

"Yes, you do," she asserted. "You *do* know how to love. I know that for a fact because we were so happy—until recently." She took his hand now and caressed it, tracing his palm with her fingertips. "So, learn from your father. Be someone different. Someone better."

He shook his head. "I tried. It took constant focus. Just too much work. Relationships shouldn't take work."

There was finality in his voice.

As though suddenly realizing Gayle needed comfort, Bella bounded off the sofa and jumped into her lap. Gayle released Paul's hands and gently stroked the cat.

"I want to be part of your life, Paul. I want to share my life with you." She drew a breath and squared her shoulders. "But I can't be in limbo any longer." She moved her head to force him to look at her. "If it's me, if I've done something to make you back away, I need to know now so I can fix it."

Paul reached for his vodka. "It's not anything you've done." He stared into the glass before downing the drink in one swallow.

Gayle stood quickly, sending Bella flying off her lap and darting behind the sofa. "Goddammit! I can't keep doing this! I just can't!"

She raised her shaking hands to her face, then slowly lowered them straight down at her sides. She looked at him and waited until he looked back at her.

"If you want me out of your life, just tell me. I'll go away."

"I want you out of my life." His voice was a monotone.

For a moment, Gayle was frozen by his words. Then she grabbed a glass coaster off his Stickley coffee table and shattered it against the wall.

Paul barely flinched.

"You know what? You're *right*!" she shouted, her face red. "You *don't* know how to love! You are not capable of loving anyone but yourself! Actually, I wonder *if* you even love yourself, Paul. I really do!"

Paul looked away. "You need to go, Gayle."

"Gladly!" She kicked a piece of the broken coaster across the room as she grabbed her coat. "By the way, good luck with the next easy fuck who comes along." She pointed down the darkened hallway to his bedroom. "I know all about the goodies in your dresser. The gifts you use to lure us all into your bed until you're tired of us. Like that scarf!"

Paul stood now, his fists balled, a wobble to his stance. "You had no business going through my things."

"That's right. I didn't. But I did anyway! And what a revelation *that* was." She pointed a finger at him. "Who was the lucky woman who got the Neiman Marcus bag? You are such an asshole!" she screamed.

She raced out of the house, slamming the door so hard that one of Paul's photos fell from the mantle.

Gayle sat in her car until she stopped shaking. She watched through the blinds as Paul slumped into his recliner, put his head in his hands, and cried.

Fuck you, Dr. Paul Thomas.

She drove away.

CHAPTER 32

P hil was just stepping in from a smoke break when Ken Zerke called.

"I've got good news, Phil."

Phil's spirits lightened. "I need some," he said. He struggled to peel out of his coat while still holding the phone. "Let's have it."

"We got excellent prints from the knife used in the Avon homicide—dozens of clear, individual characteristics. The thumbprint with the abnormality even matches the prints found earlier. We had enough to finally run an IAFIS search."

"And...?"

"Nothing came up."

Phil couldn't help but frown. "I thought you said you had good news. This better be a 'but wait—there's more' situation."

"It is!" Ken said. "As a last-ditch effort, I checked the AF database and got a hit."

Phil's frown turned to a smile. "AF? Oh, applicant fingerprints—isn't that when candidates are fingerprinted for occupations that require criminal background checks? But outside of military and law enforcement jobs, those prints are supposed to be deleted once the applicant is cleared."

Phil landed in his chair with a thud. "Wait. Are you gonna tell me our perp's in—"

"Nope," Ken quickly interrupted. "Let me back up a bit. You're right that they archive prints for applicants in law enforcement and the military. You're right too that all other print files are supposed to be destroyed if they don't correlate with a reason to deny employment." Ken paused and waited, hoping Phil was following.

"Gotcha," Phil affirmed.

"So," Ken continued, "Minnesota requires health professionals to be fingerprinted for criminal background checks in order to be licensed. Those prints are stored in a separate file in the database and are supposed to be destroyed as well."

"*Supposed* to be," Phil repeated, picking up on the emphasis.

"Right. But no one's gotten around to it. And lucky for us, because that's where we found your boy. Perfect match on all five digits—every whorl, bifurcation, island, and ridge. Even the mark on the thumb showed up, and the papillary ridges were perfectly registered. I got more than enough biometric characteristics."

Phil pounded his desk. "Bingo! Great work, Ken. Do you have a name for me?" He reached for a pen and pad.

"Sure do. David Jami Kuusisto." He spelled it out. "According to the application, he's a U of M pharmacy grad who applied for Minnesota licensure in 2009. He listed an address in southeast Minneapolis—near Eighteenth and Como Avenue."

Phil laughed out loud. Those were his old stomping

grounds. He'd managed a two-story apartment building in that neighborhood over thirty years ago, while working on his degree in criminal justice. He had good memories about the U—except for one. He would have been one of three on her divorce list, had she not broken off their engagement.

"I don't get it . . . what's so funny?" Ken was perplexed but curious.

Phil sighed away his memories. "Oh, nothing. Listen—you have no idea how much I appreciate this." He tapped his pen excitedly with each word.

"Glad to help. Hope you find your boy."

"Oh, we will. It looks like there *is* a light at the end of the tunnel after all. Thanks again."

As Phil hung up, he stared out the window at an ambulance rushing down Maryland Avenue.

A name. They finally had a name.

He didn't want to get ahead of himself, though. The perp was clearly playing some sort of cat-and-mouse game. The unsmoked cigarette butts seemed to suggest he was planting evidence just to toy with them.

But what if Kuusisto really was their guy? Maybe the cocky bastard deliberately left his own prints because he assumed he was untraceable. He correctly knew he wasn't in IAFIS—but maybe he didn't realize his prints were still on file in the AF database.

Or maybe Kuusisto was just some poor patsy who somehow ended up getting his fingerprints all over a murder weapon and shell casings. Dr. Sleeman had said this type of killer was clever—perhaps he could set up something that devious.

Even if Kuusisto was just a patsy it was still something. There had to be some link, somehow, between him and the perp. One way or another, this was their best lead—their only lead.

Phil would take whatever he could get.

The next steps tumbled in Phil's mind, cascading one after another. He could check with the DMV for Kuusisto's latest address, as he'd likely moved away from campus after this many years. If the DMV turned up nothing, he could follow up with the U of M Alumni Association. He knew Gretchen Ambler over there. The association had its ways of keeping tabs on graduates so it could beg for contributions.

But first he'd check the obvious resources.

His fingers flew across the keyboard as he typed Kuusisto's name into the Google search bar. Social media. Photos. Professional details. He wanted it all.

The light at the end of the tunnel is getting brighter, he thought. He held his breath as he hit enter.

In less than a second, the first page loaded with links to an obituary, posted in the *Grand Rapids Herald-Review* on June 2, 2009.

Phil instantly deflated, his chin dropping to his chest.

On June 1, 2009, David Jami Kuusisto died tragically in an airplane accident with his fiancée, Kristi Carlson of Rush City, MN. David was born in Bigfork on February 15, 1983. He attended Bigfork Elementary and graduated from Bigfork High School. He loved northern Minnesota and planned to return to his roots after graduating college.

David always knew he wanted to be a pharmacist and got an early start with his Gilbert chemistry set when he was a young boy. David attended the University of Minnesota College of Liberal Arts and earned a degree in chemistry, graduating summa cum laude. He then attended the University of Minnesota College of Pharmacy, graduating in May of this year.

David is sadly missed by his parents, Jami and Venla of Bigfork; his grandparents, Ville and Lida Kuusisto and Ella Ketola of Inari, Finland; his dog, Lucca; and many aunts, uncles, cousins, and friends. He was preceded in death by his grandfather Eino Ketola of Inari.

Remembrance will be Monday, June 5, 2009, 1:00 to 3:00 p.m. at Carroll Funeral Home, 284 Golf Course Road, Bigfork. It will be followed by a 4:00 p.m. memorial service at Bigfork Lutheran Church, 401 N. State Highway 38, Bigfork, MN, 56628. Interment will be at Lakeview Cemetery. Memorials are preferred to the family.

Phil stared at the accompanying photo of the handsome young man. David Jami Kuusisto died back in 2009. An elderly priest had been murdered—in broad daylight, in a public place—just days ago. And David Kuusisto's prints were all over the murder weapon.

"What in the hell is going on?" Phil asked his empty office.

Chapter 33

At seven a.m., Phil began the five-hour drive. He was heading to the home of Jami and Venla Kuusisto, in the northern Minnesota town of Bigfork. In a brief and no doubt confusing phone call to the couple the afternoon before, Phil had explained that their deceased son was somehow connected to a current criminal case. All parties agreed that an in-person discussion was in order.

It meant a long drive and an even longer day, but Phil knew the visit would be worthwhile. He not only needed insight about David; he also needed his DNA. David's prints were on that knife. Perhaps David's DNA was on the cigarette butts as well.

But if so, *how*? Logic suggested that the perp had somehow had access to David's body back in 2009. Then again, Phil had to question whether logic even applied to this case anymore.

Phil's mind wandered. While going through Moose Lake on I-35, he recalled the abduction and murder of young Katie Poirier and the difficulty identifying her remains. He shuddered, imagining what the young woman must have endured before death set her free.

From Moose Lake, he headed north on Highway 73 through Cromwell, then to Floodwood. The rural highway was in rough shape—scarred with potholes and poorly plowed. The outside temperature had fallen to minus fifteen. Phil kept turning up the heat in the Taurus.

In Floodwood, he turned west onto Highway 2, which was well cleared all the way to Grand Rapids. It was a welcome change from the snow-drifted roads he was leaving behind.

Bigfork was forty-one miles north of Grand Rapids on Highway 38. There were numerous stretches on the road where the winter sun had yet to melt the compacted snow and ice. Combined with frequent sharp curves, it made for dangerous navigating. As Phil rounded a bend by Marcell, near the Laurentian Divide, a truck loaded with logs nearly ran him off the road.

Phil reached for a cigarette. He was not the first to violate the no-smoking-in-state-owned-vehicles rule, but at least he knew better than to leave evidence behind. He reminded himself to wipe the smudges of ash along the top of the window he had cracked open.

As the miles brought him closer to Bigfork, Phil contemplated how to approach the difficult conversation with the Kuusistos. He decided to be direct yet compassionate.

He would first emphasize that the BCA did not believe their son had any involvement in the case. But he also had to tell these parents that it was possible someone had tampered with their son's remains before he was cremated. As if losing their son hadn't been hard enough on them.

Phil didn't feel like going into the situation on an empty

266

stomach. He stopped for lunch at the Bigfork Pizza Parlor on Main Avenue. When he stepped out of the car, he savored the clean, unpolluted air of northern Minnesota.

Lunch offerings were limited—pizza and more pizza. He opted for a small sausage pizza and a Diet Coke. He left part of it behind.

After lunch, Phil smoked two cigarettes back-to-back while he explored Bigfork to get a sense of the community. He was surprised at the number of lakes bordering the small town, the abundance of parks and recreation areas, and the apparent lack of turn signals in local cars. He could see why the town was known as the Edge of the Wilderness.

Steeling himself, he finally drove to Ottum Avenue, on the north side of the Big Fork River. The tree-lined street was well plowed, sidewalks and driveways were neatly cleared, and the houses were well cared for. Residents obviously took pride in their community. Several homes on the avenue were for sale. He wondered if proximity to the Big Fork River and spring flooding had prompted the decision to sell.

Partway down the street, he spotted the Kuusistos' home. It was a modest two-story structure with white vinyl siding and windows trimmed with black frames. In keeping with the neighborhood, the home was well maintained, and the angled driveway was plowed and scraped clean. Three balsam firs laden with snow framed each side of the drive, leading up to a white garage door.

Phil made his way up the concrete steps. A Christmas wreath with a red bow and silver balls still adorned the front door. A well-worn brown fiber welcome mat in-scribed with "Lucca Lives Here" lay beneath his feet.

Before he could knock, the door opened. A stocky, fair-haired man in his mid-sixties greeted him.

"You must be Agent Walker. Is that right?"

"Yes. You are Mr. Kuusisto?"

They exchanged a handshake.

"Call me Jami. Please come in."

Jami led Phil to the living room. A watercolor map of Finland and various framed Marimekko fabrics were dis-played on the walls.

"As you can see," Jami said, nodding to the decor, "we take our heritage seriously. In fact, Venla made some *pulla*, traditional sweet rolls, for you. We hope you'll like it."

Phil smiled graciously. "You really didn't have to go to all this trouble."

"We're happy to. It isn't often we get visitors from the BCA." Jami cleared his throat.

Just as Phil lowered himself into a chair, Venla entered the room, carrying a pot of coffee and a plate of browned rolls studded with almond slivers. The scent of the carda-mom spice was unmistakable.

Venla Kuusisto was a woman of thin stature, with fa-cial features sharply defined by strong cheekbones. Her hair, slightly grayer than her age would dictate, was pulled back in a tight braid wrapped into a circle and secured with a silver clip that clashed handsomely with her white belt, red blouse, and dark blue skirt.

Phil quickly rose to greet her. "And you must be Mrs. Kuusisto?"

"Yes. Venla." She spoke with her jaw slightly closed, which gave emphasis to her accent.

She quickly set her tray on the coffee table, then turned to present her hand to Phil. He grasped it softly with both of his.

"I'm Agent Walker—Phil. Thank you so much for meeting with me today."

"It's nice to meet you," she said. Her expression was pleasant but tense. "Please, sit down."

Jami and Venla both sat on the couch across from Phil. They looked at each other, faces furrowed with anxiety, then back at Phil.

"How was your drive up to our part of the world?" Jami offered, breaking the silence with small talk.

Phil knew it was a generic question requiring a generic answer. "It was fine. No problem at all." He didn't think it was necessary to detail the bad roads or the incident with the logging truck.

"Good. Good," Jami replied.

For a moment, silence again settled into the already labored conversation.

Phil scrambled to keep the small talk going. "You have a lovely home here," he said, glancing around.

"Thank you," Venla answered.

Phil had been hoping for a longer response. He didn't have a follow-up.

Jami chimed in. "Coffee?" He extended a hand to the tray in front of them.

"Oh, yes. Please."

Jami and Venla eagerly flew into action, pouring steaming mugs of coffee and plating still-warm rolls. The effect was liberating. A comfortable relief washed over everyone as they sipped and ate.

"This is delicious," Phil said with a nod toward Venla.

"Oh, thank you," she said. "It's my grandmother's recipe."

Phil took a quick sip of coffee. "I've never been to Bigfork. It's very quaint."

"It is a dying town, actually," Jami responded. "At one time, it was booming with lumber harvesting and iron mining. But that has slowed considerably. Now, tourists come through in the summer on their way to the Boundary Waters, and the deer hunters keep the bars busy in the fall. But in springtime, no one comes here. It can be very quiet."

"We used to farm the west side of town, above the river," Venla added. "We sold that land years ago to finance David's education." The lines on her face deepened. "So, here we are today. No farm and no David."

She gestured to an ornately framed photograph of a young man with a dog. Phil immediately recognized David from the obituary.

"That's David, a year before he graduated from the U. Lucca, his dog, is gone too."

Phil knew it was time to address the issue at hand. He felt uncomfortable knowing he was about to reopen an already tender wound.

"I cannot imagine the loss of a child," he began. "If there was only a way I …" His voice faltered.

"Thank you for your concern," Jami said. "We somehow got through the shock. But the pain will remain with us the rest of our lives." He placed a hand on Venla's. "Now, please tell us more about this situation with David and the criminal case…?" The statement became a question.

Venla and Jami looked at Phil with worry and apprehension.

Phil clasped his hands and took a deep breath, trying to overcome his own anxiety.

"So, you may have read in the news or heard on television that a number of priests have been murdered in the Twin Cities area."

"Yes," Venla said. The word was crisp.

Phil had no choice but to say it outright. "Somehow, David's fingerprints have been found at the scenes."

Jami's fair skin instantly reddened. Venla's hands flew over her heart.

"At a *murder scene*?" she spat. "Our son has been gone for years!"

Phil held his palms out. "Let me reassure you: we *know* David was not responsible in any way for these murders."

Jami shook his head almost violently. "No! This is a mistake!" he shouted.

Phil still held his hands up. "I'm very sorry. I understand how difficult this is. But there is no mistake. They are indeed David's prints. We found partial thumbprints on shell casings and a complete set of prints on a weapon. Our experts were able to match the prints from the weapon to the prints on David's application for pharmacy licensure. We got perfect matches on all five digits. Even an abnormality on his thumb matches."

With that, the Kuusistos crumbled. The color drained from Jami's face. Venla's shoulders sagged.

"He told us he cut his thumb on a broken pipette in the compounding lab," Venla finally whispered. "It happened just before graduation. It was a bad cut. He had to go to the clinic."

Jami lowered his head. "I'm sorry." He wiped his eyes. "It's just—this is still so painful."

"I understand," Walker said with honest compassion. "Believe me, we're as baffled as you are. *I'm* sorry this is something we even need to discuss."

"I just don't understand," Venla said. "David was cremated just a day or two after he died. How could this happen?"

Before Phil could open his mouth, Jami spoke up.

"Are you saying someone tampered with David's body—putting his fingerprints on shells and on a weapon—before he was cremated?" His eyes reflected the absurdity and horror of that prospect.

Phil paused and took another deep breath. "Unfortunately, that is a possibility. In fact, we have reason to suspect his DNA was also somehow planted, as we've found cigarette butts left at all four scenes."

"*David did not smoke!*" Venla avowed as if *this* were the greatest offense of all.

Phil's palms raised again. "I do not doubt that," he said calmly. "And I do not mean to imply David smoked these cigarettes, if indeed that is his DNA on them." He steepled his hands. "But here's the thing—we *know* the prints are David's. Now we'd like to determine if the DNA is his as

272

well. If it is, then we'll know for sure that the killer—or killers—had access to his body and DNA back in 2009."

He looked at Jami and Venla softly but intently.

"Someone seems to have gone to a great deal of effort to send this investigation down the wrong track. He's likely been planning it for years. But with your help, we might find the person behind this."

Jami lifted his chin. "What do you need?"

"What we would like, Mr. Kuusisto, is a sample of David's DNA. The ideal source would be a toothbrush."

Jami turned to Venla, who nodded.

"After the accident, David's roommates brought us all his belongings, along with some mail," she said.

She paused as tears began to fill her eyes. Venla sat quietly for a moment as Jami wrapped his arm around her. She dried her eyes with the corner of her apron, then continued.

"The things from his apartment are in boxes in his bedroom. You may go through them and find what you need. But please do not disturb anything else."

Phil nodded. "You have my word."

Jami and Venla stood. He held Venla tight to his side. They looked at each other.

"We'll show you to his room," Jami said. "We'd rather not be there when you go through the boxes, though."

In silence, the couple led Phil down the hallway to a bedroom door. Then they turned and walked away, back to the living room, leaning their heads together.

The Kuusistos had kept David's room just as it had been at the time of his death, save for the boxes of his belongings stacked on the floor. Located on the south side of the house, the bedroom was brightly decorated with a bedspread and curtains made from original Metsovaara silk screens.

Phil looked out the window. The backyard separated the house from the frozen Big Fork River. A high-water mark on an oak tree indicated the level of a spring flood.

Phil donned gloves and lifted one of the boxes and carefully placed it on the neatly made bed. The box contained books, papers, pens, Scotch tape, Magic Markers, and a University of Minnesota Golden Gophers pennant.

Taking care not to disturb the bedding, Phil returned the box to the floor and hoisted another. That box contained only clothing.

The third box held what he was looking for. Amid more clothing, he found personal items, including a toothbrush and a hairbrush. He carefully placed these items in a paper bag, hoping the DNA had not deteriorated in the closed environment.

Phil removed the gloves and returned to the living room, where Venla and Jami were still seated, staring blankly at the larch-wood floor. It took every ounce of Phil's willpower to not just bolt from the house.

He wanted out of there.

He was dying for a cigarette.

Instead, he gave them a nod. "Thank you. I have everything I need." He raised the paper bag as proof. "When we have all of this figured out, I'll make sure you know the details. Meanwhile, please be assured your son's name will not be made public as part of this investigation. You have my word on that."

"I'll walk you out," Jami said, standing up.

Venla stood too, extending her hand to Phil. "Thank you, Mr. Walker."

"The pulla was delicious—thank you," Phil said.

Her face showed she was tired, though she tried to smile.

Phil and Jami put on their coats and walked out to the Taurus together. As they shook hands, Phil thought of one more thing.

"Oh, was David right- or left-handed?"

"Left-handed." Jami looked at Phil, then shrugged when he realized Phil wasn't going to explain his question.

"Thank you again," Phil said. "Please know I'm very sorry for your loss."

Phil climbed into the car, started it, and then gave one last wave as he backed out of the driveway. As Jami and the house disappeared from view, Phil exhaled forcibly.

He had a cigarette lit before turning south onto High-way 38.

CHAPTER 34

A few days later, Phil found himself sitting at his desk, staring blankly at the DNA results from David Kuusisto's personal items. Chris was running a few minutes late for their scheduled meeting. In the interim, Phil kept wondering whether he had a lot to tell Chris or next to nothing. He also wondered how to even begin to explain the riddle.

There was a light knock at the open door. Without looking up, Phil said, "Enter."

"Sorry I'm late. I was coming from Bloomington. Had an agency-wide meeting there." Chris draped his jacket over the back of the chair, then pulled a bottle of water from his bag. He sighed as he seated himself. "The drive across the Cities in heavy traffic is terrible. I can't imagine how people do it every day."

Phil wasn't listening. He was anxiously sucking on an unlit cigarette, still staring down at the case file in front of him. The usually well-groomed graying hair on his temples was protruding in various directions as he tried to massage away a headache.

Chris shook his head. "Jesus, Phil—you look like hell."

Phil at last looked up. "I *feel* like hell." He pulled the

cigarette from his mouth, tossed it on the desk, then looked straight into Chris's eyes. "What if I told you our killer was deceased?" He held his stare to watch Chris' reaction.

Chris sprung out of the chair and put his hands on the desk. "We know who he is, but the son on a bitch *died* before we could arrest him?" The lines on his forehead furrowed as he leaned across the desk.

"No, no," Phil reassured. He sighed. "I'm just trying to figure out how to explain this to you, because I barely know how to explain it to myself."

"C'mon," Chris said, slightly irritated. "What's going on?"

"OK, here's the deal." Phil crossed his arms and leaned back. "We got excellent prints from the knife in the Avon homicide. Ken Zerke matched them to someone in the Applicant File database—a young man named David Jami Kuusisto…who died in an airplane crash in June of 2009."

Chris frowned in confusion and lowered himself back into his chair. "Is there any possibility of a mistake?"

"Not likely. Ken had a full set of prints from the knife. And remember the V-shaped impression on the thumbprint we got from the shell casing at Doyle's cabin?"

Chris nodded.

"Matches the thumbprint on the knife. And Kuusisto's parents confirmed a serious injury to his right thumb a couple of weeks before he died."

Chris finished his water and crushed the empty bottle. "I'm guessing you haven't told me the whole story yet."

A little spark came to Phil's eyes. "You're very astute."

Chris waited expectantly, giving Phil a long look. "And

now you're making me beg for it." Chris extended his hands and curled his fingers back and forth, prompting Phil to divulge more information.

"Also astute."

Both men chuckled.

Phil finally patted the case file. "The DNA from the cigarette butts…"

"Yeah?"

"Kuusisto's."

"No shit?" Chris grimaced. "So, you're telling me the prints and the DNA come from the same individual—who died in 2009?"

"Yep." Phil took off his glasses and cleaned them on his tie.

"This is unbelievable." Chris sat in silence for a moment. "Did Kuusisto know this guy way back when? What did our perp do—hand Kuusisto a knife and some shell casings and say, 'Hey, pal, can you touch these? And oh, while you're at it, put these cigarettes in your mouth, but don't smoke them.'"

"Kuusisto was left-handed. The injury was to his right thumb." Phil said this as if it answered Chris's question.

"So?"

"Think about it. Would a person firmly press his injured thumb—on his nondominant hand at that—on a shell casing?"

"Not unless," Chris added, catching on, "he couldn't feel pain."

Phil pointed his index finger at Chris. "Good catch! The perp likely had access to Kuusisto's body sometime between June 1, the day of the crash, and June 3, the day he was cremated."

Chris's cheeks filled with air before he quickly exhaled. "Medical examiner? A technician at the morgue? Someone at the crematorium?"

"Who knows? But we have to look into it."

Chris rose to his feet. "I'm on it. Maybe this is a breakthrough—the first real lead."

Phil brightened for a bit. "I'd love to believe that . . . But I can't help but prepare myself for this to be just another dead end. Literally this time. The lead begins and ends with a dead man." His face soured. "This guy is really getting to me. If that ID of him from Avon is accurate, then I picture some smug little guy laughing his goddamn ass off at us as he chews his clove gum, smokes clove cigarettes—or whatever."

Chris gathered his things and headed for the door. Before stepping out, he glanced back at Phil with a tired smirk.

"Don't forget that he's wearing a merino wool jacket," he said facetiously.

CHAPTER 35

When Chris turned onto 197th Street and saw Gayle's car in his driveway, he slowed to a stop. Kimber always told him when they were expecting company. And Gayle was never one to drop in unannounced.

He made a U-turn and drove to the community center parking lot, where he checked his cell. No voicemails or texts from Kimber.

Chris sensed it wasn't a good time to be home. As an investigator—and a husband—he deduced that something upsetting had happened to Gayle. And he had a good idea who was behind it. Letting out a sigh, Chris dialed Paul's number.

"Hey, Chris. What's up?" Paul answered. He sounded tired.

"Glad I caught ya, buddy," Chris replied. "Say, if you haven't eaten yet, how about dinner at Meyer's? My treat."

There was a pause. He could hear Paul's shaky breathing.

"Yeah, well, I suppose." He paused again. "Just got home from the office. Lemme wash up and meet you in a few minutes."

Fifteen minutes later, Chris was seated in a booth, nursing a Coors Light, when Paul sauntered into the restaurant. Immediately, Chris noticed that Paul's face lacked a healthy color; he appeared exhausted and drained. His shoulders were slumped under his jacket, making him look like a shrunken old man.

Chris slid out of the booth to greet him. "Thanks for making this work last minute. Looks like Kimber and Gayle are having a girls' night back at our place, so I thought I'd make myself scarce."

He watched for Paul's reaction. Sure enough, Paul's eyes rolled.

"Yeah, I bet she's crying her eyes out or plotting my murder. Or both." He drew an imaginary knife across his throat before hanging his coat on the hook outside the booth. "Actually, I'm surprised she waited this long. I assumed she'd been camping out at your place for a couple days now."

"Why? What happened?" Chris noticed that Paul winced a bit as he settled into the booth. "Last time I heard, you said you guys hadn't seen each other since Stella's. Did you have round two or something?"

Paul raised his hand to catch Brenda's attention from across the floor. With big gestures, he pointed to Chris's beer and then to himself. She gave him a thumbs-up.

"So, do you think the Wild will get back on track this year?" Paul said, nodding at one of the TVs. "They're not off to a good start."

Taken aback by Paul's blunt dismissal, Chris paused, then pressed on. "Paul, if something happened between you and Gayle, I'm here to listen. And help if I can. You guys must be going through something really painful."

Just then, Brenda fluttered in with a Coors Light and a big smile. "Here you go, Doc," she said. "Are you two ready to order?"

Chris picked up a menu, gave it a cursory glance, and ordered the barbecue ribs. So did Paul.

"Thanks, guys!" Brenda said, reaching over for their menus.

Paul stole a quick glance at her cleavage spilling out of her scoop-neck top.

Chris groaned silently to himself. Maybe he didn't want to know why Gayle was over at his house, seeking comfort from her best friend. Chris grabbed his beer and locked his eyes on the game.

They sat in an uneasy silence until the food arrived. Brenda gave them each a basket lined with checkered paper and brimming with ribs, french fries, and coleslaw. Chris dove into his; Paul picked, scavenging small pieces and a couple french fries.

After a few minutes, Paul pushed his basket away and looked up at Chris. "It's over," he blandly stated.

Chris grabbed a napkin and wiped sauce from the side of his mouth. "What?"

"Gayle and I. We're over. Done. She showed up at my place a couple of nights ago. Ambushed me." He flinched, holding his stomach a moment, before he continued. "Wanted to talk about 'commitment.' Started pressuring me about our relationship. Really pissed me off."

Before Chris could speak, Paul suddenly held up his

283

hand, got up, and headed for the restroom.

Chris sat with a myriad of uncomfortable thoughts until Paul returned a few minutes later, smiling. A different person had seemingly materialized.

"Are you OK, pal?" Chris asked.

Paul dried his still-damp hands on his trousers as he sat down. "Yeah. Stomach's just a little upset." He glanced around the restaurant. "Sure is nice to see this place so busy. And speaking of *busy*, how's work going for you?"

Apparently, Paul didn't want to talk about Gayle or anything of any importance tonight. Pushing him would be futile. Small talk it would be.

"Work's fine," Chris said, shrugging.

"I hear those priest murders are up to four victims now," Paul said. He made an exaggerated wince.

Chris waved his hand. "You know I can't—"

Like magic, Brenda appeared. "Who needs another round?"

"I'm in," Paul said. He pointed to Chris. "How about you?"

"Nah, I'm good."

"One Coors Light, coming up," Brenda said. She took a step away, then quickly turned back and ran her hand over Paul's coat. "Ooh, nice threads! Who's got the high-end taste here?"

Paul raised a hand and grinned. "That would be me."

Brenda gave him an impressed nod. "You didn't get that off the rack at Men's Wearhouse. That much I know." She pointed a thumb at herself. "This girl can't afford top-of-the-line stuff, but she knows it when she sees it."

Paul laughed. "Thanks, Brenda. Got it in New Zealand—the birthplace of merino sheep, so to speak."

A shock went through Chris's body. It was like slow freeze at first, but then it grew into a raging heat. He could feel his heart beating against his chest. He gripped his empty beer bottle as thoughts collided in his mind.

Merino wool. Short stature. White male. Fifties. Well-educated, respected professional. Meticulous. Clever. Deceiving family and friends. Strict Catholic upbringing. A family connection to St. Michael's.

In a blur, Chris could see Brenda leave, then return with Paul's beer. The two bantered some more. None of it registered for Chris. Sounds were muffled as though he were underwater.

Slowly, Chris raised his eyes to look at Dr. Paul Thomas, his closest friend.

Someone was brutally murdering pedophile priests. Torturing them psychologically. Making them pay for their immorality. This murderer, this serial killer—he was likely someone who had been abused himself.

Chris removed his hands from the beer bottle. They were shaking. He quickly crossed his arms, tucking his hands at his sides. Brenda smiled at him and said something. He blankly smiled back and nodded, oblivious.

No, he told himself. *No. It can't be. A million people have merino wool. It's just a coincidence. It can't be him.*

Chris took a deep breath.

It can't be Paul.

Not Paul.

"Hey, Earth to Chris."

285

In a snap, the din of the restaurant filled his ears once again. Chris glanced around. Brenda was gone, and Paul was looking at him with an amused expression.

"I said, did you see that goal?" Paul was speaking loudly to get through to him. He pointed to the TV.

Chris tried to smile as he shook his head. "Sorry. No. I was just ... just thinking about something."

At the bar, some drinkers were getting worked up as they followed the game. One rowdy guy yelled something unintelligible and slammed his glass hard on the bar.

Paul scowled. "That asshole reminds me of Matt."

Automatically, Chris's investigative instincts kicked in. He turned the segue to his advantage. Time to cease the small talk.

"Remember how Matt kept going on and on about my case with the priests?" He could hardly believe how nonchalant he sounded.

Paul looked down, scratching at the label on his bottle.

Chris was having difficulty with the thoughts galloping through his brain. Paul's hesitation only accelerated the tempo. He pushed on with his impromptu investigation, leaning forward and lowering his voice.

"You know I can't discuss the details of these homicides," Chris began, "but I can ask your opinion. You grew up Catholic, just like I did. How do you feel about these priests getting murdered? I mean, these guys were *abusers*," he emphasized.

Paul stared blankly across the bar for several seconds. There was something indescribable in his eyes. When he spoke, his voice was level but empty.

"They're not getting prosecuted. And the church hierarchy keeps covering for them. So maybe on some level, it's justice." He ended with a forced laugh, then picked up his beer and studied what remained of the label.

Chris recognized all the tells: deflecting questions, avoiding eye contact, concealing emotion.

No. It can't be Paul, Chris once again pleaded to himself. His mind was racing. Frenzied thoughts he didn't want to process were careening through his mind.

Abruptly, Paul tossed his chin toward the door. "Well, I think it's about time I hit the road. Getting late. Got a big day at the office tomorrow. I've got someone coming in bright and early with a temporary crown that's come lose."

"Cloves…" The word drifted out of Chris's mouth.

"What's that?" Paul asked, leaning forward to hear better.

Chris rubbed his forehead and forced himself to continue the thought. "Cloves. Doesn't something you use smell like cloves?"

Paul nodded. "Yep, eugenol. It's an oil of cloves product. It's used in temporary dental cement. Actually, I spilled a bunch of it on myself last Wednesday. That was another bright-and-early appointment."

Chris felt acid bubbling up into his throat. Wednesday was when Father Crowley had been murdered.

Brenda arrived with the check, which Chris accepted. His mind inebriated with confusion, he struggled to compute a 15 percent tip.

As they left the restaurant, light snow was falling and the concrete steps were slippery. Paul held on to Chris's arm and shuffled like an old man.

When they reached the Lexus, Chris grabbed Paul in a hug, gripping him tightly for several seconds.

"I'm here for you, Paul," Chris said. "No matter what."

He meant it.

"You hang out with bad company, my friend," Paul jested. The indescribable look drifted into and out of his eyes.

"You're right. You, Dr. Paul Thomas, are bad company. But I've known you so long, I can't seem to get rid of you."

As Paul drove away, Chris sat in his car, numb.

Paul was his friend. A friend who needed help. Perhaps more help than Chris could offer.

He released a painful sigh, pulled an evidence envelope from his glove box, opened it, and let a clump of gray fibers drop from his fingers.

PART III

MEA MAXIMA CULPA

The protection of minors and vulnerable persons is an integral part of the gospel message that the Church and all its members are called to spread throughout the world.

—POPE FRANCIS, MARCH 29, 2019

CHAPTER 36

*A*fter leaving Meyer's, I headed home to clear my mind. To prepare.

I have one more score to settle.

Every January, the Catholic retreat center near the little town of Marine on Saint Croix holds its Week of Silence.

Auxiliary Bishop Father Dominic McGloughlin has taken this vow of silence.

No matter. I'll be doing most of the talking tonight.

The other four were pedophile monsters. McGloughlin has not defiled an innocent child himself—at least as far as I know. But he's still a monster. He is one of the church conspirators who covered up priests' vile acts. An attorney, he engineered their movements from diocese to diocese—just far enough away so the priests' pasts couldn't follow. For decades, he's kept things quiet. Below the radar.

Of course, he made sure a substantial sum of money went to the victims' parents—those who came forward, that is. And perhaps he offered a nice annuity to the offending priests who agreed to retire. Such was the case with Father James Doyle.

I've been following McGloughlin. Studying his habits. Since arriving here in Marine on Saint Croix, he's been going on walks.

Late at night.

Alone.

It's nearly eleven o'clock. I'm wearing booties. Although nonslip, they aren't designed for walking on snow. They have little traction. The church stairway was slippery on one of my earlier missions, so I'm careful with my steps this time.

Soft light from a waxing moon bleeds through the branches. The white pines cast shadows and whisper softly in the wind. The snow glows orange in the neon-like moonlight. The river rushes beneath its icy blanket.

Tonight, the bishop is struggling along a path that meanders high above the Saint Croix. It's a popular daytime route but is rarely traveled at night.

McGloughlin is an old man. His long white hair is suspended below a black fur-lined hat with flaps covering his ears. Pronounced cheek bones, sunken eyes, and a sharpened nose accentuate his face. His spine is bent with osteoporosis. His heavy leather jacket reaches to his waist; below, his black cassock flutters gently as he walks. Small branches clutter his path. He lifts the hem of the cassock and steps gingerly over them.

He approaches a wooden bench, the boards capped with fresh snow. He brushes the snow away, unknowingly creating a place for my script.

McGloughlin sits and leans forward, elbows on his knees. He mindlessly shuffles his feet. His boots push aside the snow, revealing a carpet of pine needles hidden beneath. He's deep in thought, his eyes focused on something far away.

Is something bothering him? Does he know it's time?

He looks up at the moon, then turns. His gaze meets mine. I've been quiet, but he sensed my presence.

He breaks his vow of silence. "You've come for me."

"Yes."

Our words create clouds of vapor in the cold night air. The wind whisks them away.

His body sags, his chin lowers to his chest. "I'm ready," he whispers. "I've seen the newspapers. I know what you're doing." He clears his throat. With an impassioned voice, he continues, "And yes, the stories you've read about me are true. I've done horrible things."

For a moment—a very short moment—I feel sorry for him. I sense his remorse. He regrets the things he's done. Briefly, I consider whether letting him live with his shame and agony might be the greater punishment.

But my empathy dissolves quickly. His remorse is not enough. And it's far too little and far too late.

He made his choices.

"Kneel, Father."

Holding the arm of the bench for support, he struggles to his knees. His bent spine naturally places him in a devotional, penitent bow. He lifts his head to look at me. His eyes blink rapidly.

I don my vinyl gloves. They snap as I stretch them to my wrists. I really don't need the gloves this time, but the snap adds a little drama.

More apprehension for the hunted.

The trapped.

About to die.

"Time for Communion, Father," I say. "Hold out your hands."

A quizzical look crosses his face, but he obeys.

I remove the last rosary decade from my coat and hold it before him. "Take this and eat, for this is my body. Does that sound familiar?"

He is confused. Though he deduces his fate, he doesn't understand my ritual.

I place the beads in his gloved hand. "Think of this as the Host you raise so high before your communicants as you impersonate a holy man, fraudulently pure. So unbridled with sin, clad in your pretentious regalia."

He studies the beads. They rattle in his trembling palm. He understands now.

"This is an obscenity, a violation of the Eucharist!" His voice has dropped to a hoarse groan, barely audible over the whisper of the pines.

"A violation?" I say, my volume rising. "The children were violated. *Their trust in the Church, in the clergy, was* violated." *I pull the Beretta from my coat, point it at his head. "Do it! Swallow them—now!"*

The bishop hesitates, then places the beads on his tongue. Retching brings more tears to his already wet eyes.

"We're almost done, Father." I remove the water bottle from my pocket. "Take this and drink, for this is my blood."

"I can't," he says, crying. "Please don't make me do this." It's difficult for him to speak with the beads in his mouth.

"Do—it—now!" My voice echoes off the icy ravine below.

He takes the water and sips it. With difficulty, he swallows the beads. His retching becomes violent. I wait for him to finish.

He has swallowed the "host," and the retching subsides. He bows his head, his lips touching the tips of his prayerful fingers. His eyes look over the gold rim of his glasses. He's not pleading for mercy. He's surrendering.

The gunshot thunders across the river valley, reverberating between the cliffs.

In the distance, a dog barks. As if on cue, a brief wind picks up and causes the shadows to dance, then the valley falls silent.

It's my last kill. I have accomplished a great deal the last few weeks. My only wish is that I had more energy, more time. Time to rid the world of more of these vulgar wretches. It is a bittersweet ending, like almost having an orgasm but not quite getting there.

If I have a regret, it is molesting my friendship with Chris. I have left him with a heavy stone to look beneath.

Writing on a wooden bench is nearly as difficult as writing on cloth. His blood freezes when it touches the cold wood.

As I lay the cigarette butt beneath the seat, a memory floods back from so many years ago. An event, one that made my exterminations possible and gave the last days of my life meaning.

It was early June 2009. There had been an accident. A plane crash. Four victims.

With hopeful anticipation, I packed my bag before heading to Saint Paul that night.

I used my magnetic card to gain entry. The door clicked shut behind me, and I made my way to the autopsy suite. The disinfected floor in the morgue was still damp, as were the stainless-steel sinks and cutting areas.

Fluorescent lamps dimly lit the room. When I switched on the halogens, the steel came to life with spears of light glinting off the shiny surfaces.

Waiting for me beneath the overhead lights were four young bodies. The technician had been kind enough to remove them from the cooler and neatly line them up. Also waiting for me were four sets of dental records, for comparison.

Lucky for me, though, the plane had crashed into a lake.

Burned bodies would have been of no use to me. Fortunately, too, the bodies hadn't yet been washed.

According to the report, all four were recent pharmacy graduates.

Many secrets are divulged in morgues, but I saw no pierced genitalia, risqué tattoos, or needle track marks. These bodies looked healthy and wholesome. I assumed these young people had operated within the law. A risky conjecture, but one I was willing to make.

I chose the one I later identified as David Jami Kuusisto.

In my bag was a pack of Marlboro Reds, an MTech "Iron Mike" folding knife, and a box of Hydra-Shoks—the tools I'd use to create my master plan. I wasn't sure I'd ever choose the Iron Mike over my Beretta, but I figured a knife could come in handy in case circumstances demanded a quieter event.

Wearing vinyl gloves, I removed the cigarettes from the pack. My donor had water in the floor of his mouth, which I absorbed with a paper towel. I then lifted his cold, stiff tongue and rubbed each cigarette filter into the soft tissue beneath, ensuring I would collect a good amount of his DNA. I returned the cigarettes to the pack.

When I examined his hands, I was delighted to discover a V-shaped injury on the pad of his right thumb. It had not quite healed.

It was obvious.

It was perfect.

I dried his thumb and the area beneath his left nipple. Next, I vigorously rubbed his thumb and right index finger under his nipple in order to acquire as much skin oil as possible. I then squeezed his thumb and index finger on the casing of a

Hydra-Shok cartridge. I made sure the V wound was well rendered, but I was intentionally not so careful with the index finger.

I had a vision in mind: five mysteries. Still, you never know just how many bullets you'll need. So I repeated the imprinting process for all the cartridges before returning them to the box.

After drying the other fingers of his right hand and obtaining his oil, I squeezed his hand on the grip of the Iron Mike and slipped it into a paper bag.

Looking around the room, I spied a box of green Tyvek non-slip shoe covers. They went into my bag with the Iron Mike.

With that portion of my work complete, I at last moved on to my official reason for being there. I am the forensic odontologist for the medical examiner in Saint Paul. My job is to determine who's who in disasters like this. Give their battered remains a name.

Finished, I headed for the door. As I reached for the light switch, I had to stop and brace myself against the wall. A hot wave of arousal roiled over me, taking me by surprise. It was exhilarating.

I had what I needed. I was ready. All I had to do was wait for the right time.

I would have my vengeance. For myself. For the other innocents.

For Nick.

The memory stays with me as I crush the cigarette butt under the park bench. I take one last look at McGloughlin. Atomized blood droplets anoint the dimly lit snow. Skull fragments have melted their way into the snowbank. Only tufts of gray hair betray their presence.

He fell forward when my bullet penetrated. As he died, his last few heartbeats cast out his perverted blood.

Will the coyotes find him before morning?

CHAPTER 37

The sun rose over the valley, creating swirling orange highlights on the fog over the frozen river. Greg and Betsy Martinson were skiing along the path above the Saint Croix, enjoying their first outing on new cross-country skis since returning from a product show in Las Vegas.

Greg and Betsy were owners of a local manufacturing company and inventors of a new product designed to replace traditional caulk. The product show had been successful. Now they were looking forward to a peaceful trek along their favorite ski trail, then midmorning lunch in Stillwater at the Oasis Cafe, one of their favorite haunts.

Greg was in the lead, creating a track for Betsy. Skiing was difficult because numerous twigs and small branches had fallen on the path. Greg had to stop frequently and clear the track he was making. As he rose from hefting a large branch that had fallen on the trail, he saw the wooden bench in the shadowy distance, one of the places they frequently stopped to rest.

"Let's take five at the bench," he suggested.

Out of breath, Betsy panted in agreement.

As they grew closer, Greg could see an amorphous dark shape. He wasn't sure what it was at first, but as he got closer, he realized it was a person clad in black, bent forward, facedown in the contrasting snow. Seeing no movement of the figure, Greg knew something was seriously wrong.

"Oh my God," he exclaimed. Immediately, he released his skis and ran through the snow, nearly losing his balance as he ducked under snow-laden cedar branches that draped low over the trail.

"What is it?" Betsy called out, some distance behind him. She poled quickly to catch up. Once she, too, saw the figure, her tired arms struggled to release her bindings to follow on foot.

When Greg arrived at the bench he skidded to a stop. For a moment, his brain labored to make sense of the scene before him. The entire back of the individual's head was absent; hair and brain matter were scattered in the blood-speckled snow. Birds that were pecking on brain fragments had ascended to nearby trees, noisily objecting to Greg's presence.

"Stop!" he cried out to Betsy, holding his hands out. "Don't come any closer!"

Eyes muddled with fear and confusion, Betsy froze midstep.

Greg stared at the body, the blood. There was also blood on the bench, though not splattered. He took a tentative step forward, looking more closely.

Words? He didn't recognize the awkward characters.

"Oh my God," he repeated as he felt the blood rush from his face.

He felt faint and dizzy. With fumbling hands, he checked his cell phone. No signal.

Greg raced back to Betsy and grabbed her roughly by the arm. "Come on!" he yelled as he ran to their skis, practically dragging her along as she stumbled.

"Greg, what's going on? What's wrong?" Betsy demanded.

Without a word, Greg clicked into his skis and headed for higher ground. All Betsy could do was try to keep up.

When they topped a small hill overlooking the river valley, Greg was able to get a weak signal. Gasping for breath between words, he described the scene to the operator, having to repeat himself as the signal faded out, then recovered. Betsy listened in shock with her hands covering her mouth.

"Let's ski back to Highway 95 and wait," Greg advised.

The first responders and an ambulance from Marine on Saint Croix arrived in minutes. Greg guided them down the trail to the scene. The EMTs made no attempt to resuscitate the victim.

The Washington County Sheriff's Office soon arrived as well. Ron Grafton had just started his morning shift. He took one look at the victim's cassock and shuddered.

Déjà vu all over again, he thought.

CHAPTER 38

Chris had an uneasy feeling in his gut when he responded to Phil's page. In fact, he'd been ill at ease ever since he'd walked Paul to the car after dinner at Meyer's. The look on Paul's face was something he couldn't interpret, even with his extensive investigative experience.

Rather than calling Phil, Chris decided to drop in on him at the BCA headquarters. He had other matters to see to there anyway. Matters he hoped to keep off Phil's radar.

Marty lit up with a big smile when Chris walked in. She had a brightness that Chris had never seen. He couldn't help but comment on it.

"Wow, you look great, Marty."

"Why, thank you!" She stood and put a hand on her hip, striking a pose. "It's because I lost some weight—one hundred and sixty pounds, to be exact!" She gave a coy wink.

Chris stared at her, confused, until he put his powers of deduction to use. "Wait—are you saying what I think you're saying…?"

"Yep! I filed for divorce." She grinned, then took on a more serious expression. "You know, it's not like I didn't realize all along that he was an asshole. It just took me some time to find the strength to walk away from his emotional abuse. Sometimes it takes a while to know when you've had enough."

"That's the best thing I've heard in, well, a long time," Chris said, beaming at her.

Marty's eyes widened with understanding. "I know what you mean—this case of yours doesn't seem to be full of 'good' news…" She pointed down the hall to the cafeteria. "Boss is down there. He's not very talkative, though," she announced.

"Wanna tell me why?"

"I'll let him give you the details."

Chris smiled and nodded acknowledgment.

With every step Chris took toward the cafeteria, the lightness he had felt from Marty's good news faded. The ill feeling quickly returned.

He found Phil sitting alone at a long table, staring blankly at a half-eaten cookie on a paper plate and a cup of coffee that had long lost its steam. Rather than surprise Phil by coming up from behind, Chris hardened his footsteps so Phil would hear him approaching.

Phil turned and looked at Chris. The look on Phil's face revealed the news wouldn't be good.

"We had another one last night, Chris."

Chris blanched. "Oh, God. You don't mean—"

"Yup, I *do* mean. Your buddy Grafton called it in directly to our office. Dispatch contacted me first thing this morning. Auxiliary Bishop Father Dominic McGloughlin. He served as an attorney for the diocese. Couple of skiers found the body on a trail near the Catholic retreat center in Marine on Saint Croix. Medical examiner said the body was frozen. Investigators spoke with several priests who'd walked the trail earlier in the evening and hadn't seen anything unusual. The last priests were on the trail at eight o'clock, so we're guessing the victim died any time after that."

Feeling like his world was collapsing, Chris pulled out a chair and slumped down next to Phil. He tried to look away, tried not to show his distress.

Jesus, was that why Paul had been in such a hurry to leave Meyer's last night?

"So far, it looks like same old, same old," Phil continued. "Shot at close range, similar to all the other murders except Crowley's. Another blood message in Latin.

Chris interrupted: "The fifth—"

"Yep, 'the fifth mystery.' Another cigarette butt, which we all know will likely ping back to Kuusisto. A cartridge in the snow a few feet from the vic's body. Once the body's thawed, the ME will take x-rays. If I were a bettin' man..."

"I'd bet on it too," Chris asserted. "The last decade."

"Yeah, but is it?" Phil looked at him with probing eyes. "Is it really the last? Was this just five murders and then done? Was that the plan all along? Or will this bastard keep going? I mean, it's not like we're hot on his trail. Why would he stop now? He could be like those sickos Sleeman told us about. Dozens and dozens of victims."

A chill ran down Chris's spine.

Phil reached for his coffee and brought it to his lips before realizing how tepid it had become. He roughly set it back down. "You check with the morgue yet about who had access to Kuusisto's body?"

Chris shook his head. It took him a while to speak. "Not yet. That's on my to-do list for this morning."

"Good. Keep me posted. I'm hoping we'll get some sort of lead with that. Even if we could get just a whiff of who this guy really is…"

Chris fidgeted with the small evidence bag in his pocket, wishing he'd never found the fibers behind Doyle's cabin. Bile rose. He swallowed it back with a visible grimace.

"You OK?" Phil asked. "Christ, now *you* look like hell."

"Yeah, I'm fine. I better get back to the office." The feet of the metal chair squealed on the tile floor as he quickly pushed his chair back.

As Chris walked away, his mind was recklessly spinning, bouncing from scene to scene, correlating Paul's behavior with the homicides. No matter how hard he tried to find loopholes in his own logic, the evidence kept pointing to Paul.

He strode quickly to the restroom, yanked open a stall door, and violently threw up.

It took several minutes to gain the courage to take the next step. He cupped some water from the bathroom faucet to rinse his mouth. Then he headed for the lab to find Serena.

He caught her right before she left for lunch.

"I've got some additional fibers for you to look at," he said, trying to hold his composure, still feeling the acid in his throat. He pulled the small envelope from his pocket. "Would you be able to determine if these fibers came from the same article of clothing the previous two sets of merino wool fibers came from?"

Serena held up a finger to correct him. "I can probably determine whether the fibers are identical, though that doesn't necessarily prove that they came from the same article of clothing. If they're identical, it's *possible* they're from the same coat or sweater or whatever. We have to be careful, though, because merino wool is mass-produced. That means the three sets of fibers could be identical yet still come from different articles of clothing."

Chris nodded. He understood her explanation. *Possible* was about as good as it could get. "OK, how quickly can you get this done?"

"We're waiting on some hair samples from a rape case. If they don't come in this afternoon, I can get to it first thing tomorrow morning."

Chris didn't mean to wince, but he did. And she noticed. She laughed, then smiled, recognizing his impatience.

"Or maybe I can squeeze it in yet this afternoon! Shouldn't take long." She gave him a sympathetic smile. "Want me to send my results to Phil once I'm done?"

"No." Chris hoped he didn't say that too forcefully. "No, that's fine." His voice softened. "Just call me, and I'll fill him in later."

Serena gave him a wave as she headed to the cafeteria—where Phil was still sitting at the table all alone.

Chris didn't know whether he had been betrayed or he was the one doing the betraying.

CHAPTER 39

The wind had subsided, but small drifts remained when Chris turned off Highway 97 and into the empty parking lot adjacent to the elementary school. He needed time to process the thoughts rocketing through his mind. He also needed to make a phone call.

Chris stared at his phone. He was trapped in the shadows between the official investigation and his own suspicions about Paul. The urge to vomit was rising again.

So much evidence was pointing toward Paul: the merino wool, the clove smell, the physical description, even Sleeman's serial killer profile. And Chris still could still see that strange look in Paul's eyes as he spoke about the murders. So many pieces of the puzzle fit.

Except, perhaps, the biggest one of all.

Whoever committed these murders likely had access to Kuusisto's body in the morgue and had manipulated it to plant the DNA and fingerprints. So if Paul was, in fact, the murderer, then he would have needed access to Kuusisto's body. But how?

As far as Chris knew, Paul wasn't related to the Kuusistos and wasn't a close family friend, so there was no obvious connection. Why would Paul be in a morgue in 2009? He was a *dentist*.

That's when something clicked. *Forensic odontology.* Someone had likely done a dental ID on Kuusisto's body. Plane crash victims are often not visually identifiable.

The thought came fast, and just as quickly, Chris tried to deny it. How could Paul have done a dental ID on Kuusisto? Ann Norgren was the forensic dentist for the Ramsey County ME. Had been for years. Paul had a bustling family practice; he wasn't and never had been a forensic dentist. Again, at least not as far as Chris knew.

Or perhaps Chris didn't know much, if anything, about Dr. Paul Thomas.

Chris finally hit Call. As he put the phone to his ear, his other hand went to his mustache, stroking it while the phone rang.

"Ramsey County Medical Examiner's Office—Gorrie here. How may I help you?" It was a soft, soothing voice.

Thank God it's Gorrie, Chris said to himself.

In spite of his name—and the attendant jokes that accompanied it—Don Gorrie was an astute death investigator. Over the years, Chris had worked with him on several occasions. Because of his expertise, Don was often assigned to more-complicated death scenes.

Chris needed information that would ordinarily not be released without a heap of paperwork. But perhaps Gorrie would simply do him a solid.

"Don, Chris Majek."

"It's been a while—good thing, I guess," Don said with a chuckle. "What's up?"

Chris could barely swallow. His mouth was dry, and his tongue felt thick. "I need information on an old case of yours. Goes back to 2009. June 1, to be exact."

"Hope I can help," Don replied brightly. "What do you need?"

"There was a plane crash in Forest Lake. Believe it was in the second lake. One of the victims was a David Jami Kuusisto. That's *K-U-U-S-I-S-T-O*."

Don let out a groan. "Oh man. Please tell me this isn't going to be an exhumation case. McPhearson hates those! They cost the county so much money. You have no idea how he is about the budget."

Chris tried to let out a good-natured laugh. It failed. "No. No worries. I just need to know who had access before the body was released to the crematorium—specifically, if there was a dental identification and, if so, who did it. I know I'm supposed to file paperwork for all this, but I thought I'd skip the bureaucratic stuff and see if we can just do it over the phone…?" No matter how straight he tried to play it, his voice seemed to telegraph every ounce of his angst.

"Um … sure thing," Don said. "Let me pull it up. You said June 1, 2009?"

"Correct."

Chris could hear computer keys clicking. He drew a breath of relief.

"Got it right here. Give me a second to read through the report."

Don hummed to himself as if offering proof that he was studying the pages.

"Four people killed. Two men, two women. Kuusisto is listed here. The initial call went to Dr. Ann Norgren. It says she was out of town, though. She passed it along to one of our backup forensic odontologists at the time—a Dr. Paul Thomas."

Chris felt another wave of nausea. The air in the car was suddenly sweltering, smothering, crushing. He pawed at the power window buttons. Both front windows opened, and a waft of cold air streamed across his face. He sucked in the air and cleared his throat, pushing back the rising lump.

"Oh, I didn't know you guys had a Dr. *Thomas* working for you," he said.

He added emphasis to the name *Thomas* as if it were some foreign word. Don was nothing more than a professional acquaintance, and an occasional one at that. He had no idea Chris knew Paul personally.

"Dr. Thomas doesn't work here anymore. I think he was employed until around early 2010. Don't remember exactly when he started. I've seen his name on a few old IDs."

Chris had to fight back a groan of disbelief.

"Can you tell me what time of day he did the ID?" he managed.

"All we have here is the month and day. But the ID was done the same day as the accident, which indicates he probably came in at night, before their autopsies were completed. It's usually too busy around here to have our forensic dentist working at the same time as our examiners. By the way, did you know we added three more pathologists here?"

"Wow," Chris managed to respond. He closed his eyes and wiped sweat from his forehead. "You guys are growing," he said, trying to sound interested in Don's revelation.

"We are. Plans are in the works for a new morgue. We

sure need it." Gorrie paused. "Anything else I can do you?"

"That should do it, Don. Thanks much." His head was spinning.

When Chris disconnected, he opened his door and lurched forward all in one motion. He vomited in the fresh snow. His stomach was practically empty already, so he mostly dry-heaved.

He hung there, half inside the car and half out, breathing in the cold, fresh air. It stung on its way to his lungs.

On the seat next to him, his phone buzzed. It didn't matter who it was—Phil, Ron, even Kimber. Nothing mattered anymore.

Paul . . .

Chris wasn't sure how much time passed before he pulled himself into his vehicle, shut the door, closed the windows, and leaned back. He was weak. His stomach muscles were aching.

Several more minutes passed before he finally picked up his phone. There was a voice mail. From Serena.

Chris fumbled with the playback.

"Hey, Chris—this is Serena. Just wanted to let you know I took a look at those new fibers. There's no doubt they're identical to the ones from the two murder scenes. But as I said earlier, we can't technically prove they're from the same article of clothing. Well, hope I've been of at least a little help. Let me know if you want me to write up a lab report. I know you said you'd give Phil the details yourself."

Chris deleted the message.

There would be no lab report.

No details for Phil.

CHAPTER 40

S hortly before noon, Chris pulled into the garage at home. Numb, he left the garage door open and his car running.

Could he throw Paul to the wolves? Condemn his best friend? He sat in his car, trying to piece together his shattered sense of reality as an investigator and a friend. The pieces just didn't seem to fit anymore. He needed answers.

From Paul.

In slow motion, he moved his gaze around the garage. His eyes rested on the gas-powered auger and portable ice-fishing hut Kimber had given him for Christmas. Then he looked at his tackle box, and an idea began to germinate. It required a quick trip to a tackle shop in Forest Lake.

Next thing he knew, he was texting Paul: *Hey buddy, you free? I have new ice fishing gear I'm dying to use. Thinking the Saint Croix, Minnesota side, below the bridge. It'll be a short trip ... sunset's so early. You in?*

His heartbeat echoed in his ears as he waited for a reply. Ironically, "Under Suspicion" by Delbert McClinton began playing on the radio. Chris quickly changed the station.

His phone lit up.

Sure. Meet you there. What do I need to bring?

Just a license, Chris replied.

Wouldn't you talk the warden out of ticketing me?

Don't count on it, pal! Chris texted back. There was something comforting yet also unsettling about the banter.

Chris gathered up the auger, the hut, two stools, two poles, and his tackle box. He loaded the gear into a sled for easy hauling onto the ice. Heading inside, he layered on some warm clothes, then went into the kitchen to make some instant hot cocoa for a thermos.

He wanted this to look and feel like just another ice-fishing trek. He didn't want to raise Paul's suspicions.

As he drove to the west end of the bridge, he worried whether his plan would work. Maybe it wasn't the right tactic. He wasn't sure how Paul would react. For that matter, Chris wasn't sure how he himself would react. He had his gun tucked beneath his heavy jacket, just in case things got out of hand.

Chris parked underneath the bridge, where Paul's Lexus was already waiting. Chris could hear himself exchange a few pleasantries and small talk as the two unloaded the gear. It felt like an out-of-body experience. The man in front of him, the man his children called Uncle Paul, was likely a serial killer responsible for five grisly murders. It was too much. Every bone in Chris's body railed against it.

He took a deep breath. If he wanted this to work, he needed to stay cool, act natural. He needed Paul to open up, not shut down.

"Shall we?" Chris managed to say, sweeping his hand toward the ice. "Those crappies won't catch themselves, right?" He forced a smile.

Paul grunted. "We might not catch them either."

Chris pulled the sled filled with gear as they shuffled carefully onto the snow-covered ice. Paul seemed especially slow going. When they reached a spot near the bridge pilings, Paul grimaced and held his hands to his stomach as he waited for Chris to drill two holes a few feet apart. The new auger made quick work of the job. The biting north wind whipped down the river valley, stinging their faces, as they set up the shelter.

"They say this hut's great," Chris said. "Even on a day like this, it's supposed to stay warm inside."

"We'll see about that," Paul retorted.

Chris set a stool next to each hole inside the hut, and they took their seats. Sure enough, they were nicely sheltered from the penetrating cold. They waited for their eyes to adjust to the dim light inside the hut. Chris opened the thermos of hot chocolate, poured a cup for himself, and offered some to Paul. He declined.

Chris eyed Paul, who labored to catch his breath.

"So, how you feeling these days? You still look sapped." Chris asked. He sipped his hot chocolate.

Paul shrugged. "Not too bad. I'm OK."

Chris set the cup down and reached for his tackle box. "Grab that strainer and clear your hole," he directed. "I'll get our lines ready."

For each line, Chris chose a Gray Ghost jig, then attached a sinker and bobber. Chris cleaned ice chips from his own hole, then lowered his line into the water. He handed Paul's rig over to him.

"Wouldn't we be better off using minnows?" Paul asked, eyeing the jig.

"Nah. It's a hassle to lug a minnow bucket. Jigs seem to work about as well. Besides, I have a special lure for you to use later if this one doesn't work."

They sat in silence, jiggling their lines. Chris rubbed his mustache with his free hand. He knew what he wanted to say, but the words seemed stuck.

He cleared his throat. "Paul," he began, "there's something I want to share with you. No one else knows about this. Not even Kimber. But sometimes it really helps to get things off your chest, you know what I mean?"

Paul's eyebrows furrowed. Apprehension filled his eyes. "What is it?" His leg bounced.

Chris looked down at his line, then up at Paul. "Buddy, I did something terrible when I first started as an investigator."

Chris watched as Paul relaxed. His leg steadied. Paul leaned back and folded his arms across his chest.

"You can tell me anything," Paul said.

It was true—Chris was about to share something no one knew. Something that had filled him with shame and humiliation for years.

"There was an abandoned house in north Minneapolis a long time ago," he said. "It wasn't so much a buy-and-sell crack house as much as a crash pad for addicts and homeless. We were supposed to roust out all the occupants."

When a truck rumbled over the bridge above them, Chris paused and used the opportunity to gather his thoughts.

"It was a three-story building. I was assigned to check the third floor." He took a deep breath and exhaled slowly.

"When I opened the door to one of the tiny rooms, I found a homeless woman and her child—this beautiful little girl. All they had was a mattress, a blanket, some coloring books, a Bible, and a small statue of Jesus."

He stopped for a moment, controlling his own emotion.

"Not a word was spoken, but the woman just looked at me. Her eyes were sad, pleading for me to let them stay. That little space was the only home they had. So, I closed the door. I went back downstairs and reported the third floor clear of occupants."

Paul shook his head. "That's nothing to be ashamed of. Sounds like an act of compassion to me."

"But wait—there's more." Chris almost laughed as Phil's famous catchphrase inadvertently found its way out of his mouth. He took another deep breath. "Later in the week, that house caught fire. They found two bodies on the third floor, on the mattress."

"You can't be sure it was them," Paul reasoned. "You know what happens to bodies in a fire."

"Oh, it was them. They weren't burned. They died of smoke inhalation. I saw the pictures."

Paul grimaced. "Did you get questioned about it?"

"Oh yeah. I was in charge of that floor. I had told them no one was there. So I lied again. Said the woman and child must have taken over the space after we cleared out the house."

"I assume there was no way to prove otherwise, right?"

"That's right. And good thing. There would've been severe consequences if they had known what I did. I could have lost my job, faced a lawsuit if that woman had a family."

Chris jigged his line up and down.

"I still wonder what might have happened if I'd done things differently. If I'd cleared them out, they'd be alive today."

"You don't know that, Chris. They were homeless. That's a harsh life. For all you know, their deaths may have been less painful than the lives they were living." He reached over to put a hand on Chris's knee. "If you'd like to speak with a counselor, the pastors at my church in Marine on Saint Croix are fantastic. Pastor Joel or Pastor Hannah."

Still staring at his line, Chris tried to not to show his bewilderment. Here was Paul, encouraging Chris to speak to *clergy* about his problem.

Instead, he made a show of shrugging it off. "No, that's fine. But it's an enormous relief to just get it off my chest, you know?" Now he looked right at Paul. "I'm responsible for their deaths. Me. Two people are dead. Because of *me*. And I've kept it all to myself—until now."

Paul stared back at him for only a moment before needing to look away. Chris could see that same indescribable emotion in his eyes. Guilt. Remorse. Shame. Pain. Fear. But also resoluteness. Conceit. Conviction.

It was time.

Chris let out a sigh. "Well, these crappies aren't exactly throwing themselves onto our lines, are they? Pull out your line. I've got that special jig for you."

Chris set his pole aside so he could dig into his tackle box. His hands were oddly steady as he handed over the lure.

"Here. It's a Luhr-Jensen Hot Shot."

Paul reached over and took the lure. Still in the box with a see-through wrapper, the lure was gray, with treble hooks on the tail and midsection. The body tapered to a stainless-steel vane set just below two bright red faceted glass beads. The beaded eyes blinked at him.

Hello, Paul, they seemed to say.

CHAPTER 41

I look down at the lure in my hand. My leg begins to bounce
again. My Adam's apple quivers. My mouth goes dry.

Those faceted red beads. This can't mean what I think
it means—can it? Does Chris know? But how? No one ever
should have been able to trace the beads back to me. My plan
was infallible.

A jolt of pain moves through my midsection. It slowly dis-
sipates, though. I think the OxyContin I popped before Chris
arrived is at last taking effect.

Calm overcomes me, whether via the opiates or resigna-
tion. I begin to speak.

"Fair's fair. You shared a secret. So I'm going to tell you
something—something I am sharing only with you."

Chris leans closer. Outside, the wind beats against the
high-denier fabric. The gust makes the support poles sway and
the fabric snap loudly. Glints of bright light splash through the
seams.

"People say time heals all wounds," I say. "Sometimes it
doesn't."

I tell him I'm dying. I've been diagnosed with pancreatic
cancer. There's an avascular mass on the head of my pan-
creas, which means blood vessels haven't kept up with the tu-
mor's rapid growth. My doctor says I'm probably looking at six

months, based on averages. Maybe I'll get a little more time. Or a lot less.

Chris is dumbfounded. I can see the pain on his face.

He begins to say something about Gayle. I cut him off. I know what he's trying to say. Gayle's a nurse. She'd gladly take care of me.

But I don't want all that fuss. I couldn't bear it.

I tell him it's too late for me and Gayle anyway. I can't give her what she wants. The closer she's tried to get to me, the more I've wanted to get away. Especially now. She doesn't need to know about my cancer.

The powerful wind punches the fabric once again, testing the graphite support poles.

I tell Chris I'm a corpse. I'm emotionally dead. It's the same thing I told Gayle. I don't think he understands what I mean any more than she did.

The ice cracks and pops beneath us. That's when I find myself telling Chris about another frozen body of water. I was thirteen. It was mid-November, late afternoon. The sun was low. The sky was red. Winter had come early that year. The temperature was falling, and tiny specks of ice were falling from the sky. I still remember that they felt like needles pricking my young skin.

We'd been deer hunting. My father was coming across the lake on his snowmobile as I waited onshore. But the ice beneath the snow closer to shore was thin. There was an area of slush. I could see it; he couldn't.

I didn't say a word. Didn't warn him.

My father's sled bogged down in the slush. The rear of the sled began to slip into the water. The skis tipped up.

He jumped off the machine just as it went down. But the

ice couldn't support him. It broke away. He was chest deep and sinking, grasping at the ice. His heavy clothing was weighing him down.

He called to me for help.

I just stared at him, a smile growing on my face.

I could see his leather mitts slip off. He clawed at the ice. His fingers were bloody. They left red streaks on the thin, sharp ice.

He screamed my name again.

It felt good to watch him suffer. I enjoyed the experience, feeling no sorrow. It was about time. It was his time.

Before he slipped below the water, he made his last call for help.

I turned my back and walked away. I wanted—needed—him to see that I was turning my back on him, leaving him to suffer in fear, in pain. Just as he had done to me.

When I looked back a few moments later, my father was gone. Bits of ice were already mending the hole through which he disappeared. My smile turned to a grin.

For the first time in my life, I felt power.

Chris is shocked. Silent. Appalled. His mouth agape.

So I tell him about Uncle George. The babysitter. Father Benedict.

I tell him about Nick.

That's the hardest secret of all to pass through my lips.

The only thing I don't tell him is that yes, what he's thinking is right—I did send those feculent, depraved monsters to hell.

We're quiet for a long time. I hold my breath. Will he arrest me right here, hauling a sled full of gear and me in handcuffs back to shore? Will he let me go home, only to send the cavalry later tonight?

Chris is looking at me with an air of hesitance, as if he's afraid. He's not afraid of me hurting him. Rather, he's afraid of how I've already hurt him.

We've been close for many years now. He's the greatest friend I could ask for. I don't deserve him. Suddenly, I feel sick.

I hand the lure back.

"I think I should head home," I tell him.

He nods.

CHAPTER 42

C hris paced the house, waiting for Kimber and the kids to get home. When he heard her car pull into the garage, he met them at the door. He barely nodded a brief hello to the kids before pulling at Kimber's elbow. She was busy taking off her boots; he pulled so hard she nearly toppled over.

"We need to talk," he said. "Alone." He glanced over his shoulder to see the kids occupied with peeling off their winter gear and unloading their backpacks.

Kimber gave him a fearful look, not understanding what could be so urgent. "OK. How about we go in the bedroom?"

Without taking off her coat, she headed straight for the bedroom with Chris right behind her. As they entered, he closed the door behind them and locked it. She sat on the edge of the bed and ran her fingers through her hair. When Chris sat next to her, she reached over and rested a hand on his thigh.

"Honey, what's going on? Please tell me this has nothing to do with *us*, right?"

"No, not at all." Chris put his arm around her shoulder, pulled her close, and gave her a reassuring squeeze. "I'm sorry I scared you. But no, this isn't about us."

For several seconds, Chris stared at the floor, mustering the strength to present his thoughts. He decided to start slow and build up.

He looked directly at Kimber. "Sweetheart, Paul's dying of cancer."

She gasped. "What? Oh my God."

"Pancreatic cancer. There's nothing they can do. They say he has maybe six months."

She thought for a moment, her face wrinkled with worry and sadness. Then she nodded, mostly to herself. "That explains the weight loss. It probably explains why he's been so distant to Gayle—why he broke it off." Her eyes widened. "Why didn't he tell her? She could take care of him."

"Because that's exactly what he's afraid of." Chris sighed, forcing himself to press on. "And because there's more…"

Trepidation clouded her face. "More than him dying of cancer? It can't get worse."

"Yes, it can." Chris frowned and took a deep breath. "I think Paul's responsible for the priest murders. In fact, I'm sure of it."

The color drained from Kimber's face. She pushed herself away from Chris as if trying to escape from the words he had just spoken.

"*Paul*? What in God's name makes you think that?"

Chris reached for her hand and tried to pull her near once again. She wouldn't budge.

"It's crazy. I know. But I'm positive it's him." His words began to tumble out like a rock careening downhill. "It's a long story, but there were these merino wool fibers. And a

328

plane crash and a body back in 2009. And Paul had access to it because he used to be a forensic dentist, and he—"

"Stop! Stop!" Kimber held her hands to her temples and clamped her eyes shut. "This doesn't make any sense!"

Chris swallowed hard. "You're right—it *doesn't* make sense," he said softly. "But it's true. It's Paul. There's over-whelming evidence—real evidence—proving it."

He reached for her hand again. When she opened her eyes, he stared deeply into them. Some form of acceptance slowly came to her face, then she clapped her hands over her mouth, her face rife with worry.

"Oh my God—Gayle! Is she safe? I need to call her right now!" She began to rise from the bed.

Chris gently pulled her back. "No, she's in no danger. I promise."

"How you can tell me Paul is a murderer in one breath and then tell me Gayle is perfectly safe in another?"

Chris sighed. The only way to answer that question was explicitly. "Because Paul is the type of serial killer who targets certain people—priests. Specific priests, honey. Pedophiles. Abusers. He has a mission. He would never ever hurt Gayle or anyone else outside that sphere of de-pravity. That includes me. I know that now."

Kimber placed one hand over her midsection and another over her throat. "Oh God. This makes me sick, Chris."

He nodded. "Yeah. I know." He gently gave her an-other squeeze.

They were silent for a while.

"What does Phil say?" she finally asked.

Chris hesitated. He rubbed his mustache. "He doesn't know."

Kimber leaned forward. "So, you're going to tell him, right? You're going to turn Paul in, aren't you?" Her voice was rising.

He hesitated even longer this time. "I'm not sure what I'm going to do. Kimmy, this is the most difficult situation I've ever been in. It's not a simple matter of—"

"No, it *is* a simple matter!" Kimber balled her fists. "It's a simple matter of him being a *serial killer*." She threw the term right back at Chris. "You are a law enforcement agent. This is a simple matter of you arresting him. My God, Chris—have you disconnected from reality?" She slammed her fists on the bed.

"No. It's more complicated than that." He softly swept a tangle of disarrayed hair from her face, then held her cheeks in both hands for a moment. "Look—I've been living and breathing this case for weeks now. I *know* what Paul did was wrong. But he's my best friend. He's dying. And I now understand why he did these things, why he felt he had no other choice."

Kimber crossed her arms over her chest.

"I talked to him this afternoon, honey. We went fishing. There's this lure—" He stopped when he realized it was too complicated to explain. "What I'm saying is, I sort of hinted about the murders. I wanted to see how he'd respond. I wanted him to open up. And he did."

Chris had to pause to let a wave of emotion roll through him as he relived those moments in the hut when Paul revealed his most painful secrets.

"Honey, he told me he had been sexually abused by his uncle, a priest, and a babysitter."

Kimber's arms slowly lowered. "His uncle abused him? His own uncle? *And* a priest? And then a babysitter? My God!" She held her hands out as though pleading for an explanation.

Chris nodded. "As if that weren't enough, he was physically and emotionally abused by his father. I sort of knew that already, but now I also know that his father died right in front of him as he stood there and watched. He *enjoyed* watching his father die. That's how broken he's been his whole life. He never had a chance. Trying to live a normal, stable life has been hell for him."

Her arms crossed again. "Yeah, well, lots of people have been abused. Many more people than we'd ever realize. I see it every day at the hospital—the ones living the abuse right here, right now, and the ones now living with the lifelong effects of it. It's heartbreaking. But not every abused person becomes a serial killer on some *mission*." She scowled at the word. "People who have been abused need and deserve healing, love, validation, justice. Not murder and vengeance."

Chris rubbed his face. "You're right. But in Paul's mind, vengeance *is* justice. Or at least the closest thing to justice anyone will ever get when it comes to this epidemic with the Catholic Church. You know how it is—the whole world is learning that the church has been covering this up for decades. *Knowingly*. They've let these guys go from parish to parish, allowing them—hell, *enabling* them—to prey on innocent children. What Paul did was wrong, but he's been trying to speak for those who can't or won't speak for themselves. He knows what that pain is like. He had no one to turn to. His father punished him—made him kneel on rock salt—when he told about the priest that abused him."

There was a quiet whine and a scratch at the door. Kimber's face softened a bit as she stood up. Brodie padded into the room as soon as she opened the door. He whined again and plopped on the rug in front of them.

Chris looked at Brodie, remembering what that poor dog must have gone through that night—that night Paul murdered Father Doyle.

"There's one last thing, honey," he said.

"My God, hasn't this been enough?"

"You remember Paul's younger brother, Nick, who died when he was in college at St. Michael's?"

Kimber just nodded, bracing herself.

"It was a car crash, but it was no accident. It was suicide."

Her shoulders slumped.

"Nick mailed a letter to Paul the morning of the day he died. He said a priest at the college had been abusing him. It was ongoing. No one knew. Nick felt he could no longer live with the shame. He felt it was his fault. He knew he couldn't turn to his mother. She was a widow—Nick knew his truth would have killed her. And he certainly couldn't turn to anyone at St. Michael's. He'd been isolating himself. Suicide seemed like his only way out. So he drove into a bridge abutment east of Saint Cloud. A part of Paul died that day. He's been struggling with this for many years."

Rivulets of tears began streaming down Kimber's cheeks.

"In his suicide note, Nick named the priest. It was Father James Doyle. The priest killed here in Scandia. Paul's first victim."

Brodie stood up and put his paws on the bed and jumped up beside them. He turned round and round before lying down with a thump. Kimber leaned over, buried her face in his warm fur, and cried.

Chris felt each sob as he stroked her back.

Slowly, Kimber sat back up. She didn't wipe the tears. "Chris, what are you going to do? What *can* you do?"

He was silent for nearly a minute.

"Honey?" She put her arms around her husband and looked into his eyes, searching for answers. Brodie tried to snuggle between them.

"I'll go over tomorrow morning. I'll confront him." He paused. "But I can't be the one to arrest him. I just can't."

Kimber nodded. "Will he turn himself in?"

"That's my hope."

"But what if he doesn't? Will you call Phil?"

Chris looked down at Brodie. Somehow the dog seemed to sense their discomfort.

"I don't know," was all Chris could say.

That night, Chris's sleep was fitful. The streetlight penetrated the bedroom curtains, casting shadows on the wall. Chris lay propped on pillows, watching the shadows morph into shapes. Hideous figures danced, pointing at him, screaming. When he closed his eyes, the images remained.

He covered his face with his hands and discovered he was crying.

CHAPTER 43

I'm sitting in my recliner. The wind blows fiercely, and my house creaks with every gust. Each time the furnace ignites, the lights briefly dim.

My leg is bouncing, and I can't seem to control it. I'm nearly debilitated with pain. Not just from my insides being eaten by cancer. More than that, it feels as though something evil has crawled into my mind, burrowing into my psyche, amplifying my contempt for those who do evil against the innocent.

From the very beginning, I've struggled with the knowledge that Chris was investigating these murders. I never let it hamper our friendship, though. That's because I was certain he'd never know it was me.

But now—now it's become a betrayal. I have betrayed him. My friend, my best friend.

The fireplace is blazing. The doors are partially closed, and flames dance behind the sooted glass.

The fire reminds me of hell, the place to which I've sent several horrible people. I can see their twisted faces, contorting among the flames, flesh dripping off their bones. I hear their screams, mouths agape with pain.

There's Auxiliary Bishop Dominic McGloughlin, the attorney, the master of cover-up. With his slippery legalese, he allowed the abuse to continue by moving the pedophiles from one parish to another. I should have gotten to him sooner.

Skinny, weak Father Crowley. Even in his demented state, he knew why I'd come. I cherished the fear in his eyes when he struggled to breathe. How his eyes blinked when my knife slowly slid between his ribs. I could feel the last few beats of his heart as it struggled to sustain life.

Roosevelt Simon, hoping his boy-fuck fantasy had come true when there was a visitor at his door so late at night. Thinking about him makes me blush with satisfaction. I had plenty of DNA and prints from that David Kuusisto, but inspiration struck when I came across that wad of chewing gum in the snow across from the post office. I thought it might be fun to leave it in the saucer. Whose gum was it? I have no idea. It was like playing some sort of DNA lottery.

Next is Rodriguez, begging to say an Act of Contrition. Request denied, oh not-so-holy one. Writing in the fabric over the Communion rail was a challenge but worth the effort. Like finger painting, when we had to draw crosses in Catholic school to gain the approval of the nuns. So ironic.

McGloughlin, Crowley, Simon, and Rodriguez—those kills were necessary to avenge the faceless, nameless victims whose pain I understand.

But killing Doyle gave me the most satisfaction. I killed him for the one who shared my blood. I did it for Nick.

Doyle thought he recognized me. Nick and I did look a lot alike. As he stood there naked, repugnant, he was overcome with fear that the prey had finally turned on the predator.

Of the screams I hear coming from the flames of hell, I recognize one more. My father's. I still see him clawing at the ice, his fingers leaving bloody streaks as he loses purchase. He's begging, pleading with me to help him. I won't. I didn't.

In that moment, I knew I wanted—needed—to make men like him die.

The wind pushes a wisp of smoke down the chimney. An overhead light illuminates the twisting, smoky column from floor to ceiling.

I look at the pictures of myself on the mantle. I appear happy, so content.

A hideous monster has always been hiding beneath that fake smile.

Sitting in my lap is my Angora, Bella, my longtime companion and confidante. She knows my deepest secrets, hopes, and dreams. She knows the vile but necessary things I've had to visit upon others. She'll always keep her secrets. She doesn't judge me. Her blue eyes stare at me with understanding. We've a deep love for each other. She's going to miss me.

I think about Doyle's dog. Does he miss Doyle? Did he judge his master? I'm just glad he found a good home. Chris never said where he got his dog, but it's obvious. Where else would he suddenly find a golden retriever that had "been though a lot"? Of course Chris would rescue him. Chris has the biggest heart of anyone I know.

And it's breaking right now. I know he's suffering. In pain, conflicted about how to deal with me.

A security light illuminates. Perhaps a passing animal.

I feel a pleasurable fog roll over me. The OxyContin I took an hour ago has kicked in. My leg stops its nervous bouncing. I kick off my shoes and move my feet closer to the fire. I can feel *the heat warm them. The opiate intensifies the sensation. I rest my eyes after another deep gulp of vodka.*

A rumble rouses me. Roger Anderson is plowing. There's been another heavy snow. The headlights from his truck slice through the blinds, creating a wavering pattern of horizontal stripes on the wall each time he makes a run at my driveway.

I think about the morning he noticed I'd been out early, before he did the neighborhood plowing. That was the morning I killed Rodriguez. On the spot, I had to come up with some excuse about needing to buy gear for the hunting trip.

Which brings back even more memories. That Matt—he bothered me from the beginning. His behavior embarrassed my best friend. Jeopardized future hunting trips for Chris.

I had my own problems on that trip, and Chris knew it. But he didn't seem to know why. Not then.

The grating of Roger's blade is barely audible, and my wall is silent of his lights. He has moved on to another driveway.

As though in synchronicity, the wind settles to a gentle breeze. My house is quiet now, except for the whisper of the furnace fan and the crackle of burning wood.

Catching myself mesmerized, I shake my head to break the trance. No time for this. I've got one last job to do. Perhaps the most difficult. I'm not sure.

I slowly rise to my feet, making sure the opiates and alcohol haven't rendered my legs useless before I take a step. I stagger to shut off the security lights and move out onto the deck. I need one last foray into the cold night air. One last view of the valley.

The sky is dotted with broken moonlit clouds. Light from the moon reflects off the frozen river below my home. The moon highlights the shimmering oak leaves still clinging to the branches and casts long shadows from the tall pines.

In my stocking feet, I step on acorns that have fallen on the hard ironwood decking. Numbed, I'm aware, but it's not painful. Clad only in neatly pressed jeans and a well-ironed dress shirt, I chill quickly, but it feels good—the gentle wind brushing against my skin.

The dry oak leaves quiver with each gentle puff. The smell of burning wood drifts down from my chimney. An airplane drones thousands of feet above, its flashing lights dimming as it moves north. Where is it going? Duluth? Winnipeg?

As I go back inside, I relish the feel of the soft carpeted stairs, the heated floor. I walk through the house one final time, a goodbye to this monument to my success. My feet glide easily on the cherrywood floors. The fieldstone columns are warm to the touch.

I place another log on the fire. When it ignites, I add the remainder of the Marlboro Reds and several pairs of vinyl gloves. I watch, churning the fire, making sure it all burns completely.

Those were the last items to take care of.

I've already disposed of the forty-caliber Beretta, which I bought from a shady character in Saint Croix Falls years ago. I tossed it—along with the unused cartridges and the Tyvek shoe covers—over the bridge to Osceola. Now they're covered with snow on the frozen river. The spring thaw will carry them away when the ice begins its annual pilgrimage downstream. They'll never be found.

And my blood-stained clothing and "Arnie the Plumber" disguise have already vanished into the ashes of my fire pit.

I kept my other Beretta—a nine millimeter, the one I bought from a legitimate dealer in White Bear Lake. It will be adequate for tonight.

The meeting with my attorney went well. Everything's in order. The documents are signed and notarized. My estate and the proceeds from the sale of the practice will go to SNAP—the Survivors Network of those Abused by Priests.

I put Bella in my heated garage with food, water, her litter box, and my mother's crocheted afghan, Bella's favorite refuge. As my going-away gift, I've had something special made for her. After each priest received his unholy Communion, all that was left of the red marble rosary was the pendant with the antiphon beads and the crucifix. I threw away the crucifix but had the beads woven into a new leather collar, which I've placed around her neck.

Typical of a cat, she shows no appreciation for the seraphic adornments embellishing her collar.

I leave the garage utility door unlocked. Chris will be here first thing in the morning. I'm sure of it. He'll find her. He'll find us both.

My heart aches for him. I know he can't—and shouldn't—bear the weight of arresting me. But I also know he can't—and shouldn't—bear the weight of keeping my horrible secret.

I don't know if he'll understand my final decision. But I do know he'll do the right thing. He'll make sure the truth is revealed. The truth is justice, and I accept that justice must be served.

I return to my recliner, lower the back, and stretch my legs closer to the heat of the fire.

Will God judge me favorably? Will he understand I'm a product of those I've chosen to kill? Or will he condemn me as just another peddler of evil—like them? Soon I will know.

Or perhaps not.

I take a deep pull of vodka and wait for it to dull me fur-ther. For several minutes, I allow myself to be mesmerized by the flames.

Then I close my eyes, take a deep breath, and reach for the Beretta.

ACKNOWLEDGMENTS

A huge hats off to my editors, Janet Graber and Angela Wiechmann. To Janet, for getting me started on this mission and daring me to finish it. To Angela, for detailed editing, correcting my grammatical errors, and having the confidence in me to recommend Beaver's Pond Press for publishing.

Thank you to my brother-in-law Phil Ronning for the cover concept. And thanks to Beaver's Pond for making it real.

Special thanks to Detective Tom Romagni and crime scene investigator Jerry Reichardt for lending their expertise and making my crime scenes real.

To medical examiner Valerie Rao, a friend for many years—thank you for giving me knowledge about postmortem scenes and time of death.

Detective Ryan George, Deputy Chris Majeski, and Officers Lonn Bakke and Ryan Parker deserve a thank-you for information on police procedures.

A huge thank-you to Nicole Praska, latent print examiner for the Minnesota BCA; Ken Jensen of the BCA; and Ken Zercie, fingerprint expert at the Henry C. Lee Institute of Forensic Science. (Hopefully Mr. Zercie will forgive me for taking liberties with fingerprint procedures.)

Although they didn't know it at the time, Timothy Lynch (retired from the Saint Paul Police Department) and Bill Johnson (retired as chief of federal pretrial services) gave me plot ideas.

Too numerous to mention are my friends who continually asked, "How's the book coming?" This encouraged me to finish a job that was much bigger than I ever imagined.

The one who suffered the most during the writing process was my wife, Ruth. Never losing her smile or patience, she endured countless questions about sentence structure and listened to far too many readings before this novel went to print. Thank you, Ruth, for sticking with me throughout this project.

I wrestled with this project for nearly six years. Several false starts and a shredder filled with tossed pages finally morphed into the book now in your hands.

The book was difficult to write, given my personal experiences with abuse by Catholic priests. That said, *Unholy Communion* is not a story about me or my experiences as an abuse victim. Rather, it's a thought-provoking story about a victim of spiritual incest, who could no longer live with his own emotional defilement.

About the Author

Thomas Rumreich earned his Doctor of Dental Surgery degree from the University of Minnesota in 1973. He also holds a master's degree in psychology.

For sixteen years, he served as the forensic odontologist for the Ramsey County Medical Examiner's Office in Saint Paul, Minnesota. He is trial certified as an expert witness in forensic dentistry.

He completed his training in death investigation at the Saint Louis University School of Medicine.

Thomas lives with his wife, Ruth, in Scandia, Minnesota.

This is his first novel. Profits will be donated to Survivor's Network of those Abused by Priests (SNAP).